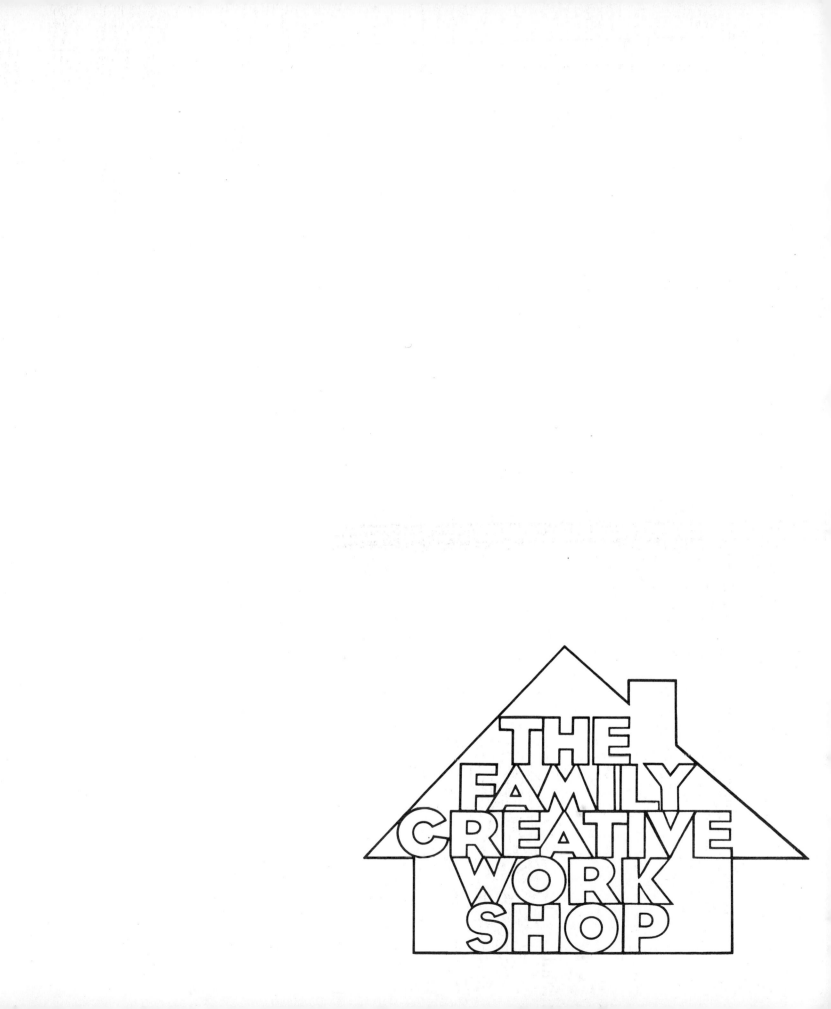

THE FAMILY CREATIVE WORKSHOP

12

Parades and Festivals, Pasta
Patchwork, Perfumes
Pet Habitats, Pewtersmithing
Photographic Printing
Pickled and Canned Foods
Piloting Small Boats, Piñatas

Plenary Publications International, Inc.
New York and Amsterdam

Published by Plenary Publications
International Incorporated
300 East 40 Street, New York, N.Y.
10016, for the
Blue Mountain Crafts Council.

Library of Congress Catalog Card
Number: 73-89331.
Complete set International Standard
Book Number: 0-88459-021-6.
Volume 12 International Standard
Book Number: 0-88459-011-9

Manufactured in the United States
of America. Printed and
bound by the W. A. Krueger
Company, Brookfield, Wisconsin.

Second Printing

Printing preparation
by Lanman Lithoplate Company.

Publishers:
Plenary Publications
International, Incorporated
300 East 40 Street
New York, New York 10016

Steven Schepp
MANAGING EDITOR

Jerry Curcio
PRODUCTION MANAGER

Originating editor of the series:
Allen Davenport Bragdon

Editorial preparation:
Tree Communications, Inc.
250 Park Avenue South
New York, New York 10003

Rodney Friedman
EDITORIAL DIRECTOR

Ronald Gross
DESIGN DIRECTOR

Paul Levin
DIRECTOR OF PHOTOGRAPHY

Jill Munves
TEXT EDITOR

Sonja Douglas
ART DIRECTOR

Rochelle Lapidus
Marsha Gold
DESIGNERS

Lucille O'Brien
EDITORIAL PRODUCTION

Eva Gold
ADMINISTRATIVE MANAGER

Ruth Forst Michel
Barnet Friedman
COPYREADERS

Editors for this volume:
Andrea DiNoto
PARADES AND FESTIVALS
PERFUMES

Michael Donner
PEWTERSMITHING
PHOTOGRAPHIC PRINTING

Linda Hetzer
PATCHWORK

Donal Dinwiddie
PILOTING SMALL BOATS

Marilyn Nierenberg
PIÑATAS

Marilyn Ratner
PASTA

Mary Grace Skurka
PET HABITATS
PICKLED AND CANNED FOODS

Contributing editor:
Lillian Gordon

Contributing illustrators:
Marina Givotovsky
Kevin Maher
Lynn Matus
Sally Shimizu

Production:
Nicholas Martori
Leslie Strong

**Photo and illustration
credits:**
PARADES: "I Love a Parade"
© 1931 HARMS, INC., copy-
right renewed. All rights reserved. Used by permission
of Warner Bros. Music. Photograph, page 1414,
courtesy U.S. Military
Academy. Page 1416: (top
right) Dick Frank, (center)
UPI, (left) N.Y. State Li-
brary at Albany, (below)
U.S. Olympic Committee.
Page 1417: Circus World
Museum, Baraboo, Wis.
Page 1418: Japan National
Tourist Organization; Swed-
ish Information Service.
Page 1419: Belgian National
Tourist Office. Page 1421:
Florists' Trans-World Deliv-
ery Service. Craftnote
drawings, pages 1424-1425, used
by permission of the T.S.
Denison Co. PET HABITATS:
Painting, page 1465, "Noah's
Ark" (1846), by Edward
Hicks, courtesy of the Phil-
adelphia Museum of Art.
PEWTERSMITHING: Photo-
graph of colonial mug by
Donald F. Eaton, Old Stur-
bridge Village.

Acknowledgements:
PERFUMES: Technical consul-
tant, Jennie Sorese, Vice
President and Director of
Odor Evaluation, Interna-
tional Flavors and Fra-
grances. PET HABITATS:
Barrel doghouse, page 1464,
adapted from plan courtesy
of the Gaines Dog Research
Center. PHOTOGRAPHIC
PRINTING: Technical consul-
tant for the drawing of the
working parts of an enlarg-
er, E. Leitz, Inc. PICKLED
AND CANNED FOODS:
Technical consultants,
Edmund A. Zottola,
Professor and Extension
Food Microbiologist and
Mrs. Isabel Wolf, Extension
Specialist, Foods and Nutri-
tion, University of Minneso-
ta, St. Paul, Minnesota. Antique scale, page 1502, from
the private collection of
Amelia Bassin.

The Project-Evaluation
Symbols appearing in the
title heading at the
beginning of each project
have these meanings:

Range of approximate cost:

¢ Low: under $5 or free
and found natural materials

$ Medium: about $10

$$ High: above $15

**Estimated time to completion
for an unskilled adult:**

⊠ Hours

🕐 Days

 Weeks

Suggested level of experience:
Child alone

Supervised child or
family project

Unskilled adult

Specialized prior training

Tools and equipment:
Small hand tools

Large hand
and household tools

Specialized
or powered equipment

On the cover:
Using the colors in the flag, this
patchwork quilt, entitled **Proof Through
the Night**, celebrates America's bicenten-
nial. The patchwork pieces were sewn on
the sewing machine; the quilting stitches,
which outline the diagonal white areas,
were sewn by hand. Designed and made
by Jeffrey Gutcheon. See the
entry "Patchwork," beginning on page
1438. Photograph by Paul Levin.

**Contents and
craftspeople for Volume 12:**

PARADES AND FESTIVALS
Here Comes Everybody

Donna Carlson, consultant for this article, first gained experience with parades as a grandstand performer at county fairs of the western states. She has degrees in both theatre and dance. As a professional dancer, choreographer, director, and designer, she has made floats, staged pageants, and participated in parades in Colorado, Wyoming, Kansas, Nebraska, New Mexico, Arizona, Oregon, and California. For six years, she was a director of Thresholds, *an off-off-Broadway theatre in New York City.*

I'd walk every step of a mile
And think it was really worth while
To see a parade come marching down
   the line.
I don't know a son-of-a-gun
Who wouldn't be willing to run
To see a parade come
Marching down the line.
Perhaps I'm what you'd call a patriot
But one thing's certain whether I am or not!

I love a parade.
The tramping of feet,
I love every beat
I hear of a drum.
I love a parade.
When I hear a band
I just want to stand and
Cheer as they come . . . .

(From **I Love a Parade**;
words by Ted Kohler,
music by Harold Arlen.)

Grab your hat, drop your chores and race to the nearest corner: a parade is coming. There are big parades and small parades, fun parades and serious parades, formal parades and casual parades—and we love them all. We love the band music, the color of uniforms and costumes, the spectacle of a moving procession. No sooner do we hear the distant beat of a drum than we run towards it to see what is going on. When we are not able to view parades in person, millions of us watch the most famous ones on television. And even viewed from an easy chair, parades have the power to stir the blood and lift the spirits, to bring that shiver of appreciation that says, "A parade is passing."

A parade can be almost any ceremonious movement of a group that is viewed by spectators. It can be as small and casual as a series of tots decked out with waterguns and cowboy hats, tugging wagons around a block, or so large that it is a wonder how the eye can encompass the multitude of horses, floats, and marching bands that are passing by. It can be military—as when cadets strut in proud review on the fields of West Point, or promotional—as when a circus parade entices spectators to buy tickets to the show by offering a tantalizing glimpse of what's inside the tents. It can be a march triumphant or a penitential pilgrimage. It can be as formal and stately as a coronation march or as casual and full of hullaballoo as a traditional New York ticker-tape parade, in which there are no marching bands or costumes, only tons of torn paper pouring down on a motorcade as it moves slowly through streets lined with cheering crowds.

But with all these differences, no one mistakes a parade for anything else. Big or small, grand or funny, all parades have three elements in common: organization, rhythm, and spectacle.

Above: the Corps of Cadets parades at the U.S. Military Academy at West Point, New York, as it has done every spring and fall since 1802. Opposite: on a New Year's Day, spectators at the Philadelphia Shooters' and Mummers' Parade are dazzled, delighted, and amused with spectacular costumes, music, and fancy footwork (pages 1421, 1423).

New-York, Nov. 24, 1783.

The Committee appointed to conduct the Order of receiving their Excellencies Governor CLINTON and
General WASHINGTON,

BEG Leave to inform their Fellow-Citizens, that the
Troops, under the Command of Major-General
KNOX, will take Poffeffion of the City at the Hour agreed
on, Tuefday next ; as foon as this may be performed,
he will requeft the Citizens who may be affembled on
Horfeback, at the Bowling-Green, the lower End of the
Broad-Way, to accompany him to meet their Excellencies
Governor CLINTON and General WASHINGTON, at the Bull's
Head, in the Bowery---the Citizens on Foot to affemble
at or near the Tea-water-Pump at Frefh-water.

ORDER of PROCESSION.

A Party of Horfe will precede their Excellencies and
be on their flanks---after the General and Governor, will
follow the Lieutenant-Governor and Members of the
Council for the temporary Government of the Southern
Parts of the State---The Gentlemen on Horfe-back, eight
in Front---thofe on Foot, in the Rear of the Horfe, in like
Manner. Their Excellencies, after paffing down Queen-
Street, and the Line of Troops up the Broadway, will
a-light at CAPE's Tavern.

The Committee hope to fee their Fellow-Citizens, conduct themfelves with Decency and Decorum on this joy-
ful Occafion.

In a 1783 broadside, an order was given for a
military parade as a tribute welcoming George
Washington and Governor Clinton to New York.
Decorum was encouraged in the ranks.

Celebrating New Yorkers welcomed Astronauts
Neil Armstrong, Buzz Aldrin, and Mike Collins
back from the moon, with a blizzard of shredded
paper and confetti.

A folk festival in New York City, Thanksgiving
Day is the occasion for Macy's parade with its
huge inflated storybook characters. It is viewed
by millions, in person and on television.

The Olympic games are heralded by contestants exhibiting their colors in a parade around the stadium.
The United States team is shown in the foreground above at the 1974 Munich games.

Of Types and Elements

If one were to take all the parades in the world and sort them into groups—a formidable task—at least four major types would emerge: parades of power, parades of enticement, parades originating in folk and religious festivals, and parades that, regardless of their origin, are so spectacular and extravagant they can really be classified only as celebrations in themselves. Each of these types has organization—a predetermined path and some separation of the units making up the parade. Each has a parade rhythm—provided by the beating of drums, the ringing of bells, the chanting or whistling of marchers, and certainly not least, the tramp of marching feet. And, of course, each has some measure of extravagance and spectacle in uniforms, costumes, and frequently, huge floats.

The Parade of Power

The parade of power is a vivid statement of condition and number. It is a tribute to the paraders themselves, and a graphic display of their strength and solidarity as a group. Such a parade may be in triumph after a victory, as was the famous parade that swept up the Champs Elysées when Paris was liberated near the end of World War II. Or it may be in anticipation of a victory yet to come, as when the Olympic contestants from each nation proudly circle the stadium before the games begin (photograph opposite). But whether the message is *I can do it* or *I have done it*, the show of power is clear.

The prototype of all such parades is the military march, and the keynote sounded is order. When West Point cadets march in review, the dazzling white and gray of their uniforms catch the eye, and the strains of martial music set feet to tapping. But the real rhythm of such a parade and the real spectacle come from the precision of the marching, the uniformity and solidity of the ranks.

Military parades are not new. Ancient cities frequently had streets that were designed especially for them. Here the statement of power was even more explicit. As the victorious legions marched, the sun caught their burnished shields and helmets, dazzling the beholders. Interspersed with the victors were their spoils—chariots laden with captured treasure, heavily chained captives trudging in a somber procession of defeat. When Rome became an empire, only the emperor could parade in triumph, but outstanding generals might be given a lesser parade, called an ovation.

The Parade Enticing

The parade of power takes its form from a full display of what has just been won (or is about to be). But the parade enticing works in almost the opposite way. It shows a bit and promises more—if you put your money down, that is. Modern-day parades of this type may generate excitement for a political rally or make you want to own a certain car or boat, but nowhere is the type of procession better exemplified than in the old-time circus parade. In the old days, when the circus came to town, it paraded down the main street, frequently to the site where the tent would be erected. The parade offered a tantalizing glimpse of what the circus offered. Clowns, ladies too-lovely-to-be-real, mustachioed muscle-men, and ferocious animals all paraded through the town to the melancholy, magical sound of the calliope.

Order was part of these parades, without a doubt. The elephants marched in proper trunk-to-tail formation; each type of performer was set apart from his brothers either by physical space or special costuming. Too, rhythm was maintained (animal marchers willing, of course). But exotic spectacle rather than uniformity and order was the keynote. The lure of this parade, its special rhythm, came from the exotic individual as much as from the massed troupe. If an elephant trumpeted unexpectedly the pleasure was increased ten-fold.

One of the most delightful of recent parades was, in fact, caused by a break-down in orderly plans. In 1971, the elephant sector of the Ringling Bros., Barnum and Bailey Circus found itself stranded in South Kearny, New Jersey (due to a railroad strike). The show must go on, of course, and the next one scheduled was at Madison Square Garden, some 20 miles away. To the joy of spectators, who showered the pachyderms with peanuts and popcorn en route, 19 elephants, one zebra and one llama hoofed from South Kearny to Manhattan. Their path included a 14-mile stretch through the Lincoln Tunnel, and for each, a tunnel toll of 50 cents was paid.

A 1911 circus parade, designed to tempt patrons in a small American town, is captured in this rare photograph. A circus wagon drawn by 16 camels was an amazing sight then and would be today.

Elaborate posters once served to announce circus parades as coming attractions, offering a glimpse of the entertainment as well as pictures of those famous impresarios, Barnum and Bailey.

A tall flower-bedecked mast, called a Maypole, is raised in Sweden's villages and towns as part of the annual Midsummer's Eve festival, which celebrates the fruition of nature and the joys of youth. Parents and children join in dances of medieval origin.

In Japan during the Shinto celebration of *Tanabata*, the Star Festival, spectators become informal paraders as they throng streets decorated with colored paper streamers.

Folk Festivals

Folk festivals, and the pageants and parades they generate, frequently add a fourth element to the order, spectacle, and rhythm that characterize other public celebrations. Overlaying these is a strong sense of ritual and tradition. The occasion may be the harvesting of crops, a change of season, the welcoming of a new year, or the re-enactment of a religious or historical event that has special meaning for the locality. Every land is rich in such celebrations. The Bavarian Oktoberfest (pictured below) began as a five-day royal wedding celebration that culminated in spectacular horse races. The races became an annual event and were combined with an agricultural festival. Spectacular opening-day parades featuring bands, horse-drawn beer wagons, and groups in traditional costumes now lead the way to the booths and beer tents.

In Sweden, a garlanded mast (left) is raised as part of the Midsummer Eve festivities, which celebrate the fruition of nature and the joy of youth. Parents and children dressed in peasant costumes dance around the flower-covered mast, and the steps they dance are of medieval origin. The maypole itself goes back to pagan rites—and whether or not each dancer knows these things, she knows the happiness she feels as she circles the maypole. A ritual of a very different nature, the Procession of Penitents in Furnes, Belgium, (opposite) is equally full of tradition. This takes place on the last Sunday in July. Since 1644, on this special Sunday, townsmen have gathered at the church where the procession begins. Hooded, wearing rough woolen robes, and bowed under the weight of crosses, the penitents walk in a solemn procession that lasts two hours. Spectators often remark on the authentic air of penitence that permeates the town. The strong sense of mystery, ritual, and sorrow is enhanced by the fact that most musical instruments are banned, as are singing and dancing. Here, spectacle is spectacle precisely because it is subdued, ordered, and somber.

In many folk festivals, however, order is thrown to the winds along with everyday cares. Spontaneity, excitement, and spectacle come to the fore. It is the thrill of being swept into the show that gives these celebrations their character.

In the Japanese Shinto festival of *Tanabata*, the Festival of the Stars (left), young people throng the lavishly decorated streets in August as informal paraders, celebrating an ancient legend, in which two stars on opposite sides of the Milky

Visitors from all over the world throng the fairgrounds at Munich's five-day Oktoberfest, since 1810 one of Europe's most colorful folk festivals. Festivities open with spectacular parades featuring bands, horse-drawn beer wagons, and groups marching in national costumes.

The solemn Procession of the Penitents is one of Belgium's great religious events, commemorating in part the time in history when the Low Countries were under Spanish domination.

In the coastal town of Oostduinkerke, Belgium, an annual shrimp festival honors the town's spectacular horseback fishermen with a sea parade featuring depictions of all kinds of water creatures like the shrimp above.

In Binche, Belgium, men called *Gilles* parade in elaborate costumes during the Shrove Tuesday (Mardi Gras) carnival. Each costume is cut from more than 15 yards of linen, decorated with 12 heraldic lions, 450 yards of white ribbon and lace, and a belt with brass bells. Their enormous headdresses of eight snow-white ostrich feathers sway to the rhythm of their special dance. They carry baskets of oranges; the fruit is tossed to the spectators.

The Year of the Hare (4673) is welcomed with a deafening display of firecrackers and a parade of dragons, large and small, down streets littered with confetti in New York's Chinatown. Adults, children, and community groups participate in the day-long celebrations. Other festivities continue through the 15th day of the Chinese New Year, marked by the first full moon.

Way symbolize young lovers whose ardor led them to neglect their duties. On the Chinese New Year (above), the festival offers a spectacular parade of paper dragons and the continual sound of firecrackers exploding everywhere. People, smoke, and confetti fill the streets with a spectacle of colorful chaos.

One folk festival that has both order and an escape from everyday self-discipline is Belgium's Carnival of Binche. This is a three-day celebration that has been called a feast of the dance. Like the Mardi Gras festivals of Rio and New Orleans, the carnival culminates on Shrove Tuesday, marking the start of the Lenten season. On that last day before Lent, there is the parade of the *Gilles*, magnificently costumed men (photograph, page 1419) who perform a demanding triple-rhythm dance, which is often echoed by the spectators en route. Ritual and order are strong. There are certain places and special times designated for each major event. Every *Gille*, moreover, is honor-bound not to change one step of his dance or one detail of his costume, from his ostrich-feather headpiece to his socks or broom. (Carnival rules state that the socks must be white wool, the twigs of the broom must be 25 centimeters long.) But in every other sense, order takes a back seat to spectacle. For three days, the streets of Binche are filled with confetti, farandole dancing, and flying oranges. The latter are tossed by the dancers to the crowd as a symbolic gift—a rather powerful bit of symbolism since the town has found it necessary to cover all lamps, windows, and signs with protective wire.

Extravagance and Spectacle

All parades seek to include extravagance and spectacles, but there are some that go so far they are in a class by themselves. Two such are the annual Pasadena Festival of Roses and the Shooters' and Mummers' Parade in Philadelphia. In the first, the point of emphasis is on grand and fantastic floats. In the latter, the splendor comes primarily from the individual costumes.

The Float Fantastic

When it comes to parades that are extravaganzas of spectacle, top prize almost surely must go to those that feature floats. Few things are as impressive as a well-constructed float. It may be as long as 40 feet, glitter with literally thousands of light bulbs, and bear any theme from the Arabian Nights to prehistoric monsters. Floats have been known to carry swimming pools (filled with live bathing beauties) or, on the other hand, to be completely animated, bearing exotic creatures that never existed in Darwin's lexicon, cunningly articulated and motorized to wave their hands (or paws) and gravely nod their heads. Floats can turn the grayest street into a spectacle of fantasy.

Jazz was the theme of the float above, created by the Florists' Transworld Delivery Association (FTD) for the 1975 Rose Parade. A typical after-hours New Orleans night club scene from the 1920s is depicted, complete with a figure of the late Louis "Satchmo" Armstrong. Approximately 25,000 roses carpet the dance floor.

Of all the parades that are devoted to lavish floats, the most famous is the annual Pasadena Festival of Roses, which takes place on New Year's day. It is viewed by an estimated 1.5 million spectators in person, about 120 million on network television, and by more than 100 million on international television via satellite. What began as a simple community flower festival in 1890 has blossomed into one of the world's most extravagant productions, with a parade of some 60 floats, 20 bands, and 200 equestrians. Since 1947, the parade has preceded the Rose Bowl football game, the progenitor of all college-bowl games in the United States. Floats for this parade, like the one shown in various stages of construction on this page, are completely covered with fresh flowers and living greenery. According to entry rules, even lettering must be created with flowers or other vegetation. Entrants using any artificial decoration—ribbon, cloth bows, tinsel, and the like—are disqualified. The cost of a Festival of Roses float averages $20,000, but many cost more than $40,000, and some require as many as 350,000 fresh flowers.

The Fanciest of All

The Shooters' and Mummers' Parade takes place in Philadelphia on New Year's Day. The Shooters' element may have been inspired by the colonial custom of shooting guns at midnight on New Year's Eve; the mummery aspect has a much older history. Mummery refers both to silence and merry-making. It has been known since the thirteenth century, and described the antics of pranksters and buffoons who traditionally paraded the streets of Europe during winter festivals, wearing masks and demanding liquid refreshment from one and all. Professional mummers performed pantomimes, always involving death and resurrection. Other masked paraders simply demanded, and gained, entry to the homes of noblemen, where they drank in silence and we can assume, good humor and contentment. The spirit of clowning was apparently an integral part of the festivals of light that were sprinkled through the dark months, when evil was rumored to be strongest.

In the same spirit, if for a different reason, the Philadelphia Shooters' and Mummers' Parade is one of the most colorful and riotous to be found anywhere. The streets, of course, are filled with marching bands and music, with humor and dancing, but the high point of the festivities is the judging of the costumes. The emphasis is on individual costumes and original themes.

Contest rules allow for three types of entrants: Fancy Clubs, Comic Clubs, and String Bands. Each group is led by a captain whose cape is of the greatest interest, especially in Fancy Club and String Band entries. At one time, these capes grew into huge trains, supported by as many as 130 page boys. But present rules limit

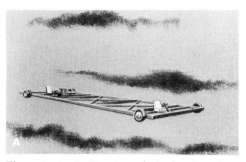

Figure A: A rebuilt motor vehicle chassis underlies the superstructure of a Rose Parade float. It must accommodate two drivers, an extra large radiator, a spare water tank, and a communications system.

Figure B: A frame is shaped close to the final dimensions of the float and secured to the chassis.

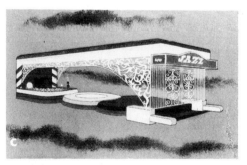

Figure C: In a process called *cocooning*, chicken wire is stretched over the frame and sprayed with a polyvinyl material that provides a surface for floral decoration.

Figure D: About 48 hours before the parade starts, the hardiest flowers are applied to the cocooning. A few hours before the start of the parade, the delicate blossoms (such as roses and gardenias) are individually placed in water vials and inserted in the cocooning. The finished float, top left, contains about 30,000 of these vials.

the number of page boys to ten. An elaborate captain's costume that appeared in the 1975 parade is shown opposite. The spectacular fan-like spreaders are built on a wooden framework that rests on the captain's shoulders. These spreaders may extend 16 feet from tip to tip, and once draped and decorated, may weigh as much as 85 pounds. Fancy Club marchers are allowed to play bongo drums, maracas, tambourines, gongs, cymbals, bells, whistles, but none of the instruments that are reserved for use in the String Bands.

The String Bands play mostly stringed instruments—banjos, mandolins, steel-string guitars, and violins, though sometimes saxophones, flutes, accordions (below), or glockenspiels are added. As in the Fancy Clubs, String Band costumes and themes are elaborate. In 1957, an award was given to a band whose theme was the syncopated clock. The band's costumes featured headpieces complete with clocks, wound up and ticking. In 1967, one of the String Band captains carried a Dutch windmill, 15 feet high and 13 feet wide, on his shoulders as he paraded. A

Members of a String Band strut and play accordions in costumes expressing an American Indian theme in the 1975 Shooters' and Mummers' Parade on New Year's Day in Philadelphia.

String Band captain in the 1975 parade remarked, "There are few things more important to a mummer than mumming."

The Comic Clubs provide much of the parade's humor. Antics and clever floats, often satirizing current events and famous people, abound. The parade's traditional theme song, *Oh, Dem Golden Slippers*, is graphically echoed by the golden slippers worn by the comics. A Fancy Club entry may be 20 blocks long, but each Comic Club is limited by the rules to one block. All mummers compete for prizes which are awarded at the end of the day on the basis of 70 percent for costume beauty and 30 percent for presentation of theme. The rules are interesting. No animals, livestock, fowl, mammals, reptiles, or fish will be allowed. All costumes must start and finish the official route of the parade to qualify for prizes. Each captain must carry his own garment (except the cape) without assistance from any other person. Any String Band marching in an old suit, or costumes renovated, shall be ineligible for any prize except the last prize.

A String Band captain in his elaborate feathered costume and golden makeup typifies the spectacle and lavishness of the parade. A captain may have 10 helpers to carry his train, but no other assistance.

Hints for simple costuming

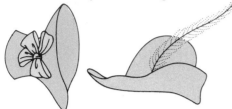

You can decorate buckram hat forms with ribbons or feathers.

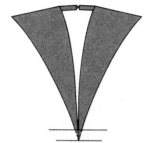

Huge buckram lapels covered with fabric or glitter add a comic note.

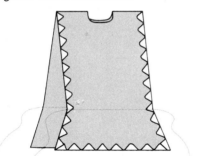

A simple rectangular tunic can be cut from a single piece of cloth, then tied at the waist with string.

Suppliers of parade floats and decorations:

Vaughn's Inc., 5050 West 78th St., Minneapolis, Minnesota 55435; or 316 So. Rome Avenue, P.O. Box 10557, Tampa, Florida 33609. Catalogs available on request.
Taffy's (costume suppliers), Offices in Atlanta, Boston, Cleveland, Dallas, Salt Lake City. "Showstoppers," a full-color catalog, available.
Circle Fabrics, Inc., 16 West 36th Street, New York, N. Y. 10018. Catalog of theatrical fabrics and accessories available. Samples included.
Dennison, 390 Fifth Avenue, New York, N. Y., 10018. Suppliers of paper products and party goods. Booklet on crepe paper decorations available.

Check local Yellow Pages under "Parade Equipment and Supplies" and "Floats—Parade."

A simple float built on a flatbed trailer (below) is designed to be pulled by a motor vehicle, usually a small tractor, which should also be decorated to complement the float. The float is constructed on a wood frame assembled to fit the chassis. The frame is bolted to the chassis at four points with the bolster stakes. Stud ties at each corner give the frame rigidity. Joists are nailed to the frame, and decking is fastened to the joists. A wood apron that frames the sides of the float is decorated to hide the wheels. The superstructure can be any shape at all; frequently figures formed from chicken wire and covered with papier mâché (see opposite page) are added. Designs can be anything, from dinosaurs to rocket ships.

Floats may also be built on trucks, cars, wagons, even boats. A sample of how a car is prepared for parading is shown opposite.

To insure a successful project, a float builder should consider the following points:

After deciding on the size and type of vehicle, a place large enough for construction is essential. Airplane hangers or sheds such as those found in lumberyards, with high ceilings and large doors, are ideal. If a float is to carry people it must be rigid, with handles for the riders to hold while the float is in motion. A float should be the same on both sides so onlookers do not feel that they are missing something. Floats are usually covered with floral sheeting, crinkled foil, or colored paper and glitter. Many embellishments such as garlands, streamers, shakers, fringes can be made or purchased from parade suppliers.

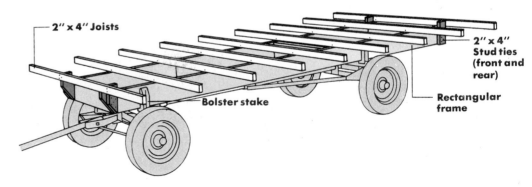

2" x 4" Joists — 2" x 4" Stud ties (front and rear) — Bolster stake — Rectangular frame

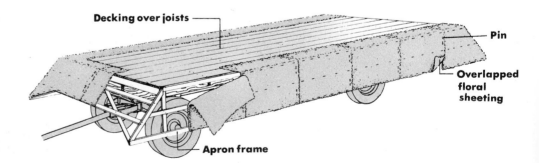

Decking over joists — Pin — Overlapped floral sheeting — Apron frame

Designs of floats are from **The Complete Parade and Float Guide** by permission of the T. S. Denison Company, publishers.

FLOATS AND DECORATIONS

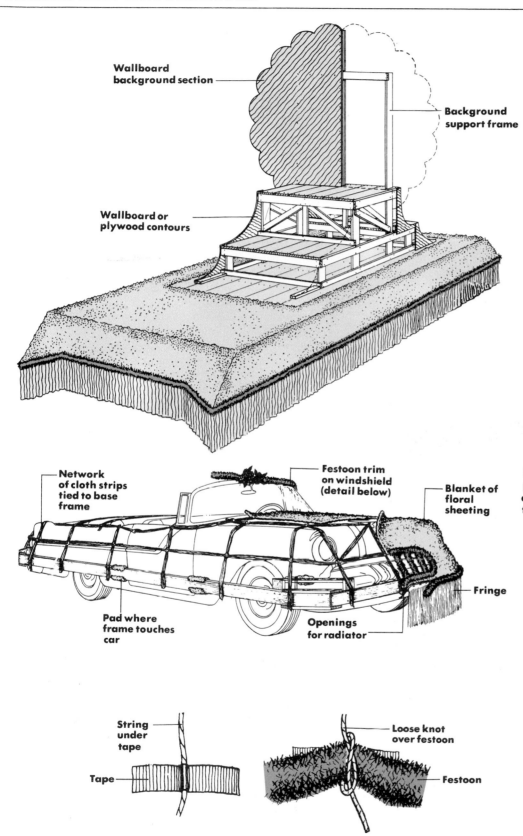

Wallboard background section

Background support frame

Wallboard or plywood contours

Network of cloth strips tied to base frame

Festoon trim on windshield (detail below)

Blanket of floral sheeting

Fringe

Pad where frame touches car

Openings for radiator

String under tape

Tape

Loose knot over festoon

Festoon

Applying papier mâché to chicken wire

A strong papier mâché can be made from wheat paste (wallpaper paste) and ordinary brown wrapping paper. Mix the paste to a creamy consistency; then tear the paper into 1-foot squares. Torn edges make smoother joints than cut edges. Use a scrap of wall board or plywood as a pasting board, and brush the first square liberally with paste, coating the entire sheet. Repeat this process about ten times, piling the paper squares on top of each other. If the stack dries out as you use it, apply more wet paste to the top piece. Tear small pieces from the

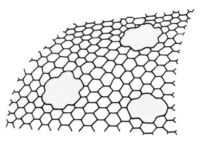

top sheet, about 3 or 4 inches square , and place them on the chicken wire, hooking the edges under the wire as shown above. Place several of these pieces several inches apart around the immediate working area. These are ties that hold securely to the wire form.

Larger pieces anchored to ties

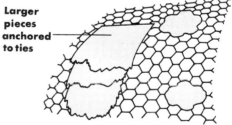

Larger pieces of paper, about 6 inches square, are applied over the ties, overlapping each piece (above). This process is repeated until the entire area has been covered once. Allow to dry. To apply a second coat of paper, brush the first dried layer with paste, and apply as above, omitting the ties. As the paper dries, it shrinks and exerts great pressure on the wire form. A large piece of paper shrinks more than several small pieces and could crush the form; so it is advisable to use smaller pieces, especially when working on detailed surfaces or on shapes where the form is completely enclosed, like a ball.

PASTA
A Plateful of Poetry

Anna-Teresa Callen is called the pasta queen by friends who have tasted her delicious Italian specialties, but her culinary skills extend to exotic foods of other lands as well. As a child, she learned many cooking techniques watching her grandmother at work in the kitchen of the family home in Abruzzo, Italy, but she did little cooking herself until she was in her twenties and living in London. Anna-Teresa manages an art gallery in New York but reserves her free time for cooking and developing new recipes.

Italians make poetry with pasta. Shaped like seashells, ribbons, stars or butterflies; colored yellow, green or red; dressed with sauces that range from delicate to hearty to indescribable—pasta is a delight to the senses.

This description bears little resemblance to the spaghetti and meatballs some people call pasta—and it shouldn't, since that dish is no more Italian than chop suey is Chinese. At its best, an Italian pasta dish is a subtle blending of flavors rather than starchy noodles buried in a heavy sauce.

Making pasta, multifarious as it is, is surprisingly easy. It takes a fair amount of time and patience, but the rewards will be waiting at the dinner table. Homemade pasta dough, made of flour and eggs, is rolled into thin sheets, then cut into different shapes, lengths and widths. In many Italian homes, this dough is made fresh each day; it is also available fresh in Italian stores. Fresh-cooked pasta can be served plain, stuffed, or baked in a casserole; there are so many possible variations that pasta need not be eaten the same way twice. But despite this incredible variety, the basic dough is always the same.

Factory-made pasta, which we Italians call macaroni, is made of durum-wheat flour and water, without eggs. Macaroni products include the familiar tube-shaped variety, all the many different kinds of spaghetti, and shapes such as shells (*conchiglie*), wheels (*ruote*), and butterflies (*farfalle*). (Of course, egg noodles can also be store-bought but they are no substitute for homemade pasta, and after eating your first batch of homemade pasta you'll see what I mean.)

The diversity of Italian cuisine results from the country's regionalism; pasta is prepared differently from town to town and even from house to house. The recipes here include specialties from several regions. Abruzzo, my region, is famous for *maccheroni alla chitarra*, thin noodles traditionally cut on a frame of closely spaced wires, dressed with a meat-tomato sauce, and served with a generous portion of grated cheese. *Tagliatelle alla Bolognese* is a classic noodle dish of the Emilia-Romagna region as is *lasagne verdi*. Other recipes here were culled from many regions of Italy, but regardless of their origin, all are time-tested and authentic.

In Italy, pasta is always served as a first course (*primo piatto*), followed by a second course (*secondo piatto*), meat, fish, or fowl, and vegetables, then by salad, and fruit. But there is no reason why pasta can't be a main dish. In fact, in days of high food prices, pasta is an excellent choice for an inexpensive and nutritious meal. An Abruzzese proverb says, *Fare le nozze coi fichi secchi*. Literally, it means to prepare a wedding feast of just dried figs, but metaphorically it suggests serving inexpensive foods, such as pasta, with great fanfare.

Cook's Advice

I learned to cook by watching women in my family, by experimenting for many years, and by using common sense and intuition. A good cook has to be flexible. You often have to adjust procedures to suit circumstances—what type of flour is being used, the size of the eggs—and this makes it hard to say precisely how much flour a well-kneaded ball of dough will absorb or how long you should cook a pot of pasta. But I have tried to anticipate the problems you might encounter and give extensive guidelines. As you become more practiced, you will discover special techniques that will work best for you.

The recipes that follow include a basic repertory of pasta shapes, fillings, sauces and know-how. You can use the recipes interchangeably. For example, *pasta verde* (spinach pasta), here used for *lasagne*, could be used for ravioli or any of the other pasta dishes. The recipes planned to serve six can be doubled or tripled for a crowd. Don't hesitate to adjust the recipes to suit your taste. The recipes in this entry invite you to be an inventive cook.

Delicate, delicious, delightful homemade pasta can be kneaded, rolled, and cut with a pasta machine into an exciting variety of noodles and other shapes.

Homemade pasta

$ ▯ ♣ ⚱

A great variety of flat and stuffed pasta shapes can be made from a basic egg-and-flour dough. A pasta machine does the work of flattening the dough and cutting it into ribbon-like noodles. Several types of machines are available; all are simple to use. They can be purchased in Italian food shops, gourmet cooking stores, and sometimes in houseware sections of department stores. Some people prefer to do all of the kneading, rolling, and cutting by hand, but this requires a great deal of practice and much more effort. Using the machine, you can make pasta that I think is every bit as good as pasta made by hand.

Using the recipe for pasta dough below, you can prepare noodles, *cannelloni*, *tortellini*, ravioli , and *lasagne*. The recipe calls for only a tiny pinch of salt; otherwise the dough would be too brittle and hard to knead. I work directly on a pastry board, but you may find it more comfortable to use a bowl.

Basic Pasta Dough (serves six)
Ingredients:

6 medium eggs

4 ½ cups of sifted all- purpose flour
Pinch of salt

Place the flour on a pastry board and make a well in the center. Break the eggs into the flour (photograph 1), beat the eggs lightly with a fork (photograph 2), then add the salt. Mix with a fork until the eggs have all been incorporated. Knead the dough until you can gather the mixture into a smooth, stiff but elastic ball (photograph 3). If necessary, add more flour. When the dough is sufficiently kneaded, it is quite elastic and smooth (photograph 4).

Let the ball of dough rest for at least ½ hour covered with an inverted bowl. This keeps it from drying out. The dough can be refrigerated overnight or frozen for later use. If you freeze it, take the dough out of the freezer the night before you intend to use it and put it in the bottom of the refrigerator.

1: The first step in making pasta dough is to break eggs into a well in a mound of flour.

2: Beat the eggs lightly with a fork; then start to knead the dough.

3: Work the dough, blending the eggs with the flour, until you can form a smooth ball.

4: The ball of dough should be smooth to the touch and quite elastic.

Basic Spinach Dough
The dough for green pasta (*pasta verde*) is made the same way as the basic pasta dough but with the addition of spinach. Use one pound of fresh spinach, or a 10-ounce box of frozen spinach, cooked and chopped. Make sure that all the water is squeezed out of the spinach and that it is very finely chopped.

Follow the recipe above for basic pasta dough, adding the spinach after the eggs. In the kneading process, you will have to add about a handful more of flour to absorb the moisture from the spinach.

Spinach pasta, which is light green, is used exactly like yellow pasta. It contributes to some of the more colorful pasta dishes in Italian cuisine.

Using the Pasta Machine

A pasta machine performs two operations. First it rolls a wedge of dough into a smooth, thin sheet. Then it cuts the dough into noodles. For this, the machine is equipped with two cylinders housing blades. One cylinder cuts the dough into ¼-inch-wide strips, the other produces noodles about ⅛ inch wide. The wider noodles, known as *tagliatelle* or *fettuccine*, are the classic flat noodles of Italy. The directions that follow show how to make *tagliatelle*, but the same procedures should be followed for rolling dough for other varieties of homemade pasta. When you make a stuffed pasta such as *cannelloni*, roll the sheets of dough by machine; then cut and stuff them by hand as the recipe directs.

Tagliatelle alla Bolognese is a classic dish of homemade egg noodles and meat sauce, ready to eat when it is topped with freshly grated Parmesan cheese. It should be served steaming hot.

Tagliatelle Master Recipe

To make these classic flat noodles, you need one batch of the basic pasta dough.

Cut the prepared dough into 12 wedges. Work with one wedge at a time, keeping the unused dough covered with a bowl so it does not dry out. Flatten each wedge into a rectangle; then cut each rectangle in half. This makes each piece of dough small enough to manage (photograph 5).

Starting with the machine set at its widest opening (No. 10 on the dial on most machines), feed the dough through the rollers several times (photograph 6). For the first few times, fold it and turn it before feeding it through again (photograph 7).

5: The dough is cut into wedges (left), each wedge is flattened (middle), and each rectangle is cut in half (right).

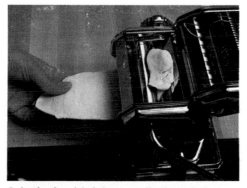

6: As the dough is fed repeatedly through the machine's rollers, and the opening is gradually narrowed, it is flattened into a thin sheet.

7: For the first few times the dough goes through the machine, fold it in half and turn it so that the dough will be kneaded evenly.

Gradually decrease the size of the opening, lowering the setting one notch at a time until you reach No. 2. After the first few times, there is no longer any need to fold the dough in half, but keep feeding it through the machine until you have a smooth, velvety strip. You may need to dust the dough with flour to keep it from sticking to the rollers, but do not overdo it or the *tagliatelle* will be too floury. After the dough is rolled into thin sheets, it needs to dry slightly. Lay it on a tablecloth (photograph 8). It is a good idea to cover the dough with kitchen towels so it doesn't become too dry. Dry sheets are hard to cut.

The sheets now can be cut into noodles. Run each sheet of dough through the wide cutting cylinder. This produces ¼-inch strips (photograph 9). If the sheets are very long and hard to control cut them in half. A good length for *tagliatelle* is 16 inches, but they can be any length.

Lay the *tagliatelle* on a flour-dusted pastry board or tray. Sprinkle flour over the strips to prevent sticking. Let the noodles dry. They can be made in advance and kept in a cool place until you are ready to use them.

Tagliatelle alla Bolognese
Ingredients:

1 recipe *tagliatelle*	1 cup freshly grated Parmesan
1 recipe *Bolognese* sauce (below)	cheese

Pasta should be eaten as soon as it is cooked, so prepare the sauces or fillings before you boil the noodles.

Bolognese sauce is typically served with *tagliatelle*. But as it is a basic meat sauce, it can be used with any kind of pasta.

Make the sauce ahead of time. It can be frozen, but when you are ready to boil the pasta, be sure to have the sauce at room temperature so it can be quickly heated and mixed with the just-cooked *tagliatelle*. For an elegant touch, add a *finanziera* to the sauce. This is a mixture of about 1 cup of chicken livers, giblets, and hearts, chopped finely and sautéed in butter. The mixture is then simmered for 15 to 20 minutes in ½ cup of Marsala wine.

Bolognese Sauce (serves six)
Ingredients:

1 slice bacon	1 pound mixture of chopped beef, veal and pork
1 sprig of parsley	Pinch of sage
1 medium onion	2 cups beef or chicken bouillon
1 stalk of celery	3 tablespoons tomato paste
1 medium carrot	¼ cup dry wine
3 tablespoons oil (olive or vegetable)	½ cup cream
2 tablespoons butter	Salt and pepper to taste

Chop the vegetables, parsley, and bacon very finely. Sauté them in the oil and butter over medium heat until quite brown. Add the meat mixture and brown it until dark in color. Add sage, salt, pepper, and wine; cook until the wine is absorbed.

In a bowl, mix the tomato paste with the bouillon and add to the mixture. Simmer, covered, for an hour or so. Remove from heat, add the cream, and mix well. If you plan to freeze or reheat the sauce, hold the cream until the last moment.

Cooking Pasta
Pasta must be cooked quickly, and homemade pasta cooks even faster than the factory-made kind. Add 2 tablespoons of coarse salt to a large pot of water, and bring it to a boil. Add the *tagliatelle*, stir gently, and cover the pot. When the water returns to a vigorous boil, cook just a few minutes; stir, and taste to see if it is done. The process should take no more than 5 minutes. To be *al dente*, the pasta should be slightly resistant to the bite. When cooked to your taste, turn off the heat, add a large glass of cold water to the pot, and drain the pasta in a colander, shaking all the while to prevent sticking.

Pour the *tagliatelle* into a serving bowl, add the heated Bolognese sauce tossing it gently, and top it with 1 cup of freshly grated Parmesan cheese. Serve immediately.

8: The rolled, thin sheets of pasta dough are placed on a clean cloth to dry slightly before they are cut into ribbon noodles.

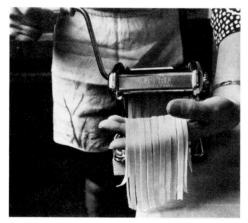

9: A sheet of dough turns into strips about ¼ inch wide when it is cut with the pasta machine's wider blades.

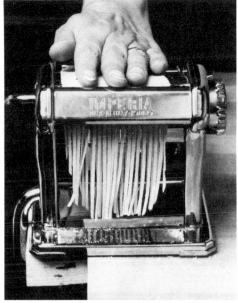

10: Making *maccheroni alla chitarra* the old-fashioned way, on a frame strung with wires, is still characteristically done in the Abruzzo region of Italy.

11: Feeding a sheet of dough through the narrower set of blades provided with a pasta machine produces noodles about ⅛ inch wide.

Maccheroni alla Chitarra

In *Maccheroni alla chitarra*, the sheets of dough are cut with a wire-strung frame called a *chitarra* (photograph 10), the Italian word guitar. These are still used in Abruzzo, but the thin noodles can be cut with a pasta machine too. They are made exactly the same way as *tagliatelle*, but the sheets of dough are cut on the narrow-cutting cylinder. These thin noodles are never called spaghetti. Spaghetti is factory-made.

I like to serve thin noodles with *ragù*, a tomato-and-meat sauce. Below is a basic recipe for *ragù*. Bolognese sauce or a cream sauce could also be used. *Ragù* goes well with all kinds of pasta.

Basic Ragù Sauce (makes about 9 cups)
Ingredients:

6 tablespoons vegetable or olive oil
2 medium onions
1 stalk celery
1 carrot
1 sprig of parsley
1 clove of garlic
1 pound chuck or rump of beef
1 pound lean pork or 3 sweet Italian
   sausages

1 pound veal shoulder
Pinch of sage
1 cup of dry wine
3 lbs. of tomato paste mixed with
   ½ glass of water
4-pound can of plum tomatoes
1 basil leaf or a pinch of dried basil
Salt and pepper to taste
1 batch of noodles (page 1428)

Pasta-eating etiquette, Italian style, calls for twirling the pasta around the fork without using a spoon.

Use a large, heavy casserole to make this sauce.

Heat the oil in a casserole. Cut a cross in the bottom of the onions, and add them to the casserole with the garlic, celery, carrot, and parsley. Prick the sausages (if used) with a fork and add them together with the other meats to the casserole. Brown well over medium heat, turning the meats and vegetables often. Add the salt, pepper, and sage and stir. Add the wine and cover.

Strain the tomatoes and the liquid from the can into a bowl. When the wine has been absorbed, add the tomato paste and water, tomatoes, and basil. Cover the sauce, and simmer very slowly for at least 2 ½ hours. Stir occasionally.

Remove all the meats and keep them warm if you want to serve them.

Strain the sauce through a sieve, squeezing the juices out of the vegetables. Discard the vegetable pulp.

Use the sauce according to your pasta recipe. Leftover sauce can be frozen.

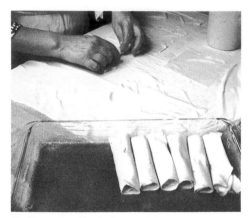

12: For *cannelloni*, sheets of homemade pasta dough are cut into 6-inch squares, boiled for a few minutes, stuffed with spinach-and-cheese filling and rolled into tubes. These are put into a buttered baking dish.

Kitchen Favorites and Celebrations
Stuffed pasta

Basic pasta dough (page 1428) can be cut into any number of shapes and stuffed with a great variety of fillings, depending on your taste. Three of the most popular types are *cannelloni*, *tortellini*, and ravioli. With these recipes you can turn simple pasta into gourmet dishes.

To make stuffed pasta, flatten wedges of dough with a pasta machine (page 1429). Then cut them by hand to the desired shape with a sharp knife or toothed cutting wheel. In the case of ravioli, a special metal tray makes the work easier. Finally, stuff the pasta as directed in the recipe you are using.

Cannelloni alla Anna-Teresa (serves six)
This is a recipe I devised, hence it bears my name. Every good cook should have at least one signature recipe. Before cutting the pasta, make the stuffing and the *ragù* sauce so the *cannelloni* can be assembled and baked quickly.

Ingredients:

1 batch of homemade dough, page 1428 (makes about 36 *cannelloni*)	2 cups freshly grated Parmesan cheese
4 cups *ragù* sauce (page 1431)	2 tablespoons butter for the baking dishes

Cannelloni Stuffing
Ingredients:

1 pound ricotta cheese	chopped and sautéed briefly in a small amount of butter
1 small Italian salami (*salamino*) or a dried sausage, finely chopped	½ pound Gruyère cheese, cut in slivers
1 pound fresh spinach (or a 10-ounce package of frozen spinach), cooked, squeezed to remove water, finely	Large egg, lightly beaten Pinch of nutmeg Salt and pepper to taste

Combine all the ingredients for the stuffing plus one cup of Parmesan cheese and a ladleful of *ragù* sauce. Mix well, taste for flavor and place in the refrigerator. The stuffing can be prepared a day in advance.

Cutting Cannelloni
Roll the wedges of dough through the pasta machine (page 1429) until they are about 6 inches wide and very thin. This usually means starting with a No. 10 dial setting and feeding the dough through, then setting the machine one notch lower each time the dough goes through until No. 1 has been passed.

Lay the strips of dough on a tablecloth or on kitchen towels. With a sharp knife or toothed cutting wheel, cut the dough into 6-inch squares.

Before Cooking
Have the stuffing and *ragù* sauce within easy reach. Butter two baking dishes large enough to contain all the *cannelloni*. Spread a thin layer of sauce on the bottom of each dish. You are now ready to boil, stuff, and bake the *cannelloni*.

Cooking
It is best to boil only a few squares at a time so the squares do not stick together. Cook in boiling salted water as directed in the master recipe (page 1430). Remove the pasta with a slotted spoon, and spread it immediately on damp kitchen towels. Boil a second batch of squares as you fill and roll the first batch.

Stuffing and Finishing
Put a tablespoon or so of filling on each square, and roll it into a tube. Line the prepared baking dishes with rolled *cannelloni* (photograph 12). Continue boiling, filling, and rolling the pasta, until you have used all the squares. Cover the pasta with the rest of the *ragù* sauce, and sprinkle it with the remaining Parmesan cheese. Top with bits of butter, and bake at 375 degrees Fahrenheit for 45 minutes.

13: To make ravioli, place a sheet of dough over the shaped metal tray and press it down firmly.

14: Use your fingertips to press dough into the tray depressions, making pockets for the filling.

15: Fill each square with a spoonful of spinach-and-ricotta-cheese stuffing.

16: Run a wet finger all around the edge of the tray and around each square. Put a second sheet of dough over the filled sheet, and press it in place to seal the edges and the individual patties.

Ravioli (serves six)

The *cannelloni* stuffing above is also delicious with ravioli. A metal tray divided into fluted-edged squares is useful for making uniform squares. These trays are available in houseware shops and department stores.

Ingredients:

1 batch of homemade pasta dough (page 1428)

½ batch of *cannelloni* stuffing (opposite page)

Roll the dough through the pasta machine, one wedge at a time, until you have long, thin sheets. Lay a sheet on the metal tray, and press the dough into the depressions of the tray (photographs 13 and 14). Place a small amount of filling in each depression (photograph 15). Dip a finger in a glass of water and run it along the lines where the ravioli will be cut. Cover the filled squares with another sheet of dough, pressing it down along the wet edges to seal the two sheets (photograph 16).

Using a rolling pin (one comes with the tray), go over the dough (photograph 17). This seals the patties completely and cuts the squares. Turn the tray over, and the squares will fall out. Separate and reserve. Repeat until you have used all the dough.

Stuffed ravioli is boiled the same way as other pasta (page 1430). It can be served with meat sauce (page 1430), or dressed with butter and sprinkled generously with Parmesan cheese. It can also be baked in heavy cream and Parmesan cheese.

17: Go over the ravioli with a rolling pin to further seal the edges and to cut the squares apart.

1433

18: A spoonful of filling goes a long way in flavoring the tiny stuffed hats.

19: If you leave enough pasta dough projecting around the filling, you can make a tight edge seal.

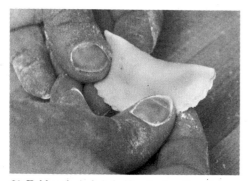

20: Fold each circle in half, and crimp the edges together between thumb and forefinger.

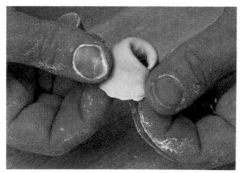

21: Press the points of the half circle together to seal the bite-sized pasta parcels into their characteristic shape.

An interesting way to serve *tortellini* is *alla panna* (with cream). The stuffed shapes are boiled, then covered with cream, and baked in a soufflé dish.

Tortellini alla Panna (with cream) (serves six)

Tortellini are also called *cappelletti* (little hats) because they have a cap-like appearance. An ancient legend says they resemble the navel of Venus. In any case, *tortellini* is a *Bolognese* specialty often served in broth (*brodo*). In Piedmont, a region of northwestern Italy, this dish is always garnished with a sprinkle of fresh truffles. Serve it with additional grated Parmesan cheese.

Ingredients:

1 batch of homemade pasta dough (page 1428)	1 cup freshly grated Parmesan cheese
1 cup heavy cream	½ stick (⅛ pound) butter

Stuffing:

1 cup cooked beef or chicken	½ cup freshly grated Parmesan cheese
½ cup cooked pork	1 egg, lightly beaten
4 slices *prosciutto*	Pinch of nutmeg
4 slices *mortadella*	2 sprigs parsley, minced
	Salt and pepper to taste

Cut the meat into chunks and put them in a blender, a few pieces at a time. Chop finely. Combine the rest of the stuffing ingredients and mix well. Set aside.

Making the Tortellini

Roll the dough into very thin sheets with the pasta machine (page 1429). Using a cookie cutter or a juice glass, cut rounds 2 inches in diameter. (This size is appropriate for *tortellini alla panna*, but if *tortellini* are served in broth, smaller rounds are better).

Put a small amount of stuffing on the center of each round of dough. Dip your finger in a glass of water, and run it around the edge of the circle. Fold the round in half and pinch the edges gently together (photograph 20). Next, press the points together (photograph 21) to make the peaked-hat shape.

Place the filled shapes on a pastry board or a clean kitchen towel until you are ready to cook them.

Cooking and Serving

For this recipe, the *tortellini* are boiled, then baked. Boil them in salted water for 8 minutes, drain in a colander, and pour them into a bowl.

Toss the *tortellini* with butter and Parmesan cheese, and transfer them to a buttered soufflé dish. Pour the cream over the pasta, dot the surface with butter, and bake for ½ hour at 375 degrees Fahrenheit. You can embellish this dish with a sprinkling of chopped *prosciutto* or a few spoonfuls of *Besciamella* sauce (page 1435).

This dish can be prepared in advance, but pour in the cream just before baking. The *tortellini* can also be served with a tomato sauce or in plain broth.

Lasagne Verdi alla Modenese (serves six)

This beautiful red, white, and green casserole comes from Modena, Italy, a city renowned for good food. The green *lasagne* is layered alternately with rich *Bolognese* sauce and cheese, then just before baking, a luscious, white *Besciamella* sauce is poured over the top. When preparing this casserole, the aim is to layer all the ingredients, not to drown the *lasagne* in sauce.

Ingredients:

1 batch of green pasta dough (page 1428)
2 cups *Bolognese* sauce (page 1430)
1 8-ounce can tomato sauce
½ cup heavy cream
Pinch of basil

Salt and pepper
8 ounces *mozzarella* cheese, cut in slivers
1 cup freshly grated Parmesan cheese
2 tablespoons butter
2½ cups *Besciamella* sauce (recipe below)

The ultimate *lasagne* comes bubbling from the oven topped with creamy *Besciamella* sauce.

Prepare the *Bolognese* sauce in advance, and roll and cut the *lasagne*. All the ingredients except the *Besciamella* sauce should be prepared and ready to work with before you cook the noodles.

Cutting Lasagne

Cut the dough in wedges and roll each wedge through the pasta machine (page 1429). The only difference between *lasagne* and *tagliatelle* sheets is that *lasagne* sheets should be as thin as you can make them. Using a paring knife or a toothed cutting wheel, cut the thin sheets into 9-by-2½-inch strips. This is the size I prefer, but lasagne can be longer or shorter, depending on your baking pan.

Cooking Sauce & Noodles

Place the *Bolognese* sauce (made in advance, page 1430) in a saucepan. Add the tomato sauce, basil, salt and pepper, and cook over medium heat. As soon as the mixture starts to boil, lower the heat and cover the saucepan. Let the sauce simmer very slowly for about an hour. At the last minute, stir in the cream and set aside. Butter a baking dish or a *lasagne* pan, and cover the bottom with a ladleful of red sauce. Try to skim off only the liquid, leaving the meat, so that it won't stick when baked. Set the pan aside and begin cooking the noodles.

Cook the *lasagne* a few at a time in boiling salted water for about 5 minutes or to your taste. Spread the noodles on a clean, damp cloth, and proceed with layering noodles, cheese, and sauce.

Layering and Finishing

Cover the prepared baking dish with a layer of cooked *lasagne* noodles. Dot with slivers of *mozzarella*, spread with some red sauce, and sprinkle with a handful of Parmesan cheese. Repeat with more layers of *lasagne*, *mozzarella*, and Parmesan cheese until you fill the pan.

At this point the *lasagne* can be refrigerated or frozen. Just before it is baked, add the *Besciamella* sauce (recipe below). Dot the surface with butter, sprinkle with Parmesan cheese, and bake the casserole for 45 minutes at 375 degrees Fahrenheit. Cool slightly before serving.

Besciamella Sauce

Ingredients:

3 tablespoons butter
3 tablespoons flour

3 cups hot milk
Salt
Pinch of nutmeg

Melt the butter in a saucepan over low heat. Before the butter browns, add the flour and stir with a wire whisk until well blended. Remove from heat and add the milk a little at a time until smooth. Return the saucepan to the heat, and stir constantly until the sauce thickens. Simmer for a few minutes; then add the salt and nutmeg. Note: *Besciamella* sauce should be a bit thin for *lasagne verdi*. If your sauce is too thick, thin it with more hot milk.

Some varieties of factory-made pasta that take their names from their shapes, origin, and use are, from left to right: *maccheroni*, *spaghettini*, *penne* (pens), *farfalle* (butterflies), long *fusilli* (twists), *rigatoni* (grooved tubes), short *fusilli*, *lumache* (snails), *cavatelli* (short curls), and *acini di pepe* (peppercorns).

Kitchen Favorites and Celebrations
Call it macaroni $ ◫ 林 ⚄

Homemade and factory-made pasta each have quite different tastes, but this does not mean that store-bought pasta should not be used. On the contrary, commercial macaroni products are used in some of the best Italian recipes. But as with home-made pasta, success depends on using fresh ingredients so the result is subtle, neither heavy with sauce nor overcooked—the most common failings. Be sure to follow the cooking instructions on the package. The recipes here, all using commercial pasta, range from the simplest spaghetti to a challenging macaroni casserole that is a specialty of many regions of Italy, including my own, Abruzzo. The first two recipes each serve six; the last serves eight. All the recipes can be doubled or tripled.

Spaghetti al Burro (serves six)
Ingredients:

1 pound of spaghetti

2 tablespoons coarse salt

1 stick (¼ pound) butter

6 tablespoons heavy cream (optional)

1 cup freshly grated Parmesan cheese

Warm a serving bowl and let the butter soften in it while the spaghetti cooks. Bring a 6-quart pot of cold water to a brisk boil. Add the spaghetti and salt and stir with a long fork. Cover and cook the spaghetti at a steady boil, stirring occasionally, for about 15 minutes or as the package directs. When it is done, it should be *al dente*, slightly resistant to the bite. Remove from the heat, add a large glass of cold water to the pot, and drain the spaghetti in a colander. Reserve some of the cooking water. Put the spaghetti into the prepared bowl and toss gently but thoroughly until all the butter is melted. Add the cream and a handful of freshly grated Parmesan cheese. If the spaghetti is too dry, add some of the reserved water. Serve with additional grated cheese.

This butter sauce can also be used for *linguine*, *vermicelli*, *tagliatelle*, *fettuccine*, and all kinds of small stuffed pasta.

Fusilli alla Franca Falcone (serves six)
The spiral pasta called *fusilli* comes in a short form (about 1½ inches long) and in a long form. Either can be used. This dish is different from any other using pasta and tuna. It is a specialty of Sorrento where my cousin Franca Falcone learned this way of preparing it from a local fisherman, who used canned tuna instead of fresh fish during the winter months.

Ingredients:

1 pound *fusilli*

1 6-ounce can of Italian tuna fish in olive oil (it is essential that Italian tuna fish be used, not a substitute)

1 8-ounce can tomato sauce

1 clove garlic

1 tablespoon chopped capers

20 small black olives, pitted and cut in circles

Handful of chopped, fresh parsley

Drain the oil from the tuna into a heavy saucepan. Add the garlic and warm over medium heat. As soon as the garlic starts to fry, add the tuna and let it cook for several minutes until it is hot. Add the tomato sauce, lower the heat, and simmer gently for about 20 minutes.

Cook the *fusilli* in rapidly boiling salted water according to the package directions. While the pasta is cooking, add the olives and capers to the sauce. Simmer until the pasta is ready. Mix the *fusilli* with the sauce, and serve it sprinkled with a handful of chopped parsley.

Timballo di Maccheroni alla Nonnina (serves eight)

This *maccheroni* casserole is my grandmother's translation of the traditional one. In our family, it is affectionately called *alla nonnina*, after our name for her. She made it for birthdays and other special occasions. It can be made in one large casserole or in individual casseroles that look attractive when unmolded.

Ingredients:

1½ pounds *maccheroni* or *penne*
½ stick (⅛ pound) butter
2 eggs lightly beaten
2½ quarts *ragù* sauce (page 1431)
2 cups freshly grated Parmesan cheese
3 hard-boiled eggs, sliced in rounds

1 16-ounce *mozzarella* cheese, sliced
4 slices *prosciutto*, chopped
1 cup tiny meat balls (recipe below)
1 cup sliced fresh mushrooms sautéed in butter
Unflavored breadcrumbs

Meat balls
Ingredients:

½ pound of ground meat (use a mixture of beef, pork, and veal)
1 teaspoon chopped parsley

Pinch of ground sage
Salt and pepper to taste
Butter

Mix all ingredients and make tiny meat balls. Fry in butter until brown.

Have all the ingredients ready before cooking the pasta. Butter a large casserole or eight individual casseroles, and dust with unflavored bread crumbs. Sauté the sliced mushrooms in butter. Cook the pasta according to the package directions but keeping it quite *al dente*.

After the pasta is cooked, drain it well and return it to the pot. Add the beaten eggs, toss, and let the mixture rest a moment before adding four or five ladles of *ragù* sauce and a handful of Parmesan cheese. Toss gently but thoroughly.

In the prepared casserole, make a layer of *maccheroni* or *penne*. (The *penne*, literally pens, are short lengths of macaroni). Sprinkle with Parmesan cheese. Distribute some of the *mozzarella* slices, meatballs, sliced eggs, *prosciutto* and mushrooms over the *maccheroni*. Ladle some of the *ragù* sauce over this, and repeat the layering until you have filled the casserole.

Top the casserole with sauce, sprinkle with additional Parmesan cheese, and dust lightly with bread crumbs. Dot with butter and bake at 350 degrees Fahrenheit for about 15 minutes. When it's done, the top will look crusty.

Let the *timballo* set for 10 to 15 minutes. For individual casseroles, loosen the sides with a knife, turn upside down, and unmold gently.

PATCHWORK
All Pieced Together

Beth Gutcheon is the author of The Perfect Patchwork Primer. *Jeffrey Gutcheon has taught architectural design at Massachusetts Institute of Technology. He participated in the design of the Hearthstone Plaza in Boston and has designed recording studios, private homes, and the bandshell in Londonderry, New Hampshire. Jeffrey is also a professional piano player. Quilts by the Gutcheons have been exhibited at the Pioneer Crafts Festival, Bear Run, Pennsylvania; the Museum of American Folk Art, New York; the Great American Quilt Festival, New York; Webb-Parsons Gallery, Bedford, New York; the Living Arts Center Gallery, Dayton, Ohio; the Galerie Mikro, Berlin; and the American Quilt Exhibition, Tokyo.*

Sleeping in a brass bed under a warm old-fashioned patchwork quilt may seem like a scene from the past, but with the revival of ancestral crafts, making a quilt has become very much a part of today's scene as well.

Patchwork quilts were very popular with the American colonists and westward-moving pioneers. Quilting, the technique of joining layers of fabric with lines of stitching, had been used since the Middle Ages, but it was particularly appreciated in bed coverings during the cold New England winters that the colonists encountered. Patchwork, the technique of making a large piece of fabric by sewing smaller pieces together, made the most of scarce and expensive goods. Whatever fabric the colonists and frontier families had, they used and reused. Clothing and bedding were used until they all but fell apart; then they were cut up and the scraps that could be salvaged were sewn together to form patchwork. The earliest colonial quilts were probably crazy quilts, a form of patchwork having no particular pattern, made of scraps of random size, shape, and color. The fact that such quilts could be beautiful made them a testimony to the taste as well as the frugality of colonial women. Quiltmaking played a large role in the social life of colonial families. The demands of rural life left little time for social gatherings without a purpose; so friendships were extended and maintained through events with a practical goal such as barn raisings and quilting bees. When a patchwork top was completed, a woman would stretch it on a quilting frame and invite her neighbors to help with the quilting stitches.

Pattern in Patchwork

Quiltmaking changed with changing times. As cotton fabric became more available, scraps could be cut into shapes to give a geometric pattern to the patchwork tops. Quiltmaking techniques had been brought from England, but the idea of sewing lap-sized blocks that could be completed individually, then sewn together, was peculiarly American. The design in each block was repeated to make an overall pattern in the quilt top. This was a change from the style of European patchwork, which had designs formed by the repetition of a single shape.

Quilt patterns became family treasures that were passed along from generation to generation long after the original quilts were worn out. Starting about the middle of the eighteenth century, two kinds of quilts were produced. Utility quilts were made for daily use; heirloom quilts, including many that can still be seen in restorations and museums, were carefully planned and painstakingly executed masterpieces. Just the fact that they have survived suggests that their owners thought they were too good to use.

During the Victorian era, toward the end of the nineteenth century, opulent fabrics such as silk and velvet came into vogue for clothing, and were used to make spectacular quilts as well. The crazy quilt made a comeback, but in a luxurious and quite impractical form as shown in the *Grand Army Quilt* (on page 1440) made by Minnie Sherman around 1880. It has no batting because the variety of fabrics used made quilting quite impossible; the Victorian quilt had become a purely decorative object made to be admired.

Minnie Sherman was the great-grandmother of Beth Gutcheon (one of the craftspeople for the eminently practical patchwork projects shown here). Beth designed the pillow (page 1443), the vest (page 1449), and the *Cynthia Ann Dancing* quilt (page 1452); her husband Jeffrey designed the crib quilt (page 1447) and the tote bag (page 1451).

This tradition-based but contemporary quilt resembles a square dance viewed from above. Called *Cynthia Ann Dancing*, the quilt is built on the design of one block (in the center) whose colors drop out until only the red and white pieces are left in the border blocks. This quilt is the work of Beth Gutcheon; instructions for making it start on page 1452.

Piecing by hand

If you want to hand-piece blocks with straight seams, rather than sewing them by machine, sew the smallest pieces to the adjacent pieces first; then add the next size, and so on until the entire block is pieced. Use a No. 8 sharp needle and quilting thread. Start each line with a knot and make very small running stitches. End with a knot and press each seam as described in the machine-stitching directions with the projects that follow.

Curved seams

Much more difficult than straight seams are curved seams, which should be attempted only by experienced sewers. If the design you are using has curved seams, there are several ways to achieve smoother seams. Before you sew one curved piece to another, carefully clip the convex (outside) curve at ¾-inch intervals from the edge almost to the sewing line. Pin the pieces together between the clip marks, starting in the center of the curve and working out to each end, smoothing the seam as you pin. Be careful not to pull the fabric—this might tear it at the clip marks. Sew the pieces together by hand or machine following the curve as precisely as possible. Press the seams open with a steam iron.

The *Grand Army Quilt*, made by Minnie Sherman of western Pennsylvania around 1880, is a crazy-quilt pattern done in the silks and velvets favored by the flamboyant Victorians. It is lavishly decorated with silk crewel embroidery, military insignia embroidered in gold, eagles, flags, stars, sheaves of wheat, and bits of ribbons from her father's Civil War medals. Thus a quilt style founded in rigorous Colonial economy became a spectacular, if unusable, work of art.

Getting Started

A quilt is a bedcover made of three layers: a top, a filling, and a backing, all usually held together with quilting stitches. The top, which is made first, is the decorative part (in these projects, the patchwork, although quilts can also be appliqued). The key to beautiful patchwork lies in choosing fabrics that go well together when cut into small pieces and placed in a particular pattern. For inexperienced patchwork-makers, this is largely a trial-and-error operation, but there are a few guidelines that help. For example, it is better not to make a first project from salvaged scraps because that limits your choice of fabric too drastically. Patchwork is always an experiment—one never really knows how well the colors, prints, and shapes will combine. So it is a good idea to gain experience by starting with a small project such as a pillow or a crib quilt. Remember, too, that the size of any project is measured not only in inches but in hours. The work involved in creating patchwork is determined by the number of pieces required. Of course, a simple four-patch design (see page 1442) will rapidly become boring. So you need to compromise somewhere between the simplest and the most complex.

How much time you are willing to spend on the project may determine whether you sew by hand or machine. Sewing by hand is much slower but it makes the project portable. Sewing by machine is faster and more uniform. The patchwork tops for all of the projects that follow were sewn by machine. The *Cynthia Ann Dancing* quilt and the pillow were quilted by hand; the crib quilt and the tote bag were quilted by machine.

Design

When you first look at a patchwork quilt, you see the whole design, not the individual blocks. When you make a quilt, however, you start with one block and by repeating or changing it, you create the design. To start a patchwork project, you can choose a geometric block from one of the projects that follow, from the traditional blocks (see page 1442), or from those you have designed yourself. To see how the design will work, draw several blocks together and fill them in with colored pencils or crayons. You can repeat one color combination in every block, or you can change it as you like. Experiment until you are pleased with the result. Save the colored sketch you like best and use it as a guide when you buy fabric.

Some traditional patchwork patterns are worked in vertical strips rather than in square blocks; two such patterns are *Picket Fence* and *Lightning Strips* (page 1442). A contemporary strip pattern has been used for the tote bag on page 1451. Strip patterns can be designed in much the same way as block patterns. Draw one strip that you like; then repeat it several times and add the colors to see how it will look as an overall design.

Fabric

Traditional patchwork was made of calico, a brightly colored cotton print that eventually faded to the muted colors you can see in antique quilts. Cotton is still the best choice—the more readily available synthetics do not have the properties that work well in patchwork. Choose pure cotton, or a polyester-cotton or rayon-cotton blend. It should be shirt weight and colorfast. If you are not sure a fabric is colorfast, wash it by itself before you use it. Avoid permanent-press fabrics; they have a stiff finish that is difficult to work with. You may want to try corduroy or velveteen to get a contemporary look, but do not mix fabrics of different weights because the resulting patchwork will not wear well. Choose your fabrics carefully, and the patchwork will last a lifetime. Buy backing fabric at the same time if it is to be color-coordinated with the patchwork pieces. However, white muslin, which wears well and is inexpensive, makes a good backing fabric for most projects. When you have purchased all the fabrics you need, preshrink them before cutting by washing them in warm water.

Calculating Fabric Needs

Most fabric suitable for patchwork comes in 45-inch widths. To determine how much of a specific fabric you will need, first decide how many pieces of what shape will be cut from it (Craftnotes, right). Put two pieces of tape 45 inches apart on a table to represent the fabric width. Lay the first pattern—called a template—between the tapes and beside one of them; then move it to see how many times it will fit in a row across to the other tape. If the template fits 15 times but you need 20 pieces, for example, you will need to buy enough fabric for two rows of the template-traced shapes. If the template measures 4 inches high (including seam allowance), you will need 8 inches of 45-inch-wide fabric. Buy a little extra, say 9 inches or ¼ yard. If more than one shape is to be cut from one fabric, repeat this procedure and add that amount to get the total needed.

Other Materials

You will also need batting and thread. Batting, the fluffy middle layer of the quilt, was originally cotton, but polyester is generally used today. It has many of the qualities of cotton batting, but since it comes in large sheets, it requires fewer quilting stitches to hold it in place. It is strong enough to withstand constant use and machine washing without becoming lumpy. The best thread to use for machine piecing is cotton-wrapped polyester because it is very strong. For hand sewing, use quilting thread, a strong cotton thread that has been treated with silicone to prevent accidental knotting. (The same effect was achieved by Colonial women when they coated cotton thread with beeswax.)

CRAFTNOTES: MAKING TEMPLATES

A template is a pattern that you use to mark fabric pieces that will be cut out for any patchwork design. You need one template for each shape and size in your design, but not for each color. Since you may be tracing around the template many times, it should be cut from lightweight cardboard, such as posterboard (available at art supply stores). Each template must be accurate; any variation in angle or width of the seam allowance can throw a block out of line; this, in turn, will throw the overall design out of line. To make templates, you will need: graph paper; sharp pencils; a draftsman's triangle of clear plastic; a ruler; glue; lightweight cardboard; and scissors.

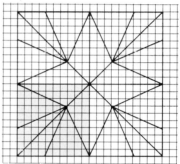

To insure accuracy, draw one complete block on the graph paper in the size you want the finished block to be. Draw it carefully and precisely, using the lines on the graph paper as guides. Make sure all the lines meet where they should; a slight error in the template will be multiplied into a large error in the quilt.

From the complete block drawn on graph paper, cut one of each of the shapes for which you will need a template. If the same shape is repeated in different colors, you will need only one. Cut carefully, following the graph lines and keeping the angles sharp. Glue these shapes onto the posterboard leaving enough space between them for seam allowances.

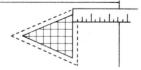

To add these seam allowances, mark a dashed line ¼ inch beyond each side of the graph paper. This line will be the actual cutting line to be traced on the fabric. The graph paper represents the finished size of the patchwork piece after the seams have been sewn. Cut out each template along the dashed cutting line using sharp scissors.

A SELECTION OF TRADITIONAL PATCHWORK PATTERNS

4-Patch Checkerboard

Picket Fence

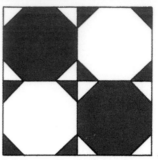
Rob Peter to Pay Paul

Drunkard's Path

9-Patch Checkerboard

Lightning Strips

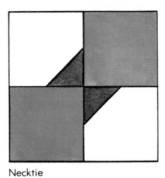
Necktie

Eastern Star

Duck's Foot—Bear's Paw

Log Cabin

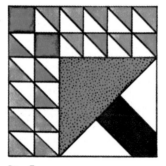
Pine Tree

Sunburst

Variable Star

House

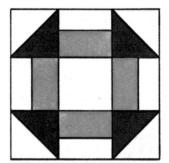
Sherman's March

Baby Blocks

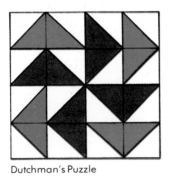
Dutchman's Puzzle

Pieced Star

Orange Peel

Grandmother's Flower Garden

From Beth Gutcheon's collection of patchwork blocks.

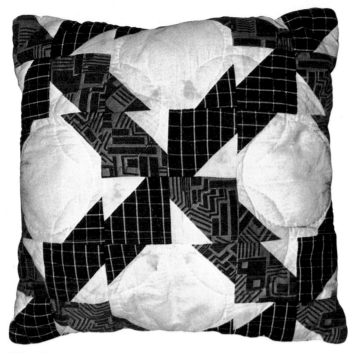

This pillow cover, with its intersecting bolts of lightning, is made with two different blocks arranged in checkerboard fashion. Different fabrics are used on the front and back; to emphasize this difference, two designs are used for the quilting stitches (page 1446).

A

Figure A: To assemble the pillow cover, arrange the nine blocks in the order shown.

Needlecrafts
Streak-of-lightning pillow

The patchwork pillow design pictured above seems to bear two streaks of lightning that cross at the center. The pillow is 15 inches square and each side includes nine pieced blocks—five pinwheels and four octagonals. These are alternated checkerboard-fashion as they are sewn together (Figure A). The design is identical on both sides of the pillow, but front and back fabrics are different.

To make the pillow you will need less than ⅛ yard each of four different printed fabrics each 45 inches wide; 1 yard of white muslin; cotton-wrapped polyester thread for piecing; No. 8 sharp needle and quilting thread for quilting; ½ yard of polyester batting; and a 15-inch knife-edge pillow form.

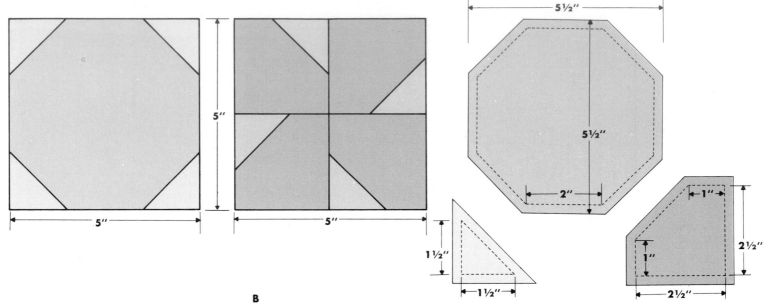

B

Figure B: The two blocks that are used to make the patchwork pillow are formed with the three templates shown. The triangle in both blocks is the same size so only one template is needed. To construct these templates, see the Craftnotes, page 1441.

The first step in patchwork is to draw and cut the templates (Figure B and Craftnotes, page 1441). Because precision in cutting each piece of fabric is important to the overall design, trace and cut each piece separately. Lay the first template on the wrong side of the fabric next to the selvage (finished) edge. Outline it with a nylon-tip pen (photograph 1). A nylon-tip pen mark will show more clearly than a pencil on dark fabrics, and such a pen does not get dull or require pressure to make a mark. But a sharp No. 2 pencil is better for marking white muslin or light fabric. Continue tracing the template, making rows of patches across the fabric until you have traced as many pieces as you need. Cut out each piece separately with sharp fabric shears. When all the pieces are cut, sort them into piles according to shape and color. (This is especially important when you work on a large patchwork project calling for many pieces in several shapes.)

Although your fabrics may vary greatly in color, one color of thread can be used for all the stitching. The cotton-wrapped polyester recommended comes in only one weight. Use a No. 14 needle in your sewing machine and set the stitch length at 10 per inch. To make a block, sew the smallest units first followed by the next size; then sew these together until the block is finished. In this case, the smallest units in the pillow are the white triangles; these are sewn onto the five-sided printed pieces. Sew these together, matching seam edges carefully (photograph 2). There is no need to backstitch or knot the thread because each seam will be crossed by another seam that will lock it. Sewing one small seam after another is time-consuming; you can speed the job by arranging all the pieces with the same seam in a row with right sides facing on each pair. As you finish one seam, feed the next one under the presser foot. When you are finished, clip the threads that join the pieces (photograph 3). After these units are joined, fold the seams to the dark-fabric side and press (photograph 4). (The seam allowance might show through on the light-fabric side.) Always press seams immediately after they are sewn so they don't get caught out of place in the next seam. The shape that results from joining the first two pieces is a square. Sew these squares to each other following the arrangement diagramed in Figure B.

With smaller pieces, you could position them simply by lining up the edges. But with larger units, as when you sew the two-block rectangles together to get a larger square, it is important that the internal seams meet exactly (photograph 5). It is a good idea to pin these rectangles together so the seams stay matched while you are stitching them. Put the pin through both seams (photograph 6) and leave it in place as you sew right over it (photograph 7). Press the seams, and this pinwheel block is finished (photograph 8).

1: On a single layer of fabric, trace around each template with a nylon-tip pen containing washable ink, as many times as the shape is needed.

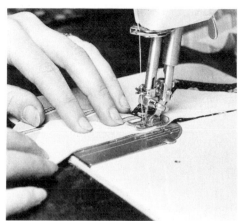

2: Stitch the smallest units to their adjacent pieces with a ¼-inch seam. Save time by stitching units of the same size in one operation.

3: To separate stitched pairs, just clip the thread that joins them. It is not necessary to knot the seams; another seam will lock each of these.

4: After each seam is sewn, press the seam allowance, turning it to the dark side of the seam so it will not show through the lighter fabric.

5: To make sure the internal seams of adjacent units line up neatly, carefully place one on top of another, matching the seams exactly.

6: Pin the assembled units together, putting the pin directly into the seams so they cannot shift position as you sew them.

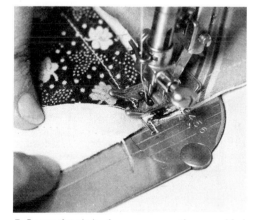

7: Leave the pin in place as you sew the assembled units together. Be careful not to hit the pin with the sewing machine needle.

8: Iron the block, pressing the seam allowance to the dark side of the fabric where possible so it won't show through the lighter fabric.

The second block is made by sewing four small triangles to an octagonal piece thus making a square (Figure B). Press all seams. When you have completed five pinwheel blocks and four octagon blocks, you are ready to sew these larger squares together to complete one side of the pillow, arranging the blocks as shown in Figure A. Make another nine-square patch for the back of the pillow.

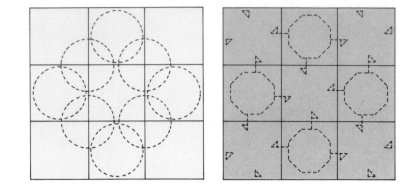

C

Figure C: The blue and red side of the pillow is quilted according to the pattern of interlocking circles (left); the quilting stitches on the beige and maroon side outline the white areas (right).

The pillow cover is now ready to be quilted. The quilting stitches hold patchwork, batting, and muslin backing together in a single unit. Lay the patchwork front and back on a flat surface, and with a pencil, draw a quilting pattern on the right side of the patchwork. In this case, a design of interlocking circles is used on the red-and-blue side (Figure C). On the maroon-and-beige side, quilting stitches outline the white areas forming octagons and triangles (Figure C). To assemble the elements for quilting, lay the backing fabric right side down on a flat work surface. Put the batting on top of this, smoothing it carefully so there are no wrinkles. Carefully place the patchwork on top of the batting right side up. Make sure that there are no wrinkles in any of the layers; then pin the layers together, putting pins where stitches will be. Use plenty of pins and check frequently to make sure that no layer has shifted out of alignment. To quilt by hand, thread a No. 8 sharp needle with a 15-inch length of quilting thread and knot one end. Bring the needle up from the muslin backing through all three layers. Pull gently but firmly on the thread until the knot passes through the backing and lodges in the batting. In this way all the

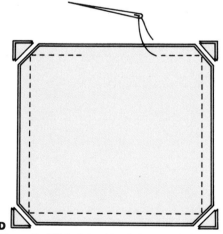

Figure D: With right sides facing, stitch the patchwork pillow's front and back together by sewing along the sides, leaving an 8-inch opening at the top. Trim the corners as illustrated and turn the cover right side out.

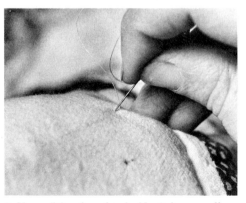

9: Use quilting thread and a No. 8 sharp needle when you quilt by hand. Bring the thread up from the back and down through all three layers—patchwork, batting, and backing fabric.

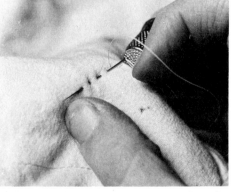

10: Make small running stitches that go through all three layers of the quilt; the purpose of quilting is to hold the layers together and to prevent the batting from shifting.

knots are concealed. Make sure you are going through all three layers (photograph 9) as you make small running stitches (photograph 10), following the penciled guideline. Keep one hand behind the work so you can make sure the needle penetrates all thicknesses. To end a line of stitching, knot the thread before the last stitch; now take the last stitch, pulling the knot through to the inside. Run the needle on the inside a bit to leave the tail of thread where it will not show. Quilt both sides of the pillow the same way. To complete the pillow, put right sides of the quilted patchwork together, keeping the edges even, and sew around three sides with a sewing machine or by hand (Figure D). Turn the pillow cover right side out and insert the pillow form. To finish the remaining seam, fold the raw edges to the inside and sew them closed by hand with tiny stitches.

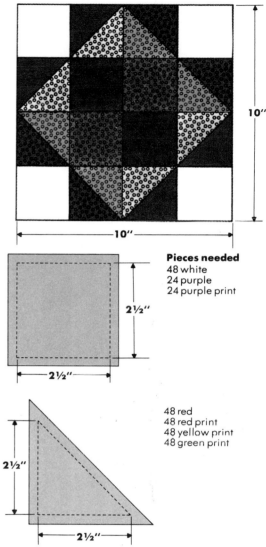

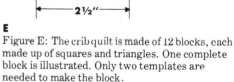

Pieces needed
48 white
24 purple
24 purple print

48 red
48 red print
48 yellow print
48 green print

E

In this crib quilt, the corners of four blocks form a white square the same size as the solid purple and purple-print squares at the center. Thus, the quilt looks like a plaid rather than a repeat of one block.

Figure E: The crib quilt is made of 12 blocks, each made up of squares and triangles. One complete block is illustrated. Only two templates are needed to make the block.

Needlecrafts
Dynamic crib quilt $ ⏱ 👤 🧵

Crib quilts are usually made in pastel colors—not so the one pictured above, made with vivid red and purple blocks. Although the quilt is a simple repeat of one block, just where the block begins and ends is not distinguishable at first. The design appears to be a red-and-purple plaid on a white background, but the white squares are actually the corners of four blocks whose centers consist of the four purple squares (Figure E).

The finished quilt measures 33½ by 43½ inches with the binding and includes 12 blocks, each 10 inches square. To make the quilt, you will need: 1½ yards of white muslin (½ yard for the patchwork pieces plus 1 yard for the backing); ¾ yard of solid purple fabric (¼ yard for the pieces plus ½ yard for the binding); ¼ yard each of purple print, solid red, red print, yellow print and green print fabric; cotton-wrapped polyester thread for sewing the pieces; invisible nylon thread for the quilting stitches; and 1 yard of polyester batting.

This design is made of two shapes, a square and a right triangle that is half the square. To make the two templates, draw a 2½-inch square on graph paper following the lines for accuracy. Then draw a second identical square and divide it in half with a diagonal line. Cut out the square and one triangle and paste them on posterboard. Mark the seam allowance ¼ inch outside the graph-paper pattern and cut out the posterboard templates on the outer line. Trace around the templates and cut out as many patchwork pieces of each color as are indicated in Figure E. When all the pieces are cut, sort them into piles according to size and shape. This will keep all the pieces organized and make piecing the blocks easier.

Assembling the Patchwork

The patchwork is assembled the same way as was described for the pillow cover (pages 1443 to 1446). To begin, make one complete block to hang near your sewing machine; it will serve as a guide for assembling the rest of the blocks. Start by sewing triangles to each other to make squares; then sew the squares together until the block is assembled. Piece each quarter of the block; then join the quarters. For example, starting with the bottom left quarter as diagramed in Figure E, sew the yellow print triangles to the red triangles and press the seams. You now have two squares. To the red side of one square, sew a white square, and to the yellow print side of the third square, sew a purple square. Press the seams. Join the two resulting rectangles, carefully matching the center seams so the squares formed of the triangles are diagonally opposite each other. Press the seams, and one quarter of the first block is complete. Piece the other three quarters the same way following the color guide in Figure E. To assemble the four quarters into a block, first sew two quarters together with a purple print square adjoining a solid purple square. Repeat with the other two quarters. Press the seams. Join the two halves, again matching the purple print squares to the solid purple squares, and press the seams. One block is complete with a four-patch purple center and four white corners. Hang this block in your work area for guidance, and use an assembly-line procedure in sewing the remainder of the blocks.

To join the blocks, place two blocks with right sides facing and carefully match all seams within the blocks. Sew these together and press the seam. Make three rows containing four blocks; then sew the rows together, again matching the seams. Press these long seams and the patchwork top is complete (Figure F).

Cut the backing fabric and the batting 30½ by 40½ inches (30-by-40-inch top plus ¼-inch seam allowances on all edges). Place the backing fabric face down on a flat work surface. Smooth the batting on top of this so there are no wrinkles. Place the patchwork on top, smoothing the layers and keeping the edges even. Pin the quilt through all three layers using as many pins as are needed to keep the layers from shifting. Thread your sewing machine with invisible nylon thread. The quilting pattern is a simple one. Imagine that the patchwork has stripes of red and purple running down and across a white background. The quilting stitches are placed ½ inch to either side of these colored stripes. They are most visible in the white areas. Machine stitch on both sides of the three stripes running the length of the quilt; then turn the quilt one quarter turn and machine stitch on both sides of the four shorter stripes.

Binding the Edges

The edges of the quilt are bound with solid purple fabric. Cut eight 2¼-inch strips (1¾-inch binding plus two ¼-inch seam allowances), four strips 34 inches long and four strips 40½ inches long. With right sides facing, sew two of the short strips together along one long side. Fold this strip along the seam so the wrong sides are facing, and press along the seam (this seam will be the edge of the quilt). Repeat for the other three pairs of strips. Open one long strip and lay it face down along the quilt edge. Matching the edges, sew the strip to the quilt, and press the seam open. Repeat on the other long side. Then sew the shorter strips onto the quilt the same way, centering the strip so it covers the sides of the quilt and the binding. Fold the bindings around the edge so the center seam becomes the outer edge of the quilt. Attach the other side of the binding to the back of the quilt, folding the raw edges under ¼ inch and taking small stitches by hand.

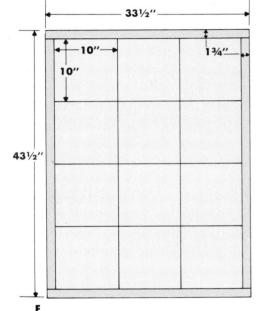

F

Figure F: The 12 blocks of the crib quilt are assembled as illustrated. After quilting, the edges are finished with binding.

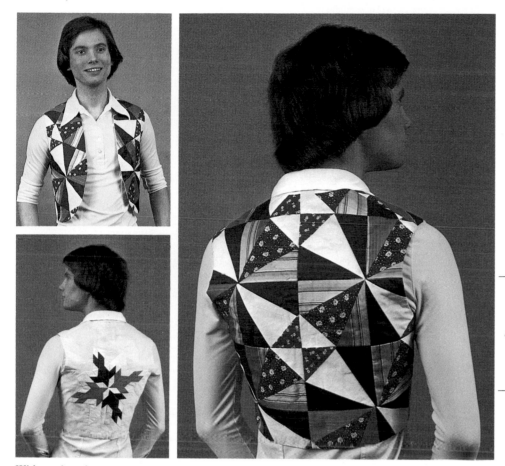

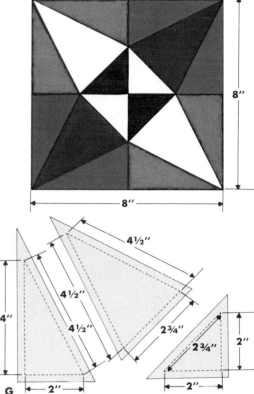

With patchwork, you can choose two designs that you like and use them to make a reversible vest—with a patchwork fabric on one side (right and top left) and one block appliquéd in the center back of the reverse side (bottom left). This vest makes a handsome addition to anyone's wardrobe.

Figure G: The *Tippecanoe* block used in the vest is a traditional patchwork block which is made of three triangles of different sizes. Patterns for the templates are shown above (see Craftnotes, page 1441). Patchwork fabric made by repeating this block is used to make an overall pattern for one side of the reversible vest.

Needlecrafts
Reversible vest
$ ● ♟ ✄

Patchwork can be used for clothing, but you must make enough yardage of patchwork so you can use it as a fabric, cutting out only what you need to make a particular garment. The garment should be lined to keep the patchwork seam allowances from fraying. A reversible vest for a man or a woman is a good patchwork project because you can use two different designs, one on each side, and the result will be two vests in one. This patchwork is not quilted, however, because that would make it too cumbersome to handle. Two traditional patchwork designs were used in the vest pictured above: *Tippecanoe* blocks (Figure G) form the overall patchwork on one side, and one patch of *Dove in the Window* (Figure H) is appliquéd on the back of the reverse side.

To start, buy a vest pattern in the appropriate size, or trace a commercially made vest to make a pattern. Lay the front and back pattern pieces end-to-end and estimate the amount of patchwork fabric needed. You will need a piece of fabric as long as the two pattern pieces and twice the width because the back pattern piece will be placed on the fold (so the back will be one piece) and the front pattern will be cut out twice. You will need the same amount of white muslin for the reverse side. The *Tippecanoe* block is 8 inches square; so you will need to make enough 8-inch blocks to equal your total patchwork fabric needs.

Make templates (Figures G and H) following the graph-paper method described in the Craftnotes (page 1441). Use the templates as guides while you mark and cut out as many pieces of each color as you need for the total amount of fabric required.

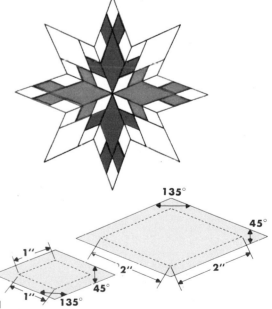

Figure H: *Dove in the Window*, another traditional pattern, is made of a small and a large diamond. Patterns for the templates are shown above (see Craftnotes, page 1441). One block with this motif is appliquéd to the back of the reverse side of the vest as shown in the photograph.

1449

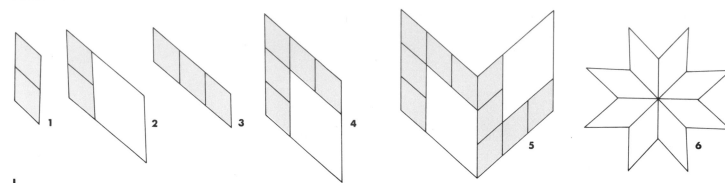

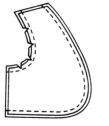

I

Figure I: To assemble the star-shaped motif, *Dove in the Window*, using only straight seams, sew two small diamonds together (step 1). Sew these to one side of the large diamond (step 2). Sew three small diamonds together in a row (step 3); attach them to the other side of the larger diamond (step 4). This completes one point of the star; repeat seven more times. Alternate the points so the large diamond points inward on one and outward on the next (step 5). Continue until four points are sewn together for one half the star; repeat for the other half. Finally, sew the two halves together at the middle (step 6).

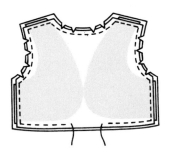

K

Figure K: To start assembling the vest, lay the patchwork front piece on the matching muslin lining piece, right sides facing. Sew around the armhole, then down the front from the shoulder to the side leaving shoulder and side seams open. Clip notches in the armhole curve and turn right side out. Repeat for the other front piece.

L

Figure L: The second step in assembling the vest is to lay the muslin back piece right side up with the appliquéd block facing you. On top of this, place the two front pieces, patchwork side up, matching the shoulder and side seams. Pin these seams. The muslin armhole seam allowance will extend ⅝ inch beyond the finished armhole seam on the patchwork fronts. On the top of the muslin back and the front pieces, place the patchwork back piece, right side down, matching all the edges. Join the back pieces by sewing around them ⅝ inch in from the edge, catching the fronts at the shoulder and side seams only. Leave about 5 inches open at the bottom edge.

To start a *Tippecanoe* block, sew one of the smallest triangles to the shortest side of a triangle that forms a star point. Press the seam. Sew a right triangle to each side of the star-point triangle. The result is a square that is one quarter of the block. Repeat to make three more squares following the color guide in Figure G. Sew two quarters together matching the small triangles. Repeat for the other two quarters. Press the seams. Sew these two rectangles—again matching the small triangles. Press the seam. This completes one block of *Tippecanoe*. Repeat to make as many more blocks as you need. Sew the blocks together following the directions given for the crib quilt on pages 1447 and 1448. Press all seams, and the patchwork fabric is complete.

For the star that is appliquéd on the back of the vest, make two diamond-shaped templates (Figure H), following the Craftnotes on page 1441. Cut out the number of pieces in each color. To sew them together using only straight seams, follow the sequence in Figure I. Turn the raw edges under ¼ inch and press. You will appliqué the star to the center of the muslin back using small hand stitches.

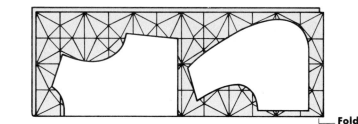

J   **Fold**

Figure J: To calculate the amount of patchwork fabric you need to make a vest of a certain size, lay the front and back pattern pieces end to end. You will need that length and twice that width.

To cut out the vest, fold the patchwork fabric in half lengthwise along the center of one square. Put the center line of the back pattern piece on that fold so one complete block will be centered on the back of the vest. Place the front pattern piece next to it (Figure J). Cut out the front in two pieces and the back in one piece. Then cut out matching front and back pieces from the muslin, and appliqué the star to the center of the back piece.

To assemble the vest, put a patchwork front piece on a muslin front piece with right sides facing (Figure K). Sew them together, stitching around the armhole and along the front and bottom edges as illustrated. Leave the side and shoulder open. Clip the armhole curve outside the sewing line. Repeat for the other front half. Turn both right side out and press.

The next step is to sandwich the front pieces between the back pieces. Lay the muslin back piece right side up so the appliquéd star faces you. On top of this, put the two front pieces, patchwork side up. Pin the shoulder and side seams. The armhole seam allowance of the back piece will extend ⅝ inch beyond the finished armhole seam of the front pieces. Place the patchwork back on top of this, right side down (Figure L), matching the edges of the back pieces. Sew around the vest as shown, stitching the front pieces to the back pieces at the sides and shoulders only. Put your hand inside to make sure that the front pieces are free at the bottom edge and at the armholes. Leave about 5 inches open at the bottom edge. Clip the armhole curves, turn the vest right side out, and press it. Turn in the raw edges of the 5-inch opening at the bottom of the back and sew it closed with small stitches.

Needlecrafts
Kaleidoscopic tote bag

The brightly colored and commodious carryall shown below is made by strip patching, a form of patchwork in which strips rather than blocks are pieced together. Each strip is the same: two small triangles and one large one are sewn together to form a rectangle that is repeated five times down the length of the strip (Figure M). The chevron effect is achieved by matching the color of the small triangles in adjacent strips. The dramatic change in the central color of each strip gives the bag a different look every way you turn it. The bag measures 18¾ by 15 by 7½ inches. To make it you will need: ¼ yard of 12 different fabrics for the patchwork pieces; 1 yard of printed fabric for the lining; 1 yard of muslin for the interlining; cotton-wrapped polyester thread for piecing; invisible nylon thread for machine quilting; and 1 yard of polyester batting. This will leave enough fabric from the patchwork for the bottom and the handles. Make templates for the two triangles (Figure M) following the directions in the Craftnotes (page 1441). Trace around the templates and cut out as many triangles of each color as are indicated in Figure M. Stack the fabric triangles by size and color for each strip. A strip patch is constructed the same way as a block patch. First sew the small right triangles on the sides of the large triangle to make a rectangle. Press the seams. Repeat four more times; then sew the rectangles together so the large triangles point downward. Press the seams, and one strip is completed. Repeat this procedure for the other five strips. Then, matching small triangles of the same color, sew four strips together to make the front and sides, two strips together to make the back.

To add a bottom to the tote bag, cut a piece of lining fabric 8 by 15½ inches and sew it to the bottom edge of the front and back pieces using a ¼-inch seam allowance (Figure M). For quilting, cut the batting and the muslin backing to the same T-shape as the patchwork. Stack the three layers with the batting between the muslin and the patchwork. With the patchwork right side up on top, pin the three layers together. Thread the sewing machine with invisible nylon thread. To quilt, follow the shape of the large triangles keeping the stitches ½ inch inside the edge. Outline the five large triangles in each strip.

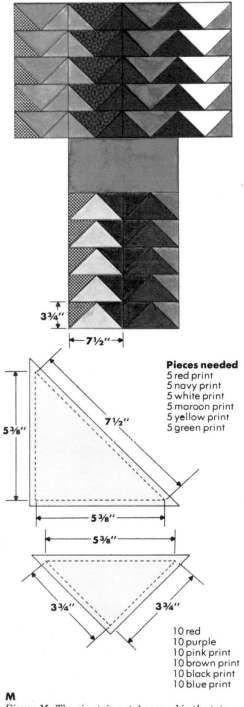

Pieces needed
5 red print
5 navy print
5 white print
5 maroon print
5 yellow print
5 green print

10 red
10 purple
10 pink print
10 brown print
10 black print
10 blue print

M
Figure M: The six strip patches used in the tote bag are arranged as shown at the top. Each strip is made of five rectangles containing three triangles, one large and two small. Patterns to use in making these templates are immediately above (see Craftnotes, page 1441).

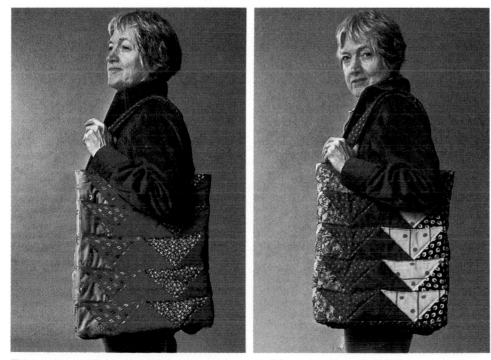

This tote bag can fit your mood and your attire because of the variety of colors used. Every way you turn the bag, you see a new color combination.

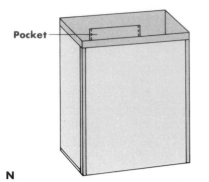

N

Figure N: Fabric cut to the same T-shape as the patchwork (Figure M) forms the lining. After a rectangle is sewn on to the front of the T to form a pocket (as illustrated), the lining is turned into an open cube by sewing the side and bottom side seams before it is inserted in the tote bag.

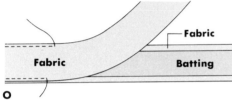

O

Figure O: Handles for the tote bag are made of two layers of cloth with batting sandwiched between them. The strips are stitched ¼ inch in from the sides, with raw edges turned inside.

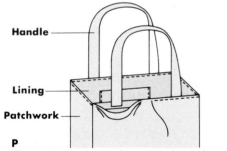

P

Figure P: By slipping the ends between the patchwork and the lining, the handles are attached to the bag as they are being sewn together.

11: Beth Gutcheon's favorite quilting position is sitting cross-legged on her bed, on top of the first quilt she made, a *Picket Fence* design.

To make the lining, cut the lining fabric into the same T-shape as the patchwork (Figure M). Cut out a 7-by-7¾-inch rectangle for the pocket. Press under a ¼-inch hem on all sides. Sew this to the center of the back of the lining by stitching around the sides and bottom of the pocket. Sew the side and bottom side seams, forming a three-dimensional rectangle (Figure N). Press the seams, and press the raw edge under ¼ inch along the top.

The handles are made of cloth and batting. Cut out four 2-by-22 inch strips of fabric and two 1½-by-21-inch strips of batting. Along the long sides, turn the raw edges under ¼ inch and press. Lay one cloth strip face down and put the batting on top of it. On top of this, lay the other cloth strip face up (Figure O). Pin the layers together along the long sides. Stitch them ¼ inch from the folded edge, being careful not to catch the batting in the seam. Repeat for the second handle.

To assemble the tote bag, sew the side seams and bottom side seams of the patchwork to form a cube open at the top. Press the seams, and press under ¼ inch of the raw edge around the top. Slip the lining into the patchwork bag with wrong sides facing. Pin the top edges together. Fold the handles in half and slip the ends between the patchwork and the lining on the front and back (Figure P). Stitch the patchwork and lining together along the top edge ¼ inch in from the folded edge, catching the ends of the handles between the lining and the patchwork.

Needlecrafts

Cynthia Ann Dancing quilt

The quilt pictured on page 1439 looks old-fashioned enough to have kept great-grandmother warm, but it is actually a contemporary quilt incorporating traditional design motifs. The patchwork starts in the center with one block of four colors and white. As the block is repeated, one color at a time is replaced by white until there are only red and white patches remaining (Figure Q). It is difficult to distinguish the individual blocks in the finished quilt because the corner patches of four blocks form a star similar to the star that is the center motif of each individual block. The placement of the four main design elements—designated squares I, II, III, and IV—and the two border elements, designated borders I and II—are mapped in Figure R (opposite).

To make the quilt, you will need fabric in the following amounts: ¼ yard of blue print; ½ yard of brown print; 1 yard of green print; 1½ yards of red print; 6½ yards of white muslin (4½ yards for the patchwork pieces plus 2 yards for the backing); and ½ yard of solid blue for the binding. You will also need: cotton-wrapped polyester thread for piecing; quilting thread for quilting stitches; and a 54-by-72 inch piece of polyester batting.

To make the templates (Figure S), follow the directions in the Craftnotes (page 1441). The blocks in squares I and II are made up of triangles of two sizes. In square III, a large white triangle replaces both the blue and the brown triangles and the white triangle between them. This is the third template. This triangle is one eighth of any block and can be cut in one piece. This saves the time it would take to piece together the same shape by sewing together three smaller triangles which are all white. This is done in square IV as well and in both the border blocks. Cut out the shapes as indicated in Figure S. Start with the smallest pieces as you sew the patchwork together. It is a good idea to complete all of one kind of block before going on to the next. You will need four blocks for square I, eight for square II, eight for square III, twenty for square IV, and four for border I and four for border II. To make a block, imagine the block as formed by four small squares. Each square in turn is made of two triangles. Each triangle is formed by sewing three smaller triangles together. So this is the starting point: sew the three triangles together following the color guide in Figure Q, and press the seams. Sew another three triangles together, also following Figure Q, and press the seams. Sew these two larger triangles together to form a square that is one quarter of the block. Repeat for the other three quarters, and sew all four together to form one complete block. The procedure is the same for the blocks of square II. For all remaining

Square I

Square II

Square III

Square IV

Border I

Border II

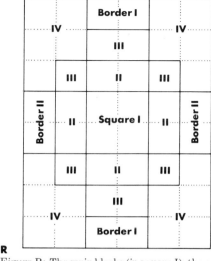

R

Figure R: The main blocks (in square I), the color variations (in squares II, III and IV) and the border blocks are arranged as shown.

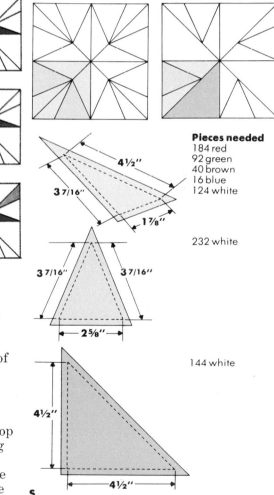

Pieces needed
184 red
92 green
40 brown
16 blue
124 white

4½″

3 7/16″

1⅞″

232 white

3 7/16″   3 7/16″

2⅝″

144 white

4½″

4½″

S

Figure S: The main square and the first color variation are made with only two triangles — cut with templates based on the two smaller patterns (see Craftnotes, page 1441). The second two variations and the border squares require a third template, a triangle formed by a combination of the other two.

Q

Figure Q: The *Cynthia Ann Dancing* quilt is made of one block motif repeated with a series of color variations. The individual blocks are shown at the right.

blocks, one quarter of each block is formed by two large triangles; one is made up of three small triangles, the other is cut out in one piece using the third template. When all the blocks are completed, sew them together following the design in Figure R. Press the seams.

To quilt the patchwork, cut a piece of muslin and a piece of batting 54 by 72 inches. Lay the muslin face down on the work surface and smooth the batting on top of it. Place the patchwork face up on top and pin the three layers together, making sure that all is secure. Roll up the quilt to make it less cumbersome and start quilting from one end. Use a needle No. 8 or 10 sharp and quilting thread to outline the irregular white shapes throughout the quilt (photograph 11). The edge of the quilt is finished with binding. Cut two strips of blue fabric 2 by 72 inches (seam two pieces together if necessary) and two strips 2 by 58 inches. Sew the long strips to the long sides of the quilt with a ¼-inch seam allowance. Press the seam open. Sew the shorter strips to the top and bottom of the quilt the same way and press open. Press the raw edges under ¼ inch on all four sides. Fold the binding to the back of the quilt, and stitch the binding to the back of the quilt with small hand stitches.

PERFUMES
Scent: A Primeval Experience

Men and women have been wearing perfume for some 6,000 years to transmit pleasurable messages to each other. Motives have remained much the same since India's high-born women first discovered the advantages of perfuming themselves with a paste of ground sandalwood and musk-scented saffron. The natural fragrance materials also remain virtually unchanged, though science has added hundreds of synthetic scents to nature's roster. Today, nearly 1,000 scents in common use offer a variety of perfume combinations, including something to please just about everyone.

Anyone can buy the essences—plant, animal, or synthetic—and blend them into original bouquets, then dilute the blend to make perfumes or colognes. To an individualist, the ultimate personal statement may be a bottle of perfume on the dressing table which was blended at home and labeled *My Own*.

The Sorcerer's Helper

Perfume is associated with personal adornment because, like beautiful clothes and jewels, it enhances the attractiveness of the wearer and stimulates an emotional response in others. The word perfume comes from the Latin words *per fumus* (through smoke). Incense, compounded from powdered spices, was the primitive form of perfume used to venerate the gods.

The language of perfume is as ephemeral as fragrance itself. Perfumers and poets borrow musical terms and the names of colors in trying to describe the effect. But the only thing certain is that a gratifying fragrance triggers reactions which can influence one's personal fortunes and can even change the course of history.

To cite one example, Cleopatra was not beautiful, contrary to popular belief. She used exotic perfumes and cosmetics to conquer Caesar and Mark Antony. According to Shakespeare's vision of her in *Antony and Cleopatra:* "The barge she sat in, like a burnished throne, Burn'd on the water; the poop was beaten gold, /Purple the sails, and so perfuméd/ that/The winds were love-sick…"

Perfume in History

Egyptians imported costly aromatics as far back as 2000 B.C. Wealthy Egyptian women used a white cosmetic paste on their faces. Over the paste went fragrant myrrh, frankincense (*olibanum*), and spikenard. Then a coating of sesame, almond, and olive oils was applied. Plutarch praised the Egyptian perfume, *kyphi*, saying it contained "things that delight most in the night". Like the Egyptians, the Israelites, Greeks, and Romans also prized perfume.

Arab merchants controlled the lucrative Eastern perfume and spice trade with such secrecy that their sources of supply (musk from China, cloves from Zanzibar, patchouli leaves from Malaya, and sandalwood, rose, and jasmine from India) remained a mystery to the West for centuries. After Rome fell, perfume use declined in Europe except, on occasion, at court and in church services.

The Crusaders reintroduced perfume to Europe during the eleventh and twelfth centuries. They discovered the most distinctive far-eastern-type perfume, *Chypre*, in Cyprus, and took it back to England and France. (*Chypre* is the French word for Cyprus.) Accounts vary as to what went into the original formula; one said it included damask roses, aloes, red sandalwood, cloves, musk, ambergris, and civet. Rose water also made its way west about that time. Rose water was obtained at first by simply steeping rose petals in warm water to force open their tiny pockets of fragrant oil. It became fashionable at court to place a container of rose water on the dining table and offer it to guests to wash their hands after meals—a necessary ablution because forks were first used in Italy in the fifteenth century and did not come into general use in England until the seventeenth century.

Scent has the power to inspire hope, desire, and poetry. Opposite, the exotic Indian goddess, Lakshmi, stands amidst once rare ancient aromatics—the Persian rose and spices from the East. Today, though such scents are available to everyone, the mystery of perfume remains.

Susanna, a former art student, was born in Grass Valley, California, an apt beginning for a career in perfumery. She now blends and sells her own fragrances in her Manhattan boutique O'Susanna. Her interest in custom-made perfumes was aroused in the mid-1960s by a chance visit to a shop that copied commercial perfumes and blended new ones at the customer's request. She learned more about blending natural oils from Steffen Arctander at Rutgers University. Susanna's recipes appear on page 1459

Perfume merchants, shown in an ancient oriental bazaar, kept their sources secret by reporting that dragons and supernatural spirits stood guard over their aromatic treasures.

The technique of distillation, used to trap the scent (called *essential oil* by perfumers) contained in miniscule pockets in one or more parts of a plant—blossoms, leaves, roots, bark, wood, seeds, rind, gum, or resin—was a milestone discovery in the science of perfumery. Scholars trace distillation to ancient India, Egypt, and Persia where, it is believed, perfumers knew how to distill the volatile oils of jasmine, rose, jonquil, and tuberose. Writing in the fifth century B.C., the Greek historian Herodotus mentioned the distillation of oil of turpentine. Avicenna, an Arabian doctor practicing in the tenth century, is said to have rediscovered the ancient art of distilling the essence from flowers such as the rose, and of producing rose water as a by-product. But the introduction of distillates to the West, other than oil of turpentine, is credited usually to a thirteenth century Catalan physician, Arnaldo de Vilanova (1240-1311).

The first known use of cologne—perfume oils in a very dilute alcoholic solution—was called *Hungary Water* and appeared in 1370. The recipe was given to Queen Elizabeth of Hungary by a hermit who claimed that it would preserve her beauty into old age. When the Queen was 72, she received a proposal of marriage from the King of Poland. Perhaps that is why *Hungary Water* remained popular for 400 years. The recipe was prepared mostly with an herb, rosemary, to which lemon, lavender or orris root was sometimes added. The most famous cologne, however, the original *eau de cologne*, was created at the beginning of the eighteenth century; Napoleon was addicted to it and used 50 bottles a month, perhaps because it contained the rosemary that grew in profusion in his native Corsica, perhaps because he could not tolerate the musky scent that Josephine favored.

In perfumery, the term *modern* describes the man-made aromatics that first were marketed about 1900. These modern aromatics can be totally new scents, such as the metallic scents currently popular in symbolizing a complex industrial society. Or they can be precise chemical duplicates of the fragrant oils of such flowers as rose and lily-of-the-valley. One of the best-known modern classics, Chanel No. 5, was introduced in 1923; it was created from aromatic chemicals blended with the natural oils of jasmine and roses.

How to Wear Perfume

Before you attempt to blend a personal perfume you should test various types and strengths to determine which suit your personal skin chemistry best. The Greeks knew that to discover whether or not a perfume is suitable, one must wear it. Appolonius explained that the warmth of the skin brings out the scent of the bouquet. "Perfumes are sweetest," he said, "when the scent comes from the wrist." He was right.

Perfume should be applied at the pulse points where the blood vessels are closest to the skin. The late French couturier, Coco Chanel, was once asked by a customer where she should apply perfume. In exasperation Chanel snapped, "Wherever you expect to be kissed." In fact, the best spots are below, not behind, the ears, at the base of the throat, the insides of elbows and wrists, and the backs of the knees.

After you apply perfume, wait at least ten minutes before trying to judge how you like it; the fragrance will not be fully developed sooner.

A drop of essential oil will last longer than the same oil in an alcohol solution. But each oil has its own optimum level; so you must experiment, and listen to the comments of others to determine whether your perfume is overpowering, undetectable, or just right.

Cologne is simply a far more dilute solution of the essential perfume oils. It is meant to be splashed on the body after bathing—as a base for the application of the perfume version. Toilet water contains more essential oil than does cologne and can be worn in place of perfume by those who prefer only a hint of scent.

Response to Scent

In perceiving odors, the human nose is 10 to 100 times more sensitive than any known laboratory test. But not everyone responds alike. On an emotional level, the scent of flowers you remember from childhood may delight or repulse you today, depending on whether the experiences you associate with them are agreeable or unpleasant.

Certain scents, such as those of narcissus, tuberose, violet, and civet, can cause physical distress if they are inhaled in close quarters or in concentrated form.

A floral clock taken from an old work on botany charts the hour of the day when each flower gives off its strongest scent, usually the time when the flower tends to open. In the center of the French perfume industry, Grasse, where flowers are cultivated for their fragrance, each type is picked in season at the most propitious hour. Clockwise, starting at 1, the flowers are: rose, heliotrope, water lily, hyacinth, convolvulus, geranium, mignonette, carnation, cactus, lilac, magnolia, and violet and pansy.

They all contain the same irritant, a form of alcohol called indol. Some voice teachers forbid pupils to wear the fragrance of violets because it can cause the throat to swell. In fact, some people are allergic to any kind of perfume oil. If you suffer from an allergy, consult your doctor before attempting to blend a perfume.

Fragrances
Homemade perfumes $ ⧖ ⚐ ⚒

To blend your own perfumes, you will need the essential oils that impart the fragrance, other essential oils called fixatives, which modify the fragrance and make the bouquet last longer, and a solvent (alcohol diluent or vodka) to reduce the concentration of essential oils. One dram (60 drops) of essential oil—fragrance or fixative—costs from less than $1 to $5.50 or more, depending on its scarcity. Alcohol diluent costs $1 or more for a 4-ounce bottle. If there are no suppliers in your area, these ingredients can be ordered by mail from the suppliers listed on page 1460. The other supplies you will need are shown in the photograph at the right.

Essential Oils
Before synthetic fragrances were discovered, all perfumes were based on essential oils found in various parts of plants and in animal products, mainly four—the ambergris of the sperm whale and the glandular secretions of the musk deer, the civet cat, and the beaver (*castoreum*). The raw materials were processed either by steam distillation, by expression (pressure), or by extraction—using volatile solvents, hot oil or fats (maceration), or cold neutral fats (enfleurage)—to obtain the concentrated fragrance or essence. The essential oils are still the basis of all perfumery, but today many natural oils, especially those from animals, are made synthetically. In addition, there are many synthetic oils that are pure chemical inventions with no counterparts in nature.

Of some 5,000 fragrant oils available to commercial perfumers, about 1,000 are commonly used; half of these are still derived from natural materials. About 100 are available for home blending, enough so you can create fragrant bouquets (a composition of several oils) to reflect your life and your moods.

These oils are quite volatile at ordinary room temperatures however; so it is important that their bottles be kept tightly stoppered to prevent evaporation. Bottles that will not be used for some time should be sealed with tape or sealing wax and stored away from sunlight and heat.

Selecting the Oils
Like any other art, perfumery combines technique and imagination. Begin by selecting several essences that you have enjoyed wearing, or that you know please you. Perhaps you enjoy the scent of certain spices in your kitchen or flowers in your garden. Essences thus chosen often blend nicely because they most likely have one or more fragrance ingredients in common. If you would rather not risk such an experiment until you have more experience with perfumery, several precise tested recipes are given on page 1459. You might not like them all; try to choose one that you think would appeal to you.

When it comes to blending the various oils, outstanding perfumes are often compared with music because each has three parts—top notes, middle notes, and bottom notes. They combine harmoniously so that no one odor overpowers the others. This assembling is known as layer blending. The top notes create the initial impression. They are always pleasing but unfortunately they evaporate fastest. Middle notes are the modifiers that link up top and bottom notes; they may be a bit nauseating in themselves but they make the perfume unique and are quite acceptable when covered by the top notes. The bottom notes, often the animal-based scents like musk or civet, are the fixatives that give the perfume life and warmth as well as tenacity, and fix the composition so its effect is long lasting. Like middle notes, they sometimes are unpleasant by themselves. Recipes No. 1 and No. 5 on page 1459 demonstrate a further point: that the very same essences can be used in different proportions to develop completely different perfumes. Once essential oils are blended, they can be worn full strength if only a drop or two is used, but usually they are diluted to make perfume, toilet water, or cologne (page 1462).

Supplies needed for blending oils to make perfumes and colognes include: essential oils (in the brown glass bottles, each with its own eyedropper attached); alcohol or vodka diluent; fixative (such as musk); sniffing strips cut from blotting paper; filter paper and funnel; and an assortment of clean glass jars like the stoppered bottle in the foreground. The measuring beaker is optional.

Outstanding perfumes blend top, middle, and bottom notes harmoniously so that no one odor overpowers another. This composition is known as layer blending.

Feminine perfumes, evocative of romance, elegance, and luxury, are usually equated with floral scents. Among the blossom fragrances in common use are essence of rose, jasmine, orange flower, tuberose, jonquil, and carnation.

Exotic fragrances are heavy, sweet, pleasantly disturbing and frankly sensuous. Their compositions include essences of rose, jasmine, violets, narcissus; animal originated musk and civet; aromatic sandalwood and cedarwood; spices such as clove, cinnamon, and ginger root; and the most penetrating of plant scents, patchouli leaves.

Fragrances
Perfume recipes

There have been many attempts to classify perfumes according to personality types but there are no rules because no two people react exactly the same way to any one scent. The recipes on the opposite page are presented in three rather arbitrary categories:

The feminine types, all floral, include a bouquet of flower scents, a wood-dominated scent, and a somewhat spicy rose scent.

The exotic types, include one with the fragrance of India, one of North Africa, and one with the heavy sensuousness associated with the Orient.

The outdoor types, are all fresh, woodsy fragrances that are popular with both men and women.

Alcoholic Solvents

To dilute the blended essential oils, you need neutral alcohol that is pure and odorless if you are to obtain a pleasing finished perfume. The drugstore variety of isopropyl alcohol will not do because it has an offensive odor, nor is the wood alcohol sold in hardware stores suitable. The most desirable commercial solvent, pure ethyl alcohol, is available only by special license. But some suppliers of essential oils are permitted to sell ethyl alcohol with fixatives added to make it undrinkable. It is called a perfume diluent. (See list of sources, page 1460.) If you use a diluent which already contains fixatives, you do not have to add more unless you are trying to create a very sophisticated bouquet.

Outdoor-type scents are clean and fresh with many green and woody notes, like the smell of crushed leaves. Citrus oils like orange, lemon, and bergamot play an important part.

Recipes for blending essential oils

Exotic types

Scent No. 1. This has the fragrance of India. Note that if you use the same oils that appear in the feminine group at center, but change the proportions, you will get a completely different result.

Sandalwood	20 drops
Tea rose	4 drops
Musk	4 drops

Scent No. 2. This is an oriental type, very heavy, very spicy, very exotic.

Gingerroot	20 drops
Sandalwood	5 drops
Orange blossom	2 drops
Musk	2 drops
China lily (narcissus)	2 drops

Scent No. 3. This is an exotic perfume of the Mediterranean-African type.

Orange blossom	20 drops
Lotus flower	2 drops
Musk	2 drops

Feminine types
(floral scents dominate)

Scent No. 4. This is a spicy rose scent. Tea rose is the top note. Carnation, the middle note and modifier, adds spice. The bottom notes, acting as the fixatives, are orange blossom and musk.

Tea rose	20 drops
Carnation	4 drops
Orange blossom	1 drop
Musk	1 drop

Scent No. 5. This is a smooth, woody scent.

Tea rose	20 drops
Sandalwood	10 drops
Musk	4 drops

Scent No. 6. This is an exotic floral bouquet, very sweet and heavy. Here, musk and orange blossom are the bottom notes and fixatives, as in the first formula. China lily is so named because the original bulbs came from China, but the scent is that of narcissus.

China lily (narcissus)	20 drops
Lotus flower	6 drops
Musk	6 drops
Orange blossom	1 drop

Outdoor types

Scent No. 7. This is a clean, fresh citrus scent suitable for men as well as women.

Bergamot	20 drops
Lemon oil	10 drops
Sandalwood	5 drops

Scent No. 8. This is a long-lasting scent for men or women. The musk, a synthetic copy of Tibetan deer musk, is reputed to be sensuous.

Vetiver	20 drops
Sandalwood	10 drops
Musk	2 drops

Scent No. 9. This is a modern, refreshing, clean-smelling combination.

Juniper oil	20 drops
Spearmint	2 drops
Sandalwood	2 drops

Benzoin

Where to get perfume oils

Aphrodisia Products, Inc.
28 Carmine Street
New York, N.Y. 10014

Caswell-Massey Co., Ltd.
320 West 13th Street
New York, N.Y. 10014

Kiehl Pharmacy, Inc.
109 Third Avenue
New York, N.Y. 10003

O'Susanna
134 East 17th Street
New York, N.Y. 10003

P. Fioretti & Co., Inc.
1470-72 Lexington Avenue
New York, N. Y. 10028

The Perfumer's Workshop, Ltd.
Suite 905
1 East 57th Street
New York, N. Y. 10022

Sherrell Perfumers of Beverly Hills
8383 Wilshire Blvd.,
Beverly Hills, Ca. 90211

Among those who will fill orders for diluent
are Caswell-Massey Co., Ltd. and P. Fioretti &
Co., Inc.

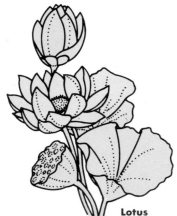

Lotus

Adjusting Vodka

Vodka can be a suitable substitute for alcohol diluent, providing you adjust it a bit (100-proof vodka contains only 50 percent alcohol). Even at its best, vodka has an earthy potato note. This can be overcome by using extra top notes or by adding musk to soften the vodka. Use 1 drop of musk to 127 drops of vodka; let it age at least two weeks, then smell it. The potato smell should be masked.

It is also advisable to add an extra 1 percent of musk, ambergris, or civet to the oil blend to give it tenacity, overcoming the low alcohol content. In practice, if you use 1 ounce (500 drops) of perfume, add 5 drops of musk as an additional fixative.

Diluting Blended Oils

The proportion of essential oil to alcoholic solvent (diluent or adjusted vodka) can be as follows:

To make perfume, dilute 1 part of essential oils with 4 parts of solvent.

To make toilet water, dilute 1 part of essential oils with 6 - 15 parts of solvent. (Some commercial toilet waters are at perfume strength, while other are diluted nearly as much as cologne; there is no legislation establishing the concentration of essential oils needed in the alcoholic solution.)

If you buy essential oils in the form called tinctures, they normally will consist of 1 part essential oil to 10 parts of alcohol diluent. Some animal-based fixatives may be sold only as tinctures rather than as essential oils. Such reduced concentration must be considered when you blend any perfume, toilet water, or cologne.

To make cologne, dilute 1 part essential oils with 20 parts of solvent. But these are only guidelines. There are some perfumers who suggest diluting 1 part of essential oils with 6 or 7 parts of solvent to make perfume. The quality of the essential oil and its degree of volatility or tenacity should be considered. But personal preferences are more important. Practically speaking, if you dilute a light floral essence, use less solvent because the delicate floral is quite volatile. In the long run, it is easier to adjust the bouquet by adding more diluent than by adding more essential oils.

Mixing and Measuring

Combine the essential oils, according to your recipe, in a clean glass or porcelain container. Both materials are non-porous and do not absorb the fragrance as would plastic or wood. Brown bottles are desirable because perfume should be shielded from light as well as heat.

Use an eyedropper to avoid wasting oils or diluent. Keep track of the proportions you have mixed so when you are satisfied with the scent, you will know what to add to increase the quantity. It is a good idea to calibrate the eyedropper. This simply means counting the drops it holds and marking it with indelible ink near the top, so you can fill it to exactly the same point each time. Then you will not need to waste time counting each drop. Use a separate eyedropper for each oil. Wash it with diluent (or vodka) after using, and discard the diluent. Then fasten the dropper to its own essential oil bottle with a rubber band.

After you have mixed the oils, stopper the bottle and set it aside for 24 hours. Then, using either filter paper or white blotting paper cut into ⅛-inch sniffing strips, dip a strip into the oil blend and smell the results. If you are not satisfied, this is the time to try an adjustment by modifying the blend in some way. But if the scent pleases you, add the alcohol diluent or adjusted vodka. Initially, do not dilute the essence more than suggested above. You can always add more solvent later if the fragrance is too concentrated for your taste.

Set the perfume (or cologne, if you have diluted the oil to that degree) aside for a week if you have used vodka as the solvent. Vodka may make the liquid turn cloudy, and you may want to filter it for appearance' sake. Be sure the container is well-corked, and set it in a cool place. After a week, the sediment will have settled to the bottom. To filter it out, put a funnel in a clean glass bottle, add an odorless filter paper, and pour the liquid through.

Stopper the fragrance bottle so it is air-tight. If you don't plan to use the perfume for awhile, heat sealing wax, and drip it around the stopper. Store your perfume in a cool, dark place. If the bottle has been opened and will not be used up in six months, store it in the refrigerator so the perfume does not turn rancid.

Musk

Jasmine

Scents: origins and descriptions

Rose

Patchouli

Sandalwood

Animal scents

Man has been on the scent of strong animal odors for centuries. Alone, such perfumes can be sickening, but they are so long-lasting they give permanence to more delicate scents, hence are used as fixatives. Since ancient times the more important animal products have been ambergris, formed in the intestines of sperm whales, and glandular secretions of the male musk deer, the civet cat and the beaver (**castoreum**). For centuries, musk was slaughtered ruthlessly for its scent, but today musk and other animal scents reproduced in the laboratory are just as prized for their strength and tenacity.

To the perfumer, these are exalting fixatives because they improve and fortify other ingredients in a bouquet and diffuse its fragrance. Only traces are needed.

Sperm whale

Ambergris: The scent is subtle, suggesting seaweed, wood, and moss, as well as animal. It has a sweet, dry undertone and unequaled tenacity. The bouquet is improved by adding musk or civet. Though synthesized today, the original ambergris was found floating at sea or washed ashore.

Musk: This odor is very persistent. It provides lift for a bouquet of essences besides acting as a fixative. There are dry and sweet musks. The original musk was a secretion contained in the abdomen of the Himalayan musk deer, but the animal is now near extinction. Today's musk is made in a laboratory.

Civet: This odor in concentrated form is obnoxious but it is very tenacious, provides lift and diffusive power. The English poet Cowper wrote: **"I cannot talk with civet in the room,/A fine puss gentleman that's all perfume."** When diluted, civet has more of a floral fragrance than musk. Originally the Abyssinian variety civet was considered the most important source of this fixative. It is now man-made.

Castoreum: This warm animal odor is leather-like and sweet; it is an important ingredient in perfumes. It blends well with ambergris, cedarwood, labdanum, oak moss, and sandalwood. The scent was originally taken from the glands of the male and female beaver, but is now synthesized.

Beaver   Civet

The plant fragrances

Popular fragrances derived from plant materials and commonly used in perfumery include the following:

Flowers

Rose: The scent is warm, deeply floral, sweet and slightly woody with spicy or honey-like notes. The effect is narcotic. **Centefolia** and **Damascena** roses are generally used in perfume. The essence is distilled from petals. The rose symbolizes perfection and romance.

Tea rose: One of many hybrids, it gives a scent of fresh green tea leaves. The fragrant oil is a delicate floral with a rose top note and a tea—like, musty under note.

Carnation: The scent is rich and very spicy and clovelike until its strength subsides or it is diluted. Then the fresh flower scent emerges. The effect is both stimulating and narcotic.

Orange blossom: The scent from bitter orange flowers is intensely floral, heavy, warm, rich, and long-lasting; it acts as a natural fixative. The effect is exalting. It is used in all kinds of perfumes, from heavy oriental types to light citrus colognes.

Narcissus: The fragrance is sweet and somewhat exotic, with spring-like notes. In Greek mythology, a youth named Narcissus who spurned Echo and fell in love with his own reflection in a pool, was transformed into the flower.

Lotus: The scent is floral and somewhat sweet, but it has a fresher, greener note than narcissus. Today's lotus oil is a complex blend of materials, partly synthetic. The fictional lotus-eaters in Homer's Odyssey were drugged after eating its fruit.

Jasmine: The odor is intensely floral, warm, rich, and highly diffusive with an unusual waxy-herbaceous, oily-fruity, tea-like undertone. The effect is sultry and stimulating. The best perfumes require jasmine, say expert perfumers who create the masterworks.

Leaves

Spearmint: The odor is very warm, herbaceous, somewhat green, powerful and penetrating, recalling the odor of the crushed herb. The plant is produced mainly in the United States. The oil is distilled from the purple tops of the plant.

Patchouli: This oil has a very rich, herbaceous, aromatic fragrance with spicy-woody and balsamic notes. The effect is hypnotic. It is a favorite in India. The odor is the strongest to be found in plants.

Rosemary: The fresh, lively fragrance provides an invigorating topnote. Rosemary keynoted two historic classics—**Hungary Water** and **eau de cologne.** Its Latin name, **ros marinus,** means **sea dew.**

Grasses

Lemongrass: This is considered one of the top ten essential oils by perfumers. The scent is lemon-like, grassy-fresh, strong, tea-like and herbaceous. The oil is distilled from the leaves of lemon grasses that grow in India.

Woods

Sandalwood: This has an extremely soft, sweet, woody fragrance. It has no strong top note, but it is one of the all-time great blenders with rose, violet, tuberose, clove, lavender, bergamot, oakmoss, patchouli, vetiver or musk, and is used as a common blender-fixative in oriental-floral and wood-floral bases.

Fruits

Juniper berry: This fragrance is fresh, warm, rich, and somewhat reminiscent of pine needles. It is distinctive for its balsamic-sweet note. It works well with modern synthetic bouquets. Juniper is one of the oldest aromatics known.

Lemon oil: This is a freshener and top note ingredient in countless perfumes, particularly in the old-fashioned citrus-type colognes. The essence is pressed from rinds by machine.

Bergamot: This clean, fresh, sweet, green-citrus scent is soothing and pleasant. It is a traditional top note and one used commonly in citrus colognes, **chypre,** and modern fantasy bouquets.

Roots

Vetiver: This is a sweet, woody, earthy scent. Vetiver belongs to a grass family that is native to India. It has sensual appeal for men and women. The Eastern perfume, **mousseline,** is made from the roots.

Gingerroot: This scent is oriental, spicy, herbaceous, pungent and aromatic. It comes from a flowering plant of southern Arabia. Roots were highly prized by the ancients because they gave off powerful scents and could be dried and stored without deteriorating.

Biblical aromatics

Myrrh and frankincense: Both are aromatic resins. Myrrh is mentioned in papyruses dated about 2000 B.C. and in directions given in the Old Testament for making holy oil. Both aromatics were among the gifts of the Magi to the Infant Jesus.

Frankincense

Recipe for Florida Water

Rose water	½ pint
Tincture of jasmine	3 ounces
Tincture of musk	1 ounce
Bergamot oil	1½ ounces
Lemon oil	½ ounce
Lavender oil	½ ounce
Cinnamon oil	⅛ ounce
Neroli oil	3 drops
Clove oil	4 drops

Lavender

Fragrances

An old-fashioned cologne

$ ⬛ 👤 🧴

There have been many variations of the original cologne created by Johann Marie Farina. The old-fashioned types were usually citrus bouquets blended with rosemary or lavender. One of the more complex blends included oils of neroli, bergamot, lemon, rosemary, oreganum, lavender, orange-flower water, essence of ambergris, and alcohol. For centuries, colognes were thought to have hygienic value and were prescribed to alleviate fatigue, strain, and to ward off illnesses.

One traditional cologne that you may wish to try is called Florida Water. Perfected in America and still popular, just as Lavender Water is popular in England, Florida Water dates back to twelfth century Europe. The recipe is at left.

Blend the ingredients; then use 2 quarts of vodka as the solvent if you cannot buy alcohol diluent. Adjust the vodka according to directions on page 1460. Filter the cologne and set it aside for at least a month before using.

Neighborly Infusions

A visitor to Thailand was charmed by an old custom that is still observed with enthusiasm on Buddhist holidays: people sprinkle perfumed water on each other as a good luck greeting. Your neighbors may or may not appreciate such a benediction on a hot August day. But even if they don't, you can infuse flowers, spices, pine needles, herbs or citrus rinds to use as a rinse for your hair, clothing or as a body splash.

An infusion consists of steeping fragrant material (without boiling it) to extract the scent. It is almost as simple as soaking a tea bag in hot water. For that matter, a water infusion of camomile tea was a popular hair rinse several decades ago, and is just as pleasant now. Besides teas, successful water infusions can be made with other spices and with dried pine needles. Blossoms yield less to water than do the other ingredients, but given enough time and fresh blossoms, satisfactory rinses can be made.

Dried plants usually give better results than fresh ones because malodorous elements disappear as plant materials are dried. Any store that sells potpourri offers a wide choice of ingredients, including rose petals to mix with lavender or carnation as well as premixed potpourri.

1: To make an infusion, pour boiling water over dried plant material, let it cool and steep anywhere from a few hours to three months; then filter it, as pictured, into another glass container.

2: Pour the filtered water into a clean carafe or decanter that can be tightly corked and set aside for a few hours before using. Packaged in recycled bottles, perfumed waters make nice gifts.

To make an infusion use a glass jar with a screw-on lid or cork stopper and a glass coffee pot. Partly fill the glass container with crumbled, crushed or ground potpourri material. Pour in enough boiling water to cover it completely (more if you are making a tea rinse for the hair). As soon as the water is cool, pour the contents into a glass container that you can cork so it is airtight. Shake the contents and set the infusion aside to strengthen. Tea is ready for use within hours. Pine needles and spices such as rosemary, clove, and cinnamon are ready in a few weeks. But leafy and woody materials like lavender and oakmoss may take up to three months. Test the infusion by sniffing saturated strips of white blotting paper about once a week. Meanwhile, shake the contents daily. If the infusion has not developed sufficient strength after a reasonable time, strain out the potpourri material and add a fresh batch. Repeat these steps until the results are satisfactory. Finally, filter the contents (photograph 1) and pour the filtered liquid into another glass container (photograph 2). Cork the container and store it in a cool dark place.

Making Tinctures

You can obtain refreshing scents with the strength of toilet water by using an alcohol diluent instead of water to extract the scents from dried plant materials. Apart from the fact that no heat is involved when the diluent is poured over the fragrant dried plants (just enough to cover) the procedure is the same as for the water infusion described above. The main advantages of solvent extraction are that you can use materials that do not respond well to water infusion and the scents will last far longer. The main disadvantage, when working with large quantities, is the cost of the diluents.

Especially for Men

Napoleon wasn't the only European male who liked to smell good. Men of European and Eastern countries have long been fond of perfume, sometimes to hedonistic excess. American men, on the other hand, have looked askance at perfumes except for vigorous splashes of bay rum. Among many men, this conservative attitude has been replaced in recent years by a willingness to experiment with almost any kind of scent, as long as it is not floral.

The record of male use of fragrances begins with the Old Testament's Song of Solomon. When the Queen of Sheba traveled 2000 miles to visit Solomon in 800 B.C., she brought him costly perfumes as a gift. By 450 B.C., Roman men used perfumes. One Ticinus Menias, a Sicilian, opened a chain of barber shops in Rome, and men of distinction came to be shaved every day with a bronze razor. Their sore faces were covered with hot towels, followed by scented unguents, and their hair was treated with perfumed pomades. Three centuries before Christ, Theophrastus, the Greek botanist, wrote that lighter perfumes were suitable for men and the more tenacious ones were appropriate for women. One male Greek bather used palm oil for jaws and chest, sweet mint extract for arms, marjoram for hair and eyebrows, and essence of ground thyme for neck and knees. Roman men must have done likewise, because Julius Caesar ordered them to stop using exotic scents. Martial, a Roman wit, criticized the excesses of young Roman bachelors thus: "He that smells always well, never does so."

Charlemagne enjoyed perfumes. Whe he was crowned emperor in 800 A.D., Caliph Harun Al Rachid of Baghdad sent him perfumes and a white elephant. Henry III of France, who ascended the throne in 1547, enjoyed scented sachets filled with orris and musk. Henry VIII, among his excesses, enjoyed wearing an overpowering blend of heavy musk and ambergris. Louis XIV went personally to his perfumer to watch him prepare his special fragrances; Louis' shirts were perfumed with *aqua angeli*, a blend of aloes-wood, nutmeg, cloves, storax, benzoin, rose water, waters of jasmine and orange flowers, and a touch of musk. He was called the sweetest-smelling monarch. Muhammad loved perfumes and promised his Muslim followers that they would be welcomed into the garden of Paradise by nymphs wearing musk, his favorite scent.

A recipe for a modern masculine scent is given at right. After you have blended the oils, either dilute the essence immediately or add a citrus top note by incorporating the undiluted recipe for Florida Water, opposite; then dilute. For related entries see "Cosmetics," and "Potpourris and Pomanders."

Dried potpourri in the large container at left is an excellent basis for brewing fragrant water. The tightly corked carafe at right contains the aromatic product that can be used to rinse hair, or clothing, or can be added to bath water.

Recipe for a masculine scent

The following fragrance for men is a dry, grassy, woody type.

Sandalwood oil	50 drops
Patchouli oil	20 drops
Musk oil	10 drops
Coumarin oil	10 drops
(or vanillin oil)	
Oakmoss oil	5 drops
Clary sage oil	5 drops

PET HABITATS
Homes, Sweet Homes

On his construction sites, Frank Ratigan designs for people; as a hobby, he designs habitats for animals. He worked for an animal talent agency for six years, designing and building carriers and displays. He also worked on the Peaceable Kingdom exhibit at the 1965 World's Fair in New York. He and his wife live in a mountainside home in Warwick, New York, with two Siamese cats; one appeared in the movie Bell, Book and Candle.

There are an estimated 81 million pets in the United States alone—36 million dogs, 26 million cats, and 19 million birds. And the number keeps growing. About 57 percent of all households include pets, and the trend is toward more than one pet to a family. If you count all the goldfish and guppies, there are three pets for every man, woman, and child in the United States.

Each of these pets needs care, affection, and the feeling of security and privacy that comes from having a place he can consider his own. A simple cardboard box or paper bag can be a special haven for a dog or cat, but making an unusual and decorative habitat for him can be an interesting project for the whole family.

Most commercially available houses, cages, and carriers are well-designed and solidly built, but many of them are quite ordinary. The habitats on the following pages are all out-of-the-ordinary, though the foremost consideration in each design is the pet's well-being and comfort. There is a house for an outdoor dog, a cardboard hideaway for a cat that is far from a plain cardboard box, a traveling tote large enough for two small pets, and an airy castle that is a delight for the birds.

Left: Noah's Ark, depicted in a painting by Edward Hicks, a nineteenth-century American artist, may have been the first animal habitat built by man. The four pet habitats that are described here are much smaller, but just as functional.

Opposite: A short-haired dachshund named Cleo proves that Saint Bernards are not the only dogs that know what to do with a barrel. A large wooden one, set on its side and remodeled to suit its new purpose, makes a cozy outdoor doghouse that could be enjoyed by almost any dog. Directions for the barrel doghouse begin on page 1466.

1465

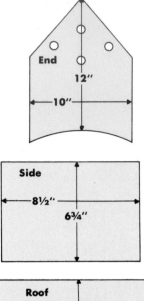

End

12"

10"

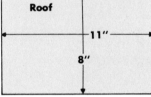

Side

8½"

6¾"

Roof

11"

8"

A

Figure A: Cut two end pieces, two roof pieces and two side pieces from exterior plywood to make the cupola for the barrel doghouse. (Dimensions can vary according to the size of the barrel.)

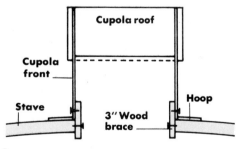

Cupola roof

Cupola front

Stave

Hoop

3" Wood brace

B

Figure B: Nail two wood braces to the staves, inside the cutout at the top of the barrel. Next, nail the cupola over these braces, resting the end pieces on top of the ¼-inch lips that extend inside the hoop ends.

Environmental Projects
Barrel doghouse

If finding a suitable outdoor house for your dog has you baffled, consider making one from a wooden barrel, perhaps one that previously held pickles or whiskey. For a small dog, you could use a nail keg. The barrel in the doghouse shown on page 1464 is a 50-gallon whiskey barrel, 36 inches long when resting on its side and 25 inches in diameter at the ends. A 30-gallon barrel is about 30 inches long and 20 inches across the ends; a nail keg is about 20 inches long and 14 inches in diameter at the ends. The size you choose depends on the size of your dog and how much room he needs for comfort. It should be large enough so he can turn around inside, yet snug enough so he can keep it warm with body heat. A well-built barrel will be virtually rain- and snow-proof, warm in winter and cool in summer. Most long-coated dogs could live in such a house all year round even in a cold climate. Short-haired dogs could use it in a mild climate or as a second home when warm weather allows them to be outdoors much of the time.

1: After all the wood parts are cut to size, soak them in a creosote solution to deodorize and protect them. Cradle ends may be cut straight or angled—both cuts are shown above.

Placing the doghouse so the door faces east or south will usually give good protection from wind and maximum sunlight in winter, along with shade and cooling breezes in summer. Situate the doghouse where the sun can reach it a good part of the day in any season; sunning the interior with the door propped open helps prevent odors and vermin. If possible, choose a site that takes advantage of a nearby building or hill to buffer strong winter winds and look for a slight slope that will allow natural drainage around the doghouse. The rounded shape of the barrel and the slanted roof of the cupola will keep rain and snow from collecting on top. High trees are best for providing shade; bushes may harbor insects that are not kind to a dog.

Bedding isn't necessary — dogs are comfortable lying on a bare floor—but if you like, you can provide a cushion of shredded newspapers, washable blankets or pleasant smelling cedar or pine shavings. Clean, dry straw is also good and is preferred by many bird-dog fanciers who believe that any material with a stronger odor will affect the dog's scenting abilities. Straw is better than hay, which is often dusty and may contain allergy-causing weeds.

Remodeling the Barrel

Because the basic doghouse is a ready-made barrel, actual construction is minimal. Start by deodorizing the barrel with diluted creosote, following the manufacturer's directions. This wood preserver will also keep the staves from drying out and shrinking away from the hoops. Use creosote on all the wood parts of the doghouse after they are cut to size (photograph 1). The strong smell will fade shortly.

Two support cradles, cut from lengths of 2-by-6 clear pine approximately equal to the length of the barrel, prevent it from rolling and hold it off the ground to keep moisture from seeping inside. The supports can be angled at the ends or cut straight. Use a jigsaw or coping saw to cut the curve from the center of each support to a depth of 2 inches in front and 2½ inches in back. Trace the curve of one end of the barrel to the right depth on each side of the support; then cut out the slant-edged half-circle piece. Use a rasp to further shape the curve to fit the part of the barrel which the cradle will hold. Make one support first; then trace the exact curves onto the second board. You will reverse the second support under the barrel so the deeper part of the curve is toward the middle. To hold them in place, drive flat-head screws or nails through the barrel staves and into the supports.

A cupola set over a hole cut in the barrel insures proper ventilation, no matter what the weather. For the cupola, first cut a rectangle out of the barrel around the bunghole. If there is no bunghole, cut the rectangle anywhere using staves and hoops as measuring guides. Cut out as many staves as necessary (four in the doghouse pictured) between the center hoops, leaving a ¼-inch lip at each end near the hoops to support the cupola. Build the cupola of ¼-inch thick exterior plywood to fit on top of this cutout, matching the barrel curve with the end pieces (Figure A), and drill ventilation holes (photograph 2). To secure the cupola to the barrel, nail one 3-inch-wide scrap of wood across each hoop end of the cutout so that half extends above the barrel. Fit the cupola over these two braces and nail it in place (Figure B).

To make the area around the door weather-tight, cut a circle of ¼-inch exterior plywood with a coping saw or sabre saw, and nail it in place to make a recessed cover for the front end. (If the barrel is open on this end, use ½-inch thick plywood and toe-nail it to the lip of the barrel.) Saw a square door from the barrel end, making it as large as possible (drill corner holes so you can start the coping-saw or sabre-saw cut). Cut a door the same size from the plywood circle, and trim ⅜ inch off the top of the door piece to allow a two-way swing. Attach the door with lengthwise strips of thin leather tacked inside and out, or use two-way hinges at the top (Figure C). Attach the plywood circle to the barrel end with contact cement or waterproof adhesive and brads.

For additional ventilation, drill holes above the door (you can plug them with corks in very cold weather). Cover the roof of the cupola with tar paper, and use tar paper to make a rain shield over the doorway (Figure C). For the shield, cut a semicircle of thin metal, with the straight edge equal to that part of the barrel end circumference which is above the door. Make an inch-deep fold along the straight edge, and clip it every inch or so for a smooth-fitting curve. Fit the visor underneath the lip of the barrel and staple it to the plywood front.

You can paint the finished doghouse or coat it with a plastic resin, or you can paint the hoops with rust-resistant paint and let the wood weather naturally.

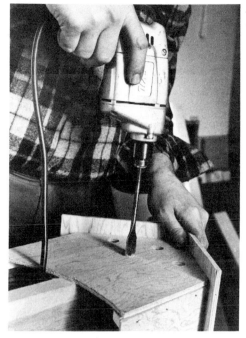

2: Drill ventilation holes through the front and back end-pieces of the cupola, with a power or hand drill.

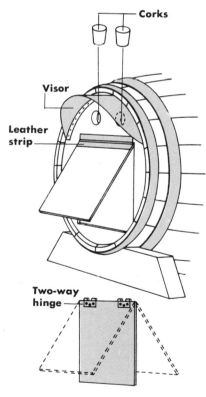

C

Figure C: In cold weather, ventilation holes drilled above the door may be plugged with corks. The swinging door is attached with strips of thin leather or two-way hinges, leaving a ⅜-inch clearance. A visor shields the entry from the elements.

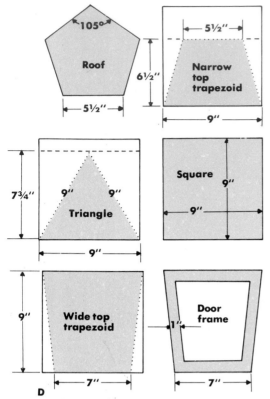

D

Figure D: Cut the cardboard pieces for the cabaña as follows: one pentagon for the roof, five narrow-top trapezoids for the upper wall, five squares and five triangles for the lower roof, and eleven wide-top trapezoids for the lower wall (two are cut out and layered for the door frame).

Bop's cabaña is landscaped with edible shrubbery for cats. With different decorative paper, the basic cardboard structure could easily become a rustic cabin, a mighty castle, or a circus tent.

Environmental Projects
Cat cabaña

This cat cabaña is just as easy to make as it is colorful. Corrugated cardboard, masking tape, and adhesive-back paper are the main materials. The outside can be wiped clean, and the lower roof slopes to keep the cat from perching there. If you like, you can add luxury touches such as carpeting, a sun lamp (actually a low-wattage light bulb), and pots of edible greens for cats outside the front door.

Start by cutting 27 squares of single-ply, double-faced corrugated cardboard, each 9 inches square, and one 24-inch square of the same kind of cardboard for the floor. You can buy such cardboard or salvage it from used boxes. If you recycle cardboard, select strong, straight pieces of equal thicknesses.

You will need a metal-edged ruler and a craft knife for cutting the pattern pieces (Figure D). Cut one pentagon for the roof, five small narrow-top trapezoids, five squares, five triangles, and 11 large wide-top trapezoids. Measure and cut carefully; the masking tape will cover minor errors, but the strength of the construction depends on how accurately the pieces fit together.

Start assembly with the upper wall of the cabaña (Figure E). Align the five small narrow-top trapezoids with tops facing the same direction and edges touching, and tape them together along the full lengths of the seams with 1½-inch-wide masking tape. Turn the taped seams to the inside, and tape the two end pieces, forming a narrow-top cone. Retape the seams on the outside. This double-taping of all the seams makes the cabaña very sturdy, and is done each time pieces are joined. Place the pentagon on top of the cone and tape it in place, inside and out. If the sun lamp is to be added, glue a pentagon of aluminum foil to the inside of the roof. Punch a small hole in the center of the roof, push the electrical cord through with the socket on the inside, and knot the cord loosely on the outside to keep it in place. Screw a 40-watt light bulb into the socket after the cabaña is finished, and plug in the cord when you want to turn the light on (Figure F).

To make the lower roof, alternate the squares and triangles as shown in Figure E, and tape all the seams. Tape the two end pieces together forming a cone; then double-tape as before.

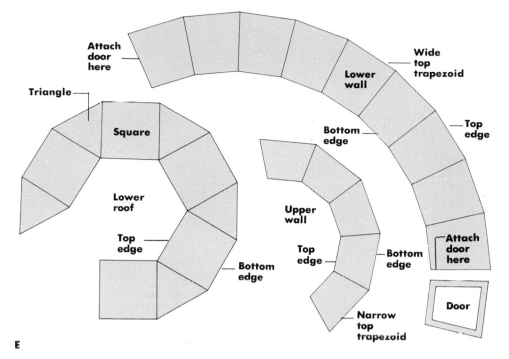

Labels on Figure E diagram:
Attach door here
Triangle
Square
Lower roof
Top edge
Bottom edge
Lower wall
Wide top trapezoid
Top edge
Bottom edge
Upper wall
Top edge
Bottom edge
Attach door here
Narrow top trapezoid
Door

E

Figure E: Assemble the upper wall, lower roof, and lower wall of the cabaña as shown, butting the edges of the pieces and taping the seams on both sides for extra strength.

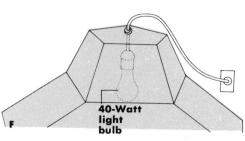

40-Watt light bulb

F

Figure F: A low-wattage light bulb can be suspended inside the cabaña to act as a sun lamp. Knot the cord loosely on the outside and line the roof with aluminum foil.

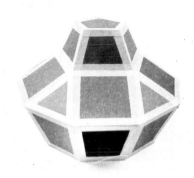

3: The cardboard structure, with all seams taped and the floor attached, is ready to be decorated with adhesive-back paper.

4: Make a cardboard pattern for the scallops that trim the cabaña, using a circular object such as a coin to keep them even and of equal size. Trace the pattern with a pencil onto a narrow strip of adhesive-back paper.

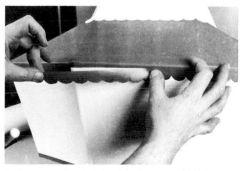

5: Cut out a short strip of scallops, peel off the backing, and press into place over the narrow straight-edge overlap.

For the lower wall, line up nine of the large wide-top trapezoids as shown in Figure E and tape them into a row. The two remaining trapezoids will be used for the door frame. Cut out the centers of both pieces, leaving a 1-inch frame on all sides. Layer these two pieces and tape them together. Join the door frame to the end pieces of the lower wall, taped seams inside, forming a wide-top cone. Retape all the seams on the outside. Join the lower wall to the lower roof, double-taping as before. Finally, double-tape upper and lower units together. (This requires a little maneuvering.)

Place the cabaña on the 24-inch square of cardboard, trace around the bottom edge, and cut out the floor. Tape the floor to the cabaña, inside and out.

To add carpeting, place the cabaña on top of a carpet remnant (backing side up), and trace the shape as you did for the floor. Cut out the carpet, making it ¼ inch smaller all around than the outline. Roll the carpet, push it through the door, and spread it flat. Because it is not attached, it can be removed for cleaning.

Now you are ready to decorate the structure (photograph 3) with adhesive-back paper. You can make it look like a cabaña with white walls and red scalloped roofs, as shown in the photograph opposite. You will need 18-inch-wide adhesive-back paper, about 1½ yards of red and 2 yards of white. Leave the backing on until you are ready to use each piece, and be careful not to stretch or wrinkle the paper. The results will be better and there will be less waste if you cover each shape individually rather than trying to fit the paper over an entire section at once. Cut the pieces one at a time, allowing a ¼-inch overlap on the right edge, and a 1-inch overlap top and bottom. Start with white for the lower wall. No bottom overlap is needed for this because a narrow trimming of red covers the bottom edge and is tucked beneath the floor. Cover the lower roof with red and the upper wall with white. The roof, with a bottom overlap, is red.

As you press each piece into place, align the left edge with the seam, and let the piece overlap the shape on the right by ¼ inch. The succeeding pieces are attached in the same manner so there is always a ¼-inch overlap at the seams.

The bottom overlaps of the roof, upper wall, and lower roof are cut straight. Make the scallops by cutting them from an extra strip, depending on the depth of the scallops you want. Make a pattern of thin cardboard, using a coin or other circular object to keep the scallops even and of equal size. Trace the outline of the scallops with pencil on a strip of the paper (photograph 4); then cut and press them in place over the existing overlap (photograph 5).

If you prefer, you could also make the cabaña look like a castle by covering it with stone-pattern paper or like a cabin with wood-grain paper.

If a cat comes on the scene causing a ruckus, or it is time for a nap, a fabric cover with squares of self-gripping fastener tape is quickly attached to the tote, and covers the vinyl roof.

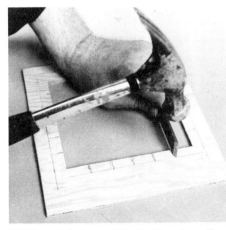

6: Make 1-inch-long notches for the wire grillwork in the windows by hammering the side of a chisel into the wood around the cutout.

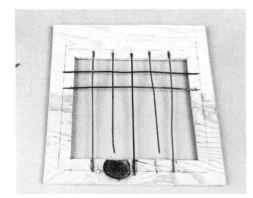

7: With a staple gun, attach five wires in the notches on one side. Next, weave five more wires through the first group, stapling these at both ends. Finally, staple the free ends of the first set of wires in their respective notches.

Pekingese twins, China and Tai-Tai, travel contentedly in a tote built for two. The clear vinyl observation roof lets them sight-see along the way and the wooden framework is strong enough to support their combined weight. Wire grillwork windows at both ends provide ventilation.

Environmental Projects
Two-in-one tote

Two pets who are seldom out of each other's sight at home will feel more secure if they can be together when they travel. Because their combined weight and movement can put great stress on a carrier meant for a single occupant, the tote for the two pictured above is solidly built with wooden ends, floor, and crossbar for strength. But since most pets feel safer if they can see where they are going (with their master at their side), the main part of this carrier is of transparent vinyl. For timid types and for rest periods, there is a separate fabric cover.

This carrier is designed for cats or small dogs whose combined weight is 25 pounds or less; heavier pets would be hard to lift. Of course, if you have just one pet, you can adapt this plan to suit his space needs. Construct a cardboard mock-up to try on for size if you are uncertain about the measurements. You may discover that adding an inch to each side means the difference between being comfortable and being crowded. This carrier is 14 by 23 by 17 inches, about 2 inches larger all around than a cardboard container from a pet shop. It is strong enough to be used as a shipping container on a commercial airliner.

Materials
You will need a 23-by-43-inch sheet of 3/32-inch clear vinyl. A plastics supplier may cut it to size for a small charge; otherwise, buy a piece 2 feet by 4 feet and cut it with a fine-toothed saw. (Leave the extra inch on one long side as an allowance for error; it can be trimmed later to fit precisely.) You will also need: ¼-inch-thick exterior plywood, 4 feet by 8 feet (or individual pieces cut to the sizes in Figure G); a 22-inch length of ¾-by-1-inch clear pine for the crossbar; 8 feet of ½-by-¾-inch pine cut into two 13-inch, two 22-inch, and one 21-inch lengths; a 5-inch leather handle with rings or posts; two surface-mounted hinges and a spring-loaded cabinet latch; five wire hangers; four packages of ½-inch round upholsterer's tacks; a carpet remnant; contact cement; and a small can of polyurethane finish. Tools needed are wire cutters, staple gun, hammer, chisel, drill, jigsaw or coping saw.

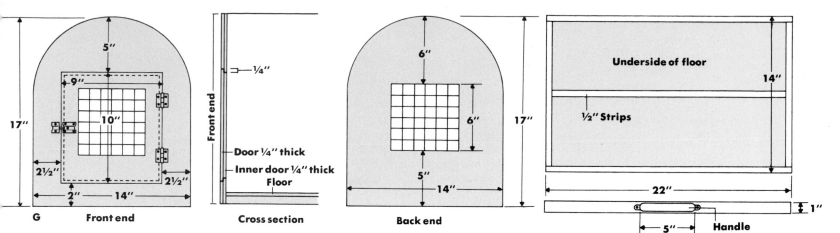

Figure G: Cut the two front end pieces, two back end pieces, and crossbar to the dimensions given above. The cross section of the double-thickness front end shows how making the inner door piece ¼ inch smaller than the outer door piece creates a door stop.

The Wooden Framework

Cut all the pieces from the sheet of plywood if they have not been cut to size. Notice that there are four end pieces and two door pieces; these parts will be glued together to double thickness for added strength. Cut the door and windows from the end pieces by drilling holes at corners and cutting pieces with a jigsaw or coping saw.

Frame the bottom of the floor piece with wood strips, and add a center strip for added strength (Figure G, far right). Nail through the floor into the strip to avoid sharp points on the inside of the tote.

Cut twenty 8-inch lengths from the wire hangers with wire cutters. On what will be the inside of one door piece, make 1-inch long notches an inch apart all around the window cutout. Do this by hammering the side of an old chisel into the wood (photograph 6). Attach five wires at one side with a staple gun, fitting them into the notches. Then, weave five more wires through the first wires, and staple them at both ends (photograph 7). Finally, staple the free ends of the first wires into their notches. Make window bars on one back end piece in the same manner. Next, laminate the two back end pieces, and the two front end pieces with contact cement. Let them dry. If there is a gap in any of the edges, such as one caused by a knot hole (photograph 7), fill it in with wood plastic.

Attach the door to the front end (both are now double thickness) with two surface-mounted hinges. The ¼-inch lip on the inside will act as a door stop. Screw on a two-piece cabinet latch (Figure G).

Nail the front and back ends (now ½-inch thick) to the floor board, keeping all bottom edges flush. Fit the crossbar between the top of the two end pieces so it spans the case, and nail in place. Drill the holes for the handle screws at this point, before the vinyl is attached, so you can clear away the sawdust, but do not attach the handle. Sand all wooden parts smooth and cover them with two thin coats of polyurethane, letting each coat dry thoroughly. This finish will darken the wood slightly, giving it a stained look. If you prefer, paint the wood with exterior paint.

The Vinyl Observation Roof

The vinyl roof starts at the bottom edge of the floor, curves over the top, and continues down the other side. All edges are fastened with ½-inch round upholsterer's tacks hammered into the wooden frame at 1½-inch intervals. To be sure of even placement, measure and drill tiny holes for the tacks before starting to attach the vinyl (Figure H). One way to do this is to place a long strip of ½-inch-wide masking tape on the bottom of an overturned cardboard carton. Mark the lengthwise center of the tape for a ¼-inch guide. Mark 1½-inch intervals along this line. Keep the paper backing on the part of the vinyl that is not being drilled, to protect it from scratches. Align the edge of the vinyl with the edge of the tape; drill holes at the marked intervals on the center line so they are ¼ inch in from the edge, and 1½ inches apart. Drill through the vinyl and into the carton. Move the vinyl sheet when you reach the end of the tape.

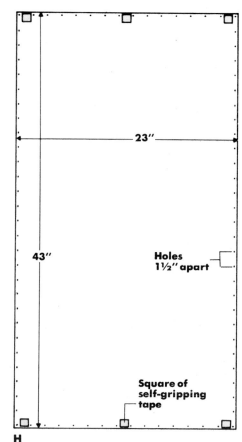

Figure H: The observation roof is cut from a sheet of 3/32-inch-thick clear vinyl. To assure even spacing, tack-holes are drilled in the vinyl before the roof is attached. Squares of self-gripping fastener tape are glued in place to hold the fabric cover in place (Figure I, page 1472).

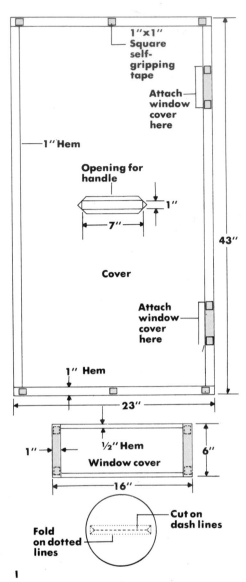

Figure I: The removable fabric cover has an opening for the handle, and squares of self-gripping fastener tape that correspond to the tape on the vinyl roof (Figure H, page 1471). A separate cover for the back window can be attached to prevent drafts in cold or wintry weather.

Remove the paper backing and tack a short edge of the vinyl sheet to the floor on one side of the carrier, aligning the bottom edges. Next, tack along the curving ends, alternating between them to keep the tension even. Finally, attach the second bottom edge. If there is any excess vinyl on the last edge, cut it away with a coping saw.

Attach the handle by drilling holes in the vinyl to correspond with those in the crossbar, and joining them with bolts and washers. If the bolts extend beyond the bottom of the crossbar, file them off to avoid injury to your pets. Use a leather handle for comfortable carrying; a strong handle is needed to support the weight of the carrier and its occupants.

Cut a carpet remnant slightly smaller than the floor piece, and lay it loosely inside so it can be removed for easy cleaning.

The Coverup

Make the cover (Figure I) of any lightweight, washable fabric. You need a piece 25 by 45 inches. Machine-stitch a 1-inch hem on all sides. Cut six 1-inch squares of self-gripping fastener tape from a strip or buy individual pieces; glue the burr side to the bottom edges of the vinyl—one each between the two end nailheads and one in the center on each side (Figure H, page 1471). Sew the fuzzy squares to the inside of the cover, matching those on the case.

Make an opening for the handle in the center of the cover (Figure I); fold under all four sides and machine-stitch close to the edge. For cold weather, you may want to make a removable window cover for the back end, too. Cut a separate piece 7-by-18 inches. Machine-stitch ½-inch hems on the long sides and 1-inch hems on the short sides. Sew 1-inch squares of self-gripping fastener tape at all four corners, and sew corresponding squares to the under side of the main cover.

Environmental Projects
Room to fly

A birdcage five stories high gives small birds plenty of room in which to fly. Finches, though tiny, need such space to spread their wings. Because the cage is made of wood, it is best suited for finches and canaries. Such small-beaked birds can resist the temptation to nibble on a cage; members of the large-beaked parrot family usually cannot. If you have a parakeet who has never shown an appetite for wood, he might be happy in this cage if you give him a cuttlefish bone to chew on. A sprayed-on coat of white non-toxic enamel makes the cage easy to wipe clean and gives it a charming Victorian look.

To make the cage, you will need the materials listed in the column at right, opposite page. You will be cutting and assembling dowels, square strips, and hollow tubes for five roofs and a floor (Figures J and K, page 1474), and for 12 walls (Figures L and M, page 1475). You will also be making a tray (Figure J). In putting the pieces together, evenly-spaced ⅛-inch holes are drilled through all the square strips. Where a dowel joins only two strips, the strips are not completely drilled through. If by mistake you drill through a strip when you should not, use a little wood plastic to fill the hole remaining in the strip after the dowel is inserted. You will find it easier to keep track of the units if you cut and assemble one piece at a time.

The Roofs and Floor

The first four roofs (pieces e, g, i and k in Figures J, page 1474, and N, page 1475) are similar, sloping down from two side peaks formed by the hollow tubes, and open in the center to fit around the cage walls. The only differences occur in the overall dimensions and the number of short (2-inch) dowels used. The roof sections are connected to the tubes to form the peaks. In this process, the last dowel on each side is put in place after the sections are fitted into the notches cut out for them in the tubes. These dowels are inside the tube section and are indicated by the dotted lines in Figure J. A detail of the joining is shown in Figure K.

Long dowels, indicated by yellow in Figure J, are continuous pieces; they are inserted through the square strips of the side sections and pass through additional

This airy environment is almost too pretty to be called a cage. Though the feathered friends in the photograph aren't real, a couple of finches or a lively canary could be very happy here. Even if you didn't own a bird, this would make a decorative room accessory.

Materials

To make the birdcage, you will need:

Enough ¼-inch-square wood strips to total 72 feet for the horizontal bars. This is not a standard size but can be cut at the lumberyard from ¼-by-¾-inch finishing strips. Be sure the wood is soft; the bars at the peaks of the walls must be soaked, bent into curves and left to dry in a vise. Straight bars can also be used if you butt the ends that meet in the center;

For the vertical bars, ⅛-inch round dowels to total approximately 265 feet;

For the bottom of the door and the cage feet, 12 inches of ¼-by-½-by-¼-inch wood strips;

For the peaks of the roofs, 40 inches of round hollow tubing (1 inch outside diameter)—bamboo, acrylic plastic, PVC plastic pipe, or heavy cardboard (if the cage is to stand, not hang);

For the tray, a sheet of 1/16-inch plywood, 9½ by 11¾ inches;

Finally, you will need: 21 small screw eyes; two cans of spray paint (be sure it is non-toxic); white glue; and a drill with a ⅛-inch bit.

short square strips that are evenly spaced across the center sections of the roofs. The tubes are notched to fit over the peaks of the walls below as well as to hold the side sections of the roofs together. When the cage is assembled, the peaks of the roofs alternate directions (see photograph, above, and figure N).

For each of these roofs, drill the holes and insert the dowels as indicated; then glue. The red lines indicate where short attachment dowels will be added later; drill holes here as for the other dowels. These attachment dowels connect the roofs to the walls of the cage and are threaded through a screw eye attached to the wall

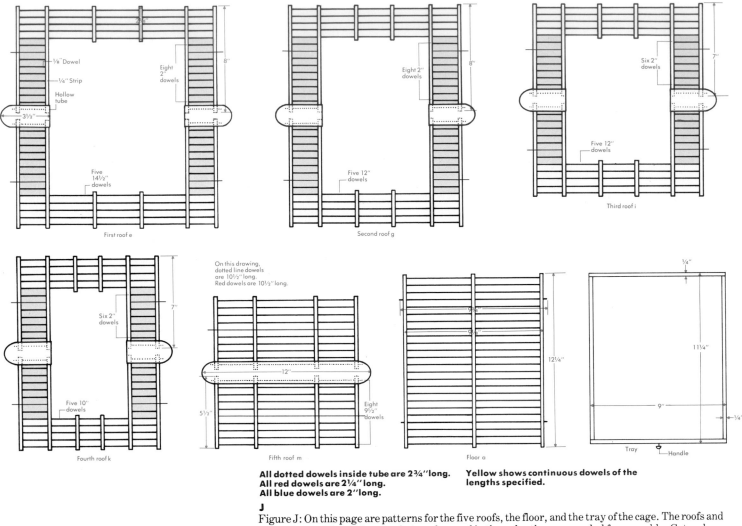

On this drawing, dotted line dowels are 10½″ long. Red dowels are 10½″ long.

All dotted dowels inside tube are 2¾″ long.
All red dowels are 2¼″ long.
All blue dowels are 2″ long.

Yellow shows continuous dowels of the lengths specified.

J

Figure J: On this page are patterns for the five roofs, the floor, and the tray of the cage. The roofs and the walls (see Figure L, opposite) are lettered in the order they are needed for assembly. Cut and assemble the dowels, strips, and tubes for one piece at a time to avoid confusion. The red lines indicate the position of the dowels that will be inserted through screw eyes extending from the walls below, attaching the sections to each other (see Figure M). The tubes are shown in detail in Figure K (below).

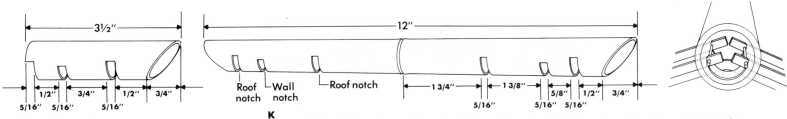

K

Figure K: The hollow tubes at the peaks of the roofs are slanted at the outer ends and are notched to fit over the peaks of the walls below and to hold the side sections of the roof together. One long tube is cut for the fifth roof at the very top (piece m); eight short tubes are cut for the remaining roofs. At right is a detail of the tube with the two halves of the roof in place. The last two short dowels are inserted inside the tube, locking the sides in place.

below (see Figure M). They are then glued in place. Because they are ¾ inch longer than the other short dowels, they will extend beyond the outside edge of the roof.

The fifth and top roof piece (m) consists of two rectangular shapes, joined by one long tube section (Figure K). Two long dowels, indicated by the red lines, join the roof to screw eyes in the top wall. For balance, let them extend at opposite sides. The floor piece (a) consists of 24 evenly spaced long dowels threaded through three strips. Twenty-two of these dowels are equal length. The two longer ones fit into holes inside the bottom square strips of the front and back piece of the cage.

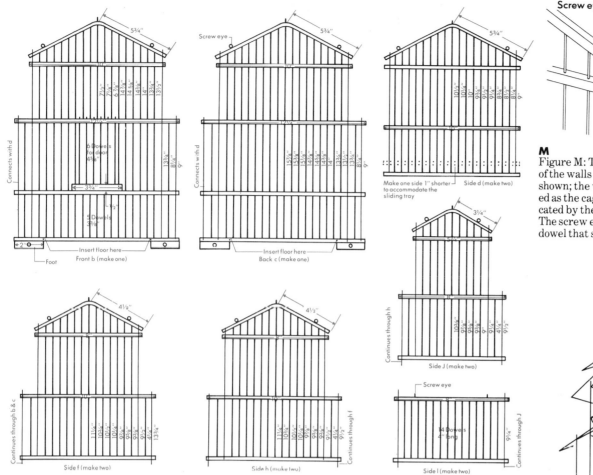

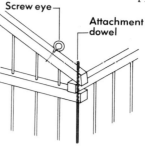

M

Figure M: The horizontal and slanted strips of the walls of the cage interlock at the corners, as shown; the vertical attachment dowels are inserted as the cage takes shape. These dowels are indicated by the red lines in Figures J and L. The screw eye holds the horizontal attachment dowel that secures the roof above.

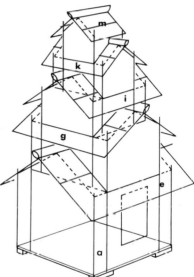

L

Figure L: On this page are patterns for the twelve walls of the cage. Like the roofs (Figure J, opposite), the walls are lettered in the order they are needed for assembly. Lengths of all the dowels and strips are given; the red lines indicate the attachment dowels that will be inserted through holes at the corners (see Figure M for detail). Cut and assemble the dowels and strips for one piece at a time to avoid confusion.

The Walls

There are 12 walls (pieces b, c, d, f, h, j and 1 in Figure L). All but the top two walls (pieces 1) are two stories high and have sloping tops that fit perpendicularly under the sloping roofs. Make one front wall (piece b) and one back wall (piece c). Note that the door section on the front slides upward through holes drilled in the square strip directly above the door. The dowels above and below the door are short; all the rest are long and run continuously from the top to the bottom of the piece.

In all other cases, make two identical copies of each wall unit shown. The one exception is piece d, where one unit is 1 inch shorter than the other to accommodate the sliding tray. The walls interlock at the corners and are connected with vertical dowels (Figure N). Some joining dowels extend the height of one story, and others extend the height of two stories (Figure L). They are indicated by the red lines in Figures L and N.

Assembly

The pattern pieces are lettered in the proper sequence of assembly, starting with the floor (piece a) and ending with the top roof (piece m). The attachment dowels are inserted in the empty holes as the cage takes shape. A swing and hanging ring may be added to the center of the top tube section with wire.

When the cage is completed, give it two coats of spray enamel, letting each coat dry completely. Wait 24 hours before using the cage for live birds. To control mites in this wooden cage, sprinkle mite powder in the joints.

For related entries, see "Ant Farms," "Birds and Birdhouses," "Insects," "Tropical Fish" and "Vivariums."

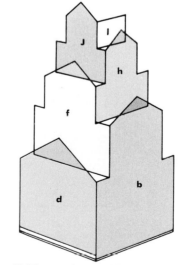

N

Figure N: The cage is assembled from the floor upward. The pieces are keyed in consecutive order, and the letters correspond to the pattern pieces given in Figures J and L. The top drawing shows the alternating roofs in yellow and the attachment dowels in red. The bottom drawing, with parts also keyed, shows the wall sections in alternating colors.

A cast pewter owl perches on an acrylic plastic base. The feet are assembled from solder strips. You can make figurine paperweights like this using only a few special tools and the heat of a kitchen range.

PEWTERSMITHING
Colonial Crafts for Today

Pewter is surrounded by an aura of glamor and elegance that makes it unique among base metals. It evokes visions of tankards, candelabra, serving trays—and a quieter way of life. Until the coming of inexpensive pottery in the nineteenth century, the satinlike sheen of pewter graced the homes of rich and poor alike on both sides of the Atlantic. In colonial and federal times, many domestic utensils were made of pewter because it was the most economical and workable material available. Now a wide range of materials from plastic to steel serves in its place. But nostalgia has led to a revival of interest in pewter crafts.

Pewter is a mixture of a number of metals, and the recipe has varied widely over the years. The great bulk of it—usually about 91 percent—is tin. But pure tin is too brittle to be worked easily and cannot withstand everyday use. In the past, small amounts of lead were added to the tin. Lead is poisonous and its use, as was subsequently learned, made pewter risky indeed for a dining utensil. Today, lead in pewter utensils is prohibited by law, and antimony (7 or 8 percent) is generally used instead. The result is a metal somewhat harder and whiter than the colonial version, but one that is safe and tarnish-resistant. A small amount of copper, usually 1 or 2 percent, is added to improve the working properties of the alloy.

Thanks to this threefold composition, modern pewter can be stretched, compressed, pounded, bent, or cast into almost any shape desired, and it does not harden or stiffen while being worked. These properties, in addition to its low cost, make it ideal as an introduction to metalsmithing. Mistakes can usually be corrected easily. Scraps and rejects can be melted down on the kitchen range. The four common ways of working pewter are: casting in a mold, handworking with a mallet, piecing together, and spinning on a lathe. The projects that follow include examples of all but spinning, which requires costly machinery and considerable skill.

Pewtersmith William Gerard is president of Contemporary Innovations, Inc., Jackson Heights, New York, designers and producers of cast figurines. He attended the Museum School in Philadelphia and later left a career in advertising to devote all of his time to designing in pewter and leaded glass.

A colonial mug (above left) and its modern-day counterpart (right), though separated by two centuries, have in common the singular warmth of pewter. Curiously enough, both were made in Middletown, Connecticut, one by Joseph Danforth who worked there from 1780 to 1788, the other by Stephen Strait, whose instructions for working with pewter begin on page 1480.

Tools and materials for pewter casting

Pencil
Stiff cardboard
Carbon paper
Tracing paper
Craftknife or scissors
Wood scraps
Saw
Non-hardening modeling clay
Pin or needle-point scribing tool
About 16 two-penny finishing nails or brads
Hammer
Soap and water
Old paintbrush
Metal-casting plaster
Raw pewter in any form
Commercial iron ladle
Asbestos padding
Asbestos work gloves
Stove or hot plate
Cooking oil
Pumice

Optional:
Solid-core wire solder
Epoxy glue
Plexiglas or wood base

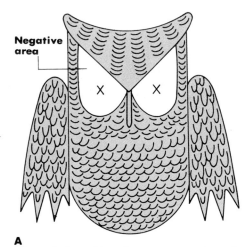

Negative area

A
Figure A: Copy this owl pattern onto a sheet of tracing paper; then use carbon paper to transfer the pattern to a stiff piece of cardboard. With a craft knife or scissors, cut out the cardboard pattern, including the open areas of the eyes that are marked "x" on the pattern.

Carving and Molding
A kitchen-cast figurine $ ● 👤 ✈

Early casting molds were expensive and hard to make; only a few survive from Colonial times. But you can easily make your own mold by pouring a special heat-resistant plaster over a clay model. After the plaster hardens, the clay is removed and molten pewter is poured into the recess—thus making an exact copy in pewter of the clay model. With this technique you can make figurines, paperweights, mobiles, or small utensils. The instructions that follow are for making the owl pictured on page 1476, but the technique can be used for any casting.

The Clay Model
To begin, transfer the owl pattern in Figure A to a sheet of stiff cardboard such as bristol board. Cut the design out of the cardboard with a craft knife or scissors, removing all the internal spaces that will become openings in the casting, such as the eyes of the owl (or a hole at the top for attaching string if you plan to hang the figurine). To back the clay model, cut a rectangular piece of scrap wood at least ½ inch larger in all directions than the design.

Knead a piece of modeling clay until it is smooth and soft, and flatten it on the wood backing to a height of ½ inch. Center the cardboard pattern on the clay. The moisture in the clay will hold the cardboard in place while you outline it with a pin or needle-point scribing tool (photograph 1). Trace lightly at first; then remove the cardboard pattern and cut on the lines to the full depth of the clay. If you want a reusable mold, slope all cuts slightly outward from the top surface. Undercutting the clay would force you to break the plaster mold when you remove the pewter casting. Gently separate the outer waste from the clay design. Remove negative areas such as the eyes, and be sure the outline of the figure is sharp (photograph 2).

Use a pin or toothpick to draw further details on the clay surface, such as the feathering of the owl, and build up projections such as the beak. For a freestanding figure, add sufficient clay at the base—in the form of protruding feet, for example—to give you a well-balanced, bottom-heavy casting. (This was not done with the owl.) Hide your initials in the design.

The Plaster Mold
Build an open-topped wooden box 2½ inches high (on the inside) to hold the plaster that will be poured over the clay model. Make the bottom of the box the same size as the wood backing. Cut the sides to length and nail them to the base and to each other with small finishing nails or brads. Seal the joints of the box with clay so the plaster will not seep out. Gently remove the clay model from its base and center it on the bottom of the box. Make sure the model is still intact and cleanly delineated.

Before the plaster is poured, the clay model must be treated so it will not stick to the hardened plaster. Paint it with a strong soapy-water solution, and let it dry.

1: To make a clay model for the mold, place the cardboard pattern on a bed of clay ½ inch thick, and trace its outline with a needle-point scribing tool (pictured) or a straight pin.

2: Remove the waste clay from around the design and from the open areas within it. With a pointed tool, sharpen the outlines and draw in details. Add clay in raised areas—here, the beak.

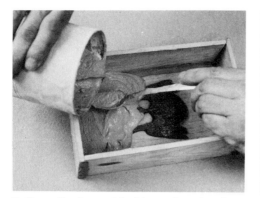

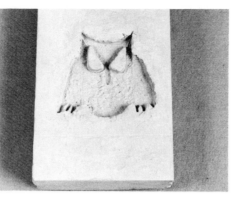

3: Cover the clay model with metal-casting plaster, filling the box almost to the top. Be sure the box is level while the plaster hardens.

4: When the plaster mold is hard, disassemble the box and remove the clay. The result is a plaster block with a recessed impression of the model.

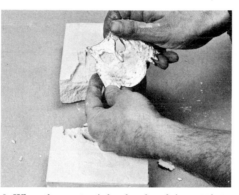

5: Pour the molten pewter slowly into the recess in the plaster cast. Fill it, but do not let it overflow. Be careful to avoid splashing.

6: When the pewter is hard and cool, invert the mold. If the figure does not come free, break the mold in half by hammering it on the bottom

Where to buy pewter

Raw pewter is not always easy to buy. Craft supply shops and metal mills are possible sources, but they often require large orders or charge dearly for piecemeal purchases. One alternative is to see if an established local metalsmith will sell you a fraction of his pewter supply at a reasonable price. In addition, the following firms sell raw pewter by mail order:

Anchor Tool & Supply Co., Inc.
231 Main Street
Chatham, N.J. 07928

Allcraft Tool & Supply Co.
215 Park Avenue
Hicksville, N.Y. 11801
Or: 22 West 48th Street
New York, N.Y. 10036
Or: 204 North Harbor Blvd.
Fullerton, Calif. 92632

Alan Bell
105 Saxonwood Road
Fairfield, Conn. 06430

William Dixon & Co.
750 Washington Ave.
Carlstadt, N.J. 07072

T. B. Hagstoz & Son
709 Sansom St.
Philadelphia, Pa. 19106

Mix enough metal-casting plaster (available at craft-supply stores) to fill the wooden box. (It is better to mix too much than too little.) Follow the manufacturer's mixing instructions. The plaster should be thick but free-flowing. Put the box on a flat surface and fill it almost to the top with plaster (photograph 3).

Bake the plaster dry in a 250-degree oven for 12 hours (longer for thicker castings). When cool, turn the box upside down and gently remove the sides and bottom. Remove the clay, leaving a sharp, reversed image of the model (photograph 4). To melt and pour pewter into the mold, you will need an iron ladle with a strong handle, available in craft supply stores. Do not work with a kitchen ladle; it is too light and increases the risk of dangerous spills. The ladle must be large enough to hold the metal needed to complete the casting in a single pour. The raw pewter may be in ingot (block) form or just a collection of scraps small enough to fit within the ladle before melting. (For where to buy pewter, see listing, above right.) With the recess side up, set the plaster mold on a level, uncluttered, asbestos-covered surface near a range or hot plate. Be sure the room is well ventilated. Wearing asbestos gloves, melt the metal in the ladle over low heat. Move cautiously so you don't splash or spill the molten pewter. Have a bucket of water nearby in case of an emergency. Pour the molten pewter slowly into the mold (photograph 5). Fill the recess completely but not to overflowing. Do not cover the plaster peaks that represent open areas in the finished work. When the pewter in the mold is cool to the touch (wait 10 minutes before testing), turn the mold upside down and tap the figure out (photograph 6). If necessary, crack the mold in half by hammering on its sides and bottom. Polish the finished figurine with a mixture of cooking oil and pumice in equal proportions; then wipe it with a clean, dry cloth.

If your design is to be freestanding, the feet or base can be made separately, and attached with epoxy glue. You can make them in a second casting or, as here, glue them together from pieces of solid solder. For stability and a finished appearance, glue the figurine on a base of wood or acrylic plastic.

Trees lend themselves well to the clay-model, plaster-mold technique described here for the owl figurine. By cutting away some clay areas and building up others, the craftsman can make a pewter casting with an airy form.

Tools and materials for making a handwrought bowl
Raw pewter, 16-gauge, in sheet or disk form
Tracing paper
Carbon paper
Graph paper
Pencil
Masking tape
Felt-tipped pen
Old towel
Coping saw or jeweler's saw, blade with 32 teeth to the inch
V-shaped wooden jig for sawing support
C-clamp
Metal files, fine and coarse
Scrap of wood
Paper mallet (available at craft-supply stores)
Rubber mallet
Sandbag
Any hard, round form such as a dumbbell
Tin snips
Pen knife
Wet-or-dry sandpaper, 400- and 500-grit
Liquid soap
0000 steel wool

Jewelry, Lapidary, and Metalwork
A handwrought bowl

$ $\boxtimes$ ⛷

Stephen Strait, with his wife Christina, owns and operates Strait Designs, a Middletown, Connecticut, crafts shop for his pewterware and her weaving. After earning a master's degree in applied physics at Cornell University and spending two years as a researcher, Strait decided to devote himself entirely to handcrafting pewter. The Straits have a daughter, Selin, and live in a nineteenth-century carriage house.

Working in pewter with a different technique, one not involving heat, you can make a flat-bottomed oval bowl. Gentle persuasion with a paper mallet made especially for pewter work does the job. Start with a flat sheet or disk of the metal. A range of sizes and thicknesses is available; for the present project, use 16-gauge pewter (about 1/20 inch thick) in a 12-by-12-inch sheet or a 12-inch disk. This will make a bowl that is quite substantial, weighing about 11 ounces.

The Pattern
To make a pattern for cutting the pewter oval, fold an 8½-by-11-inch sheet of graph paper into quarters, align the folded edges with those in Figure B, and draw the two curved lines indicated. (You can trace the full-size figure directly onto tracing paper; then with carbon paper transfer the figure to the folded graph paper.) Working from this pattern, you will get a finished bowl about 1 inch deep, 4½ inches wide, and 10 inches long.

A handwrought pewter bowl, shaped from a sheet of metal in an afternoon, makes an attractive serving dish. Modern pewter, which contains no lead, is a safe container for food and drink.

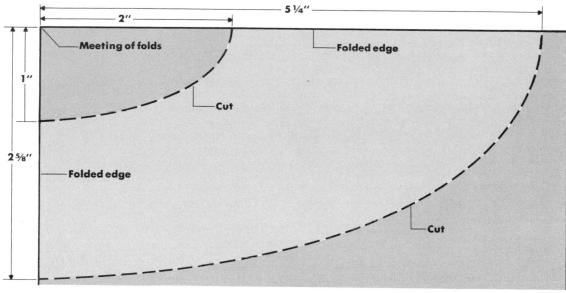

B

Figure B: To make the pattern for the pewter bowl, fold an 8½-by-11-inch sheet of graph paper in quarters and draw the two curving lines indicated. Cut along the curved lines (not the folds); then open the paper to produce the oval doughnut shape partially shown in photograph 7.

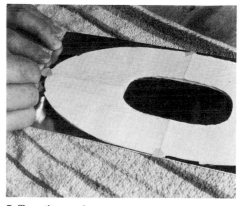

7: Tape the graph-paper pattern to a sheet or disk of pewter, and use a felt-tipped pen to trace the outlines of both the inner and outer ovals.

If you want a bowl of a different size, revise the dimensions accordingly. Cut the graph paper along the curving lines, unfold, and you will have a symmetrical oval with a similar oval cut out of its center. Save the smaller oval for later use.

Tape the large pattern to a sheet or disk of pewter, and outline it with a felt-tipped pen (photograph 7), maintaining a continuous, flowing curve. Trace the inner oval, too, before removing the pattern. The ink will be removed during the finishing process. Protect the pewter here and at all stages possible by keeping an old towel between it and the work surface. Cut the outer oval from the pewter sheet with a coping saw or jeweler's saw (photograph 8); use a notched wooden jig clamped to the workbench (as illustrated) to help hold the metal steady as you cut. The ideal saw blade for work of this kind has 32 teeth to the inch, but you can use any blade that engages at least two teeth in the pewter edge at all times. To forestall surface scratches, blow metal fragments away frequently.

To avoid damaging your mallet later, file down rough edges left by the saw (photograph 9), but do not try to make the oval perfect at this point.

From any scrap of hardwood such as oak or maple, cut a piece the size of the inner-oval pattern, using a coping or jigsaw. File its edges smooth (photograph 10). This wooden form will be used later to flatten out the base of the pewter bowl.

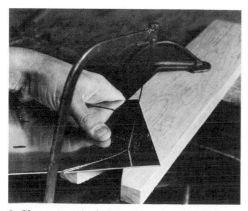

8: Clamp a notched piece of wood to the workbench, and use it as a jig to support the pewter while you cut the outer oval. Here, a jeweler's saw is being used to do the cutting.

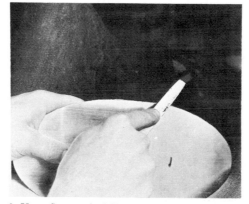

9: Use a fine-toothed file to remove rough edges left by the saw cut. Hammering on such sharp edges can ruin a paper mallet. (You needn't round off irregularities in the curve at this point.)

10: Trace the outline of the smaller graph-paper oval on a hardwood scrap and cut out this shape with a coping saw or jigsaw. Then file the edges of the block smooth.

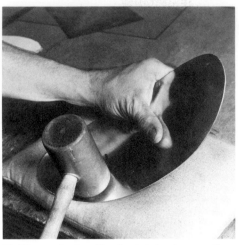

11: Begin shaping the pewter oval by placing one end on the sandbag and striking it gently two or three times with a paper mallet. Then turn the pewter to hammer the next area, following the sequence in Figure C.

12: The pewter bowl begins to take shape as the sequence for shaping the ends of the oval is completed (Figure C). At this stage, most of the rounding occurs at the narrow ends.

13: Using a paper mallet, round the sides of the bowl gradually by making a series of light overlapping blows around the circumference. The curve should be gradual and uniform.

14: To increase the curvature of the bowl still more, hold the edge of the pewter at a slight angle against padding on the flat workbench, and hammer lightly so the ends don't buckle.

15: To finish rounding the bowl, hold it upside down on top of a hard, round object (such as a dumbbell) clamped to the workbench; then tap on the bottom with a rubber mallet.

C
Figure C: To raise the ends of the bowl when you start to shape it, hammer gently two or three times in each of the numbered areas, using a paper mallet and following the sequence indicated. Note that the circles overlap slightly.

The Hammering Process

Pewter dictates its own tempo; the bowl must form gradually as a unit rather than being forced into shape area by area. With a sandbag—a small canvas pillow filled with beach sand—and a paper mallet made for pewter work (available at tool and craft stores), begin slow and gentle hammering according to the following sequence: the area labeled "1" in Figure C is centered on top of the sandbag—it lies flat. Then strike two or three mallet blows in this area (photograph 11). Do likewise with the area marked "2" in Figure C. Note that area "2" slightly overlaps area "1". Repeat with areas "3" through "8". By this time, the pewter will have become slightly rounded as the surface begins to resemble the inside of a bowl (photograph 12). Next make a series of light overlapping hammer blows around the circumference of the outer oval, always centering the work area on the sandbag, and continue circling until the bowl has acquired a gradual and even curve (photograph 13).

To raise the sides, hold the pewter at an angle against the towel-covered workbench (photograph 14), and hammer gently, so the ends do not buckle. To increase the curve, hammer the bowl against any hard, rounded object (such as a dumbbell or the end of a baseball bat) clamped to the workbench (photograph 15). Use a rubber mallet to raise the edge against the rounded object. Let the raising of the sides proceed gradually from sandbag to workbench to rounded object.

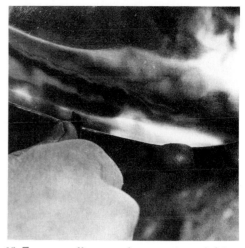

16: With the bowl back on the sandbag, place the wood oval (photograph 10, page 1481) in the center of the bowl and form a flat base by hammering on the wood with a rubber mallet.

17: Using tin snips, cut away irregular areas that have formed at the edge of the bowl during the hammering process. With a little care, the rim will again become a perfect oval.

18: To scrape off any rough spots or burrs left by the snips, drag the blade of a penknife, held perpendicularly to the edge, around the circumference of the bowl.

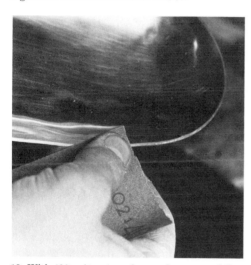

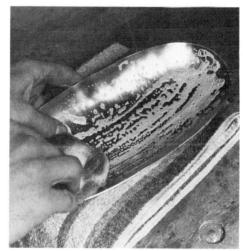

19: With 400-grit wet-or-dry sandpaper sand the edges of the bowl smooth. But do not sand the surface unless there are large accidental gouges to be removed.

20: Polish the bowl to a warm glow with 0000 steel wool dipped in soapy water. Move with the contours of the metal as much as possible. Rinse and dry carefully.

When the bowl has taken on a well-rounded shape and you are satisfied with its contour, place it on the sandbag again, concave (top) side up. Set the wooden oval in the center of the bowl within the pen marks, and hammer the wood gently using a rubber mallet (photograph 16). When the center of the bowl is partly flattened, place it on a hard, flat surface, and continue hammering the wooden oval center, until the bottom is perfectly flat.

Finishing Touches
Examine the overall curve of the edge. Some areas will have expanded more than others during the hammering, leaving irregularities. Use tin snips to cut off any gross imperfections (photograph 17), and drag the blade of a pen-knife along the fresh cuts to smooth them further (photograph 18). Then with a fine metal file, smooth the entire edge, and sand it with 400-grit wet-or-dry sandpaper used dry (photograph 19). Any gouges in the surface can be removed by first sanding with 400-grit and then upgrading to 500-grit paper. If there are no gouges, do not touch the surface with the sandpaper, only the edge. Polish the finished work with liquid soap and 0000 steel wool, moving with the contours of the metal, and removing the ink marks (photograph 20). Rinse and dry the finished bowl carefully with a smooth, clean cloth.

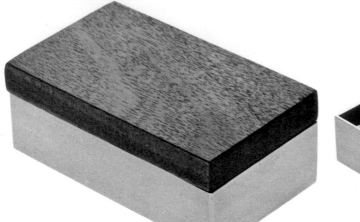

A simple but elegant box is a good introduction to fabricating pewter. A lid of Honduras mahogany (left) or a pewter top (right) are handsome finishing touches for the plain box (center).

Jewelry, Lapidary, and Metalwork
Fabricating a box

If you become interested in pewtersmithing, sooner or later you are likely to embark on a project that cannot be made in a single piece. With pewter, joinery presents few problems. It readily lends itself to piecing and patching without telltale joints because it is so similar in composition to the solder that is used to fasten it. A good introduction to fabrication—the art of piecing metal together—is making a simple pewter box.

Cutting and Bending
First decide on the dimensions you want your box to be. The instructions that follow are based on a box 4 by 2¼ by 1 inches, and measurements are computed for 16-gauge pewter (less than 1/16 inch thick) when the thickness of the material affects construction. If you use other dimensions or pewter of a different thickness, adapt the diagrams accordingly.

With a machinist's square and a metal scribe, mark a 4-by-4¼-inch rectangle on a sheet of pewter (to serve as the bottom and sides of the box) and two 1⅛-by-2½-inch rectangles (for the ends). Cut out all three pieces with a hacksaw or sheet-metal saw, and file all the edges to remove roughness. With the square and scribe, score the larger rectangle to indicate where the sides will be bent up from the bottom (Figure D and photograph 21). Be careful not to scar the pewter in this and

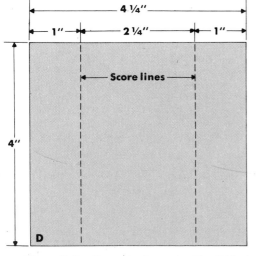

Figure D: For the pewter box, cut a 4-by-4¼-inch rectangle from a sheet of pewter, and scribe two lines to guide the scoring along its shorter dimension, 1 inch in from each end.

21: To insure square corners in the box, scribe lines in the pewter using the guidance of a machinist's square held tightly against the edge of the metal sheet.

22: Using a piece of wood as a straightedge, score grooves with a hard, sharp tool such as an awl, ice pick, or the end of a triangular file honed to a 90-degree wedge-shaped edge.

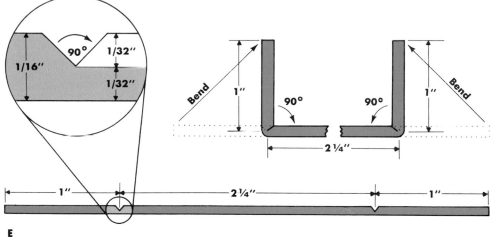

E

Figure E: On the scribed lines, score a 90-degree groove halfway through the metal (shown in profile enlargement at top left). Then bend the sides along the grooves until they form right angles with the bottom (above right).

any other procedure in which tools touch the metal. Use a large nail, awl, ice pick or the end of a triangular file sharpened to a 90-degree V-shape, to continue scoring along the scribed lines (photograph 22) until you have made a V-shaped notch 1/32-inch deep (half the thickness of the pewter sheet) as shown in Figure E. If you make the V as illustrated, the corner will be well defined and of small radius. Smooth the groove with a penknife and the side of a file, taking care not to scratch the surface.

Cut the second groove; then clean the surface of the pewter rectangle with 500-grit wet-or-dry sandpaper followed by 0000 steel wool and a mixture of equal amounts of cooking oil and pumice (photograph 23). Remove the polishing abrasive with soap and water and dry the metal. (It is necessary to prefinish the inside of the box because once the sides are bent up, the corners become inaccessible to the finishing materials.)

To bend the box sides, first tape a piece of paper to the edge and top of the workbench. Put the pewter rectangle on the paper face-down, with one groove lining up with the edge. Using the bench as a form, slowly bend down one side of the box by pressing on the projecting section with a wood block while with a second block, you hold the rest of the rectangle flat on the bench top (photograph 24). Continue bending until a right angle is formed. Follow the same procedure to bend the other side, but insert a wood block at least 1 inch thick under the pewter to compensate for the side already formed (photograph 25). The angles of the sides can be checked with the machinist's square.

Tools and materials for fabricating a pewter box
Raw 16-gauge pewter in sheet form
Machinist's square or try-square
Metal scribe
Hacksaw or sheet-metal saw
Metal files, fine and coarse
Large nail, awl, ice pick or triangular file sharpened to a 90-degree wedge-shaped edge
Penknife
400- and 500-grit wet-or-dry sandpaper
0000 steel wool
Cooking oil
Pumice
Soap and water
Paper towels
Masking tape
Scrap wood
Pewter flux
Old paintbrush with a fine point
Solid-core wire solder, 63 percent tin and 37 percent lead
Propane gas torch
Asbestos mats
Double-cotton work gloves
Pane of glass or similar hard, smooth object
Tin snips

Optional:
Rottenstone (for fine polishing); felt-tipped pen; walnut, teak or mahogany for box top; saw; all-purpose white glue

23: Polish the rectangle with 0000 steel wool and a fine abrasive made of equal amounts of cooking oil and powdered pumice. Then wash the pewter with soap and water, and dry it carefully.

24: Place one groove above the edge of the workbench and bend the pewter by pressing against the projecting section with a wood block while holding the rest in place with a second block.

25: To make the second bend, insert a wood block beneath the pewter to compensate for the height of the side already formed, and bend with two blocks as before.

1485

Soldering

The next step, attaching the ends to the box, requires soldering—the joining of two or more metal parts with heat and another metal alloy, solder. Because solder melts at a lower temperature than pewter, it can be used in molten form to join two pieces of pewter. The solder mixes with the pewter only on the surface; upon cooling and hardening, they form a continuous piece of fused metal. A good solder for this and most other pewter projects is a solid-core wire of 1/16 inch diameter that comes wound on a spool and consists of 63 percent tin and 37 percent lead. Before soldering, flux is applied to the pewter to clean it and keep it from forming oxides that would prevent proper fusion. Buy special flux for pewter.

There are a number of possible heat sources for soldering, but the most convenient and inexpensive device I have found is a small, fuel-in-hand, propane gas torch. Although this torch is safe when properly used, it is important to be constantly aware of the flame and of any materials in a molten state. Have a bucket of water nearby in case of an emergency. In using this or any other torch, protect your work surface with asbestos mats. Work in bright light so you can readily observe changes in the metal, indicating overheating. If the pewter begins to take on a hazed, slightly wrinkled appearance, withdraw the flame immediately.

Although soldering adds a small deposit of metal, it will not compensate for a poorly-fitted joint; so test the fit of the box ends against the sides and bottom, and adjust the angles of the bends if necessary. All parts to be joined must be smooth, flat, and clean; so gently hammer the ends flat and sand the edges of the formed box body (see Figure E, page 1485) by rubbing them over 500-grit wet-or-dry sandpaper placed on a sheet of glass resting on the workbench (photograph 26). Finish the end pieces with 0000 steel wool, or cooking oil and pumice; then wash and dry them.

Cut 16 wire solder snippets about 1/16 inch long with tin snips (photograph 27). Cover the work area with asbestos mats. Place one end-piece flat on the asbestos and set the body of the box on it. Position the box so it is flush with the endpiece at the top, leaving a slight overlap or ledge at the sides and bottom (see Figure F). The dimensions of the ends leave about a 1/16-inch overlap on the sides and bottom. With a small brush, spread a coat of flux around this ledge (photograph 28). Put the solder snippets on the ledge at ½-inch intervals (photograph 29), using the moist tip of the flux brush to pick them up and position them.

Wearing double-cotton work gloves, light the propane torch according to the manufacturer's instructions. The proper flame for soldering pewter has a pointed, bright blue cone within a less distinct outer cone. Moving the point of the inner cone continuously over the pewter to avoid scorching or melting it, heat the surfaces to be fused until the flux boils and the solder snippets round out and begin to flow into the joint (photograph 30). At this point, firmly press the box down on the end piece with a gloved hand. Attach the other end of the box, following the same sequence.

When the box is cool, wash away any flux residue inside and out with soap and water. Shear away the excess ledge with tin snips (photograph 31). Then file the joints, first with a coarse file, then with a fine one, to make the ends blend with the

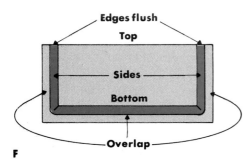

F

Figure F: Place the body of the box on end atop one end piece, viewed here from above. When the top edge of the box is flush with the top edge of the end piece, and the rest of the box is centered, a small ledge for soldering remains along the other three sides.

26: Place a sheet of 500-grit wet-or-dry sandpaper on a pane of glass, and smooth the pewter edges by rubbing them over the sandpaper.

27: With tin snips, cut solid-core solder into 1/16-inch snippets. Sixteen such pieces should be enough to hold the ends of the box in place.

28: Spread flux liberally along the ledge, using a small brush to clean the metal thoroughly and forestall harmful oxidation.

29: At ½-inch intervals, place snippets of solid-core solder on the ledge. Asbestos padding protects the workbench surface.

30: Focus the inner-cone tip of the torch flame on the ledge, moving it back and forth until the flux boils and the solder begins to melt.

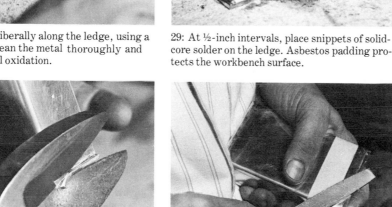

31: With tin snips, cut away as much of the projecting ledge as you can. But be careful not to mar the box by shearing too close.

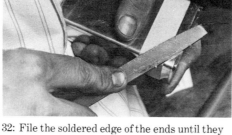

32: File the soldered edge of the ends until they merge into the profile of the box. Masking tape keeps the file from scratching the side.

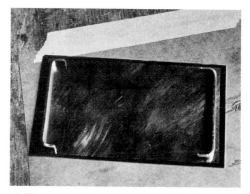

33: The pewter lid is a rectangle, slightly larger than the box. Two thin guides soldered on it fit inside the box. The black border, a felt-tipped pen tracing of the outline of the box, shows where guides should be placed.

profile of the box (photograph 32). Stretching a piece of masking tape across the box, as in the illustration, will prevent marring; the thickness of the tape will guide the file at the slight angle necessary for rounding the edge. Sand the outside of the box with 400-grit, then with 500-grit wet-or-dry sandpaper. Smooth off the top edges on sandpaper over glass. Polish the box with oil and pumice or 0000 steel wool—or use even finer rottenstone to achieve a satin finish. Wash and dry the box carefully.

A Cover

Three options arise at this point: you can consider your box completed, you can make a pewter top, or you can make a wooden top.

A pewter top can be cut in three pieces and assembled by soldering. Let the top rectangle overlap all four sides by about ⅛ inch to make it easy to remove. To it, attach two small guides which just fit inside the opening of the box and thus keep the top in place (photograph 33). For the guides, cut two strips of pewter 2½ by 3/16 inches and without scoring, make the bends ¼ inch from each end. Place the box upside down on the lid and center it. Outline the overhang of the box top with a felt-tipped pen so you can place the guides properly (photograph 33). Place them inside the inked borders, allowing for the thickness of the box sides and ends. Prefinish and solder as before, fluxing and placing the snippets against the inner side of the guides in this case.

For a wooden top, cut a block of wood as wide and as long as the box (or larger to create a slight overlap) and up to ¾ inch thick. Walnut, teak, and mahogany work well with pewter. To this block, glue a smaller thin block cut so it will fit easily into the box and hold the top in place. When dry, smooth the wooden cover—and remove excess glue—with fine sandpaper. Finish it with finishing oil and wax, or polyurethane varnish.

For related projects and crafts, see "Colonial Crafts," "Silversmithing," "Tin and Pierced Work," and "Wrought Iron."

Paul Levin, Director of Photography for the Family Creative Workshop, worked on University of Maryland publications and was a news photographer for the Baltimore Sun. His photographs have appeared in a number of national magazines and have won two William Randolph Hearst photojournalism awards. His work is represented in the permanent collection of New York's Metropolitan Museum of Art.

If photography means more to you than casual snapshots, sooner or later you are likely to want to develop and print your own pictures. Handling the entire process opens a new dimension of craftsmanship for you. The cost of equipping a home darkroom is substantial, but ultimately you will save money. A photographer shooting one roll of black-and-white pictures per week can make a home darkroom pay for itself in a year.

How to set up such a darkroom is described on the pages that follow. The mechanical processes involved in working with black-and-white film are easy to master. (Color printing is more complicated, though new techniques are simplifying the process.)

How Photography Works

Black-and-white film is a transparent plastic coated with gelatin that contains fine, uniformly distributed particles—several billion per square inch—of light-sensitive silver salts. When a photographer trips the shutter, letting light reach the film, the particles undergo an invisible change. During processing, this change is made visible. Chemicals cause the particles exposed to light to blacken, but wash away particles not struck by light. Since the particles look black, the image is reversed, a *negative* in which light areas appear dark and vice versa. Figure A illustrates this process. The developing chemicals affect mainly the exposed particles of silver

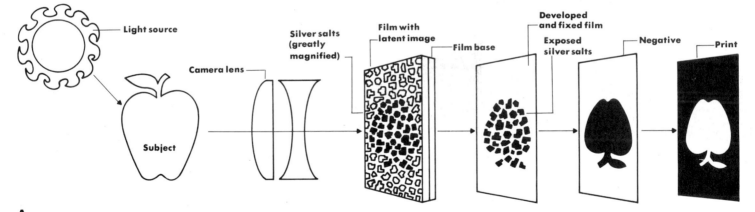

A

Figure A: A picture is made when light reflected by the subject passes through a camera lens and strikes light-sensitive particles of silver salts suspended in gelatin on a plastic film. Particles that have been exposed to light are modified so chemical processing can create a negative photograph. The dark and light tones of the negative are then reversed to produce a positive print.

salts, but they eventually act on the unexposed ones; thus, if the developer were allowed to work indefinitely, the result would be a totally black negative. To prevent this the chemicals are neutralized at the proper time with a *stop bath* that ends the chemical action. Then the negative is fixed (that is, made permanent) by treating it with another chemical, to dissolve unexposed particles that would otherwise darken in time. A final wash removes the fixing chemical.

In the darkroom, you first develop a negative, bringing out the reversed negative image. In a second stage, you use the negative to expose paper that is coated—much like the film—creating on the paper a positive copy of the image (dark areas appear light and vice versa).

Transferring the negative image onto printing paper may be done in two ways. When negative and printing paper are in physical contact as light is projected through the negative, same-size contact prints result. But when the negative image is projected onto the printing paper by an enlarger, the image can be enlarged many times. In either method, the exposed paper is processed by the same steps employed on film—developing, stop bath, fixing, washing, and drying.

Opposite: Photographic processing in a home darkroom starts with developing a roll of exposed film to get reverse-image negatives (top). These can be printed as positive-image same-size contacts (middle) as a guide in selecting those you want to print as finished enlargements (bottom).

The Darkroom

The term *darkroom* is something of a misnomer. Of all the steps involved in turning exposed film into pictures, only one brief operation—transferring the exposed film from its camera container to a small developing tank—must be done in total darkness. Any light-tight closet will serve for this step. Other steps in film-processing are done in ordinary light. The exposing and developing steps of printing require dim illumination from a *safelight* (an ordinary low-wattage light-bulb with a special filter to block colors that will fog the film).

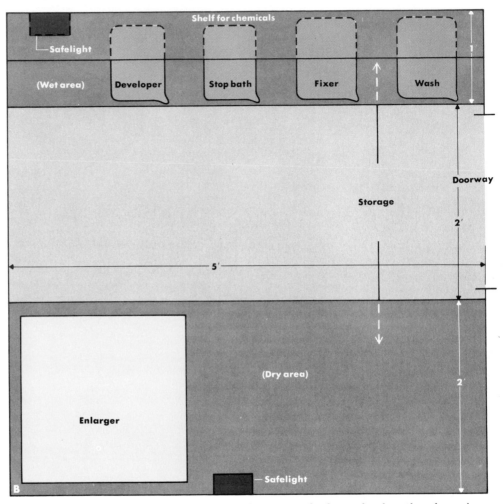

Figure B: The basic darkroom should have two work areas, one for dry work, where the enlarger is placed, the other for wet work, where the developer, stop bath, fixer, and wash trays are lined up in that order. A shelf for chemicals above the wet area, safelights near the enlarger and developer tray, and storage space below both complete the basic requirements. All items will fit into a 5-by-5-foot area.

Your darkroom need be no larger than 5 feet square. A bathroom, kitchen, attic room, or basement corner will do, as long as a temperature of about 68 degrees Fahrenheit can be maintained and light can be excluded. Light leaks through a window are difficult to block entirely in daylight. It is easiest to start out by working at night. Be sure to block light coming under a door from other rooms. A common belief that darkroom walls should be black is unfounded. When no light is present, there is no danger of reflection. When a safelight is being used, maximum reflection is desirable.

A minimum-space arrangement for basic darkroom equipment is shown in Figure B. Note that wet and dry processes are separated by the aisle so the chemicals cannot contaminate the printing paper. Ordinary electrical outlets are adequate for the enlarger lamp, the safelights, and the timer. A source of hot and cold running water is a great convenience but not essential—developed and fixed negatives and prints can be taken to a nearby sink for washing, which does not require darkness.

Graphic Arts
Developing negatives

Once your darkroom is ready and you have some exposed film which you are willing to risk in experimentation, you are ready to develop your first set of negatives. You should get a good result on the first attempt.

The steps are simple. In a totally dark room you load the film onto a spiral reel and put it in a light-tight developing tank. Then with lights on, you will pour chemicals in and out of the tank, following a set time schedule. Finally, you will wash the negatives and hang them up to dry.

The equipment and materials you will need for developing negatives are listed at right. All items are available at photographic supply stores.

All photographic chemicals should be handled with care. Those containing acid can cause painful burns, especially in the more concentrated solutions. Too, the chemicals can stain clothing—wear a plastic apron. Use the proper tools to avoid touching the chemicals, and wash any splashes off skin at once. Keep chemicals away from children (many of them are poisonous) and read the labels carefully so you will know the proper antidote in the event of an accident.

Preparing the Chemicals

Prepare the film developer solution in a bottle or other container, following the label instructions. Many developers come in powder form and have to be dissolved in hot water. If your developer is of this type, put ice cubes in a plastic bag that you can suspend in the solution, thus lowering the temperature quickly (photograph 1). Many powdered chemicals are mixed first with water to make a stock solution, which can be stored in a brown bottle. This stock solution usually is further diluted with water to make the working solution actually used. When you have prepared a working solution, measure the capacity of your developing tank by filling it with water; then set aside exactly that amount of developer to avoid a messy overflow.

Have a second container holding the same amount (developing tank capacity) of the stop bath. Then put the same quantity of fixing-bath solution in a third container. The temperature of all these liquids should be as close to 68 degrees Fahrenheit as possible. Any temperature between 65 and 75 degrees will work, provided all liquids are at the same temperature, and the times recommended for that temperature are followed. (The film can be damaged by the rapid expansion and contraction that occur with drastic temperatures changes.) Uniform temperatures can be achieved by setting all three containers in a single large tray of 68-degree water (photograph 2).

Equipment

A film-developing tank and reel to fit your film
Film developer
Stop bath
Fixing bath
Wetting agent, to keep film from water-spotting as it dries
Soft, clean sponges for drying negatives
Photographic thermometer
Scissors
Can opener for 35mm film, to remove film from its container
Spring-type clothespins or clips to hang film on a wire to dry
Plastic stirring rods
Plastic graduates for measuring chemicals
Plastic funnel
Containers for holding and storing chemicals
Timer (a watch with a second hand will do)
Water tray for equalizing chemical temperatures
Glassine envelopes for storing negatives

1: If the developing chemicals you plan to use have to be dissolved first in hot water, you will have to wait for them to cool to the required temperature before using them. But you can speed the process by suspending a watertight plastic bag of ice cubes in the solution.

2: To maintain a uniform temperature in the developer solution, fixing bath, and stop bath—ideally 68 degrees Fahrenheit—set all three (as well as the developer tank) in a single container of warm water. After a short while a thermometer reading taken for one will apply to all.

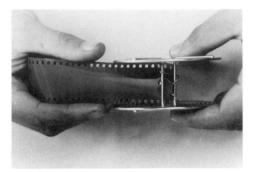

3: Loading film onto a developer reel in total darkness is difficult at first; so practice with a junked roll of film in daylight until you can do it with your eyes closed. If you use a spring-type stainless-steel reel, bow the last few inches of the film by pressing from the sides with your thumb and index finger. Insert the end of the film into the clip at the center of the reel.

4: Once the film is attached, rotate the reel with one hand and unroll the roll of film held in the other, thus drawing the film onto the reel's spiral track. Too much tension between reel and roll will pull the film end from the clip; too much slack will let the film wander from the track.

5: In a properly threaded reel, the film is rolled up like a carpet except that adjacent layers do not touch. If, when you view the reel from the side in daylight, space can be seen between each loop in the spiral, you have mastered loading the reel and are ready to develop an exposed roll of film.

The Developing Tank and Reel

The hardest darkroom task for beginners is loading the film onto the reel of the developing tank (photographs 3, 4, and 5), a task that must be done in total darkness. Practice this operation first. It pays to sacrifice a roll of junked film to perfect your technique—first in light, then with your eyes closed, then in the dark. Pry open the film container, if there is one, pull out the spool, pull loose the end of any paper backing (such as that on 620-roll film) and cut off the leader with scissors so the end is straight. The means of attaching the film to the reel vary, but the objective is to put the film in grooves without any parts touching. If your reel is the stainless steel kind with a spring clip in the center (a common type), use one hand to hold the rolled film by its edges (never its face), and use the other to depress the spring clip. Slightly bow a short length, about 3 inches, at the end of the film between your thumb and forefinger, and insert it beneath the clip. Let the clip spring back, pinning the film to the core. When the film is attached, keep turning the reel counterclockwise, gradually feeding the film into the reel's spiral channel. Too much tension will pull the film out of the clip, too little will make it leave the channel (and the negatives will come out with spots and kinks). Plastic reels, while not as durable as the stainless steel kind, are less expensive and easier to load. The film is started at the outer edge of the reel and is easily wound into the center by turning the sides back and forth.

When you have mastered the art of loading a reel, you are ready to develop an exposed roll of film. After making sure your developing tank and reel are clean and

6: When the film is fogged by inadvertent exposure to light during the developing process, a print made from it will have a gray cast.

7: An unfogged negative will produce a print such as this one, with a wide tonal range, bright highlights, and good shadow detail.

dry, turn the lights out. The room must be totally dark. If you can see anything at all after being in the room a few minutes, it is not dark enough. Light leaks can ruin film (especially the high-speed types) causing overall fogging, and graying all the highlights (see photographs 6 and 7). In darkness, load the film onto the reel, put the reel in the developing tank, and close the tank. Only then should you turn the room lights back on.

The Developer Solution
Depending on what film and developer you use—there are thousands of different combinations—developing time will vary from 2 to 30 minutes. Follow the manufacturer's guidelines for your film, being sure to make any adjustment needed for temperature. A typical time and temperature table is shown below right. This is not a minor detail; for one kind of film, the developing formula requires 5½ minutes to work at 75 degrees Fahrenheit and twice that time at 65 degrees Fahrenheit. Start timing the developer when you begin pouring the developer into the tank. Tilting the tank slightly (photograph 8) will shorten the pouring time because it allows air to escape on the top side. Continue pouring quickly until the tank is filled, bringing the tank to an upright position as it gets full.

Agitation
The tank contains enough chemicals to complete development, but if it is left undisturbed, the developer solution touching the film will become exhausted. You can keep the developer working with a gentle movement called agitation. Cap the tank and slowly turn it upside down, then restore it to its original position (photograph 9). A complete turn should take about five seconds. Start agitation as soon as the tank is filled, and repeat once a minute through the developing process. After the first agitation only, give the tank a sharp rap to dislodge any air bubbles that might be trapped in the solution. When the time is up, uncap the tank and pour off the developer.

You can reuse many film developers, but keep track of the number of rolls developed. The manufacturer's instructions tell how many rolls can be developed in one batch of solution and what compensation through replenishment may be necessary. Also note the date you mixed the solution so you will not use it beyond its recommended life. Used developer should be strained at room temperature just before reuse—pour it through a funnel stoppered with absorbent cotton or lined with filter paper.

The Stop Bath
Pouring the developer solution out of the tank does not entirely end the development process. It is necessary to rinse the film to stop its action. Check the temperature of the stop bath to be sure it is still the same as the developer solution was. Start timing the 30-second stop bath as you begin to pour it into the developer tank. Agitate the tank slowly and continuously. When the time is up, pour the stop bath back into its storage container.

The Fixer
Chemical development of the exposed silver salts has been arrested, but the unexposed particles must still be removed by the process called *fixing*; the chemical that accomplishes it is sometimes called *hypo*. A second chemical in the fixer hardens the emulsion.

Check the temperature of the fixer, and pour it into the tank as you did with the developer and the stop bath. Let it work for the time recommended (usually two to ten minutes). Agitate the tank for at least half the fixing time. When the time is up, pour the fixer back into its storage container. You can reuse fixer many times.

If, after you reuse a fixer several times, your film emerges from the developing tank with a milky color, your fixer has lost some of its strength. All is not lost, however. Return the film to the tank with the *same* fixer solution and let the fixer work for twice the time it takes the milky color to leave the film. To tell when it is gone, check once a minute. Then discard the fixer. You can use a fixer check to tell you when the fixer nears exhaustion; if a milky precipitate forms, discard the solution.

8: Tilt the developing tank while pouring chemical solutions into it. This shortens the time it takes you to fill the tank, and allows you to control the timing more precisely.

9: Gently agitate the tank holding developing film by inverting it slowly and then returning it to an upright position. This maneuver, lasting about 5 seconds, keeps the developer circulating. (Some tanks cannot be inverted without leaking; these should be agitated with a circular motion.)

Time and temperature chart

Name of Film	Normal Developing Time in Minutes		
	65°F	70°F	75°F
Kodak Tri-X	6	5½	5
Kodak Plus-X	6	5	4¼
Kodak Panatomic-X	4½	3¾	3
Ilford FP-4	7	6	5
Ilford HP-4	11	8	5½
Ilford Pan-F	5¼	4½	3¾
GAF 125	7	5½	4½
GAF 500	8½	7	5¾

The Final Wash

The chemicals have done their work. All that remains is to rinse and dry the developed film. The simplest way to rinse the film is to remove the reel from the tank and set it under running water for 30 minutes. The water should be adjusted to the temperature of the other solutions. If you like, you can speed the rinsing process by using a *clearing agent* to remove the fixer residue. Such agents do the job in about three minutes and can be reused. But a final short running-water wash is still recommended.

The Wetting Agent

Before unloading the film from the reel, immerse the reel in a commercial wetting agent (a sudsy mixture that keeps water spots from forming on the film as it dries). Remove the film from the reel, holding it by the edges, and squeeze water from the film by running it between two soft, damp photographic sponges. Attach one end of the film to a spring-type clothespin or clip on an overhead wire in a dust-free place, and put a second clip on the bottom to make it hang straight.

When the negatives are dry, cut the roll into short strips and store each one in a glassine envelope (photograph 10). Handle the negatives only by the edges. Store in a cool, dry place.

Graphic Arts
Making contact prints $ ▨ ⚦ ⚴

There is little room to exercise creative options when you develop negatives. Results depend on how accurately you follow set procedures. But once you have the negatives, judgment and handcrafting skill have a role to play.

Printmaking is usually done in two stages. First, prints the same size as the negative, known as contact prints, are made. Their purpose is to let you see exactly what you have on film so you can check the quality of your pictures, and choose the best ones for the more costly and time-consuming work of making enlargements. Contact printing is not essential in arriving at the finished product, but unless you are able to judge a picture from a negative, it is a valuable detour to take on the way to obtaining the best results. Too, contact prints provide a means of reference within your files, and simplify finding any particular negative.

Contact prints are so named because they are made with the negatives held directly against the printing paper. After exposure to light, the development of the pictures is the same for contacts as for enlargements.

The equipment and materials you will need for making contact prints (in addition to those listed on page 1491 for developing negatives), are listed at left.

Setting Up

Since much of the printing process takes place in semi-darkness, advance preparations are necessary. Mix the developer, stop-bath solution and fixer as you did for the negatives, but increase the quantity to fill the trays about halfway. Mix only enough working solution of developer for one session (it does not keep well at diluted strength). A fourth tray containing water holds prints after fixing until you are ready to rinse them. At the end of the session, all prints can be rinsed together. Arrange the trays in this sequence: developer, stop bath, fixer, and holding tray (so you can move easily from one step to the next). If you are using an enlarger, place it away from the chemicals—on the other side of the room if possible. (If you don't have an enlarger, you can substitute an ordinary lightbulb, as explained below.)

To make contact prints, use a hinged contact-printing frame (photograph 11) to hold the negatives flat against a sheet of printing paper. Clean both sides of the glass top; then open the frame, taking care not to get fingerprints on the glass. Take the negatives out of the glassine envelopes, holding them only by the edges. Notice the direction that the negatives curl; they always curl toward the dull emulsion side. Since this emulsion must face the paper during printing and the negatives will be between the glass top and the printing paper, position them in their slots with the concave (dull) side facing up (photograph 11).

Equipment

An enlarger for your size of negatives, or a 15-watt incandescent bulb

Print developer

Two 2-inch-deep stainless steel or plastic trays, 11 by 13 inches, one for the developer, the other for the stop bath

Two 13-by-16-inch trays, 4 to 6 inches deep, one for fixing, the other for rinsing

Hinged contact-printing frame

Photographic printing paper

Timer with a range up to 60 seconds

15-watt safelight with an amber filter

Two pairs of tongs for handling prints

Tray siphon to be attached to a sink faucet for rinsing prints

Hypo clearing agent to speed rinsing (optional)

Print-flattening solution to limit curling (optional)

Blotter books, blotter roll, or an electric dryer

Magnifying glass and grease pencil for examining and marking contact sheets

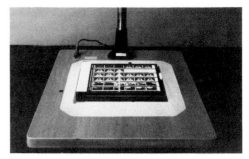

10: Store and protect negatives in glassine file sheets (above) or individual glassine envelopes. Hold negatives by the edges while inserting them into their containers. To help locate negatives for printing, attach a matching contact-print strip to the glassine compartment.

11: To insert negatives into the contact-printing frame, hold a strip at the corners without touching the emulsion, and slip it into the horizontal slots in the frame. The dull, concave side should face up because the emulsion must be in contact with the paper during the printing process.

12: To prepare for contact printing, turn on the enlarger lamp and adjust the height of the head on the supporting column until the light covers the contact printing frame. But be sure to turn off all lights except a safelight before putting photographic paper in the holder.

Close the loaded contact frame and put it on the base board of the enlarger (Figure C). Adjust the height of the enlarger until the light covers the contact frame (photograph 12). Note the position of the contact frame, set the lens in the enlarger at f/11, then open the contact frame again.

Making the Contact Prints

Turn off all lights, including the enlarger light, and turn on the safelight. Remove one sheet of printing paper from its light-tight box or envelope, and reseal the container. This paper is coated with a light-sensitive emulsion, and like film, it curls toward the emulsion side. But this emulsion may be shiny or dull, depending on the kind of paper. Because this concave side must face the negatives, slide the paper, emulsion side up, into the slot on the side of the contact frame that will be beneath the negatives. Then close the contact frame. The weight of the glass presses the negatives against the paper. Make sure the frame is in the right position under the enlarger.

Determining the Exposure Time

You will have to discover the best exposure time by trial and error. To start, set the timer for 10 seconds and turn on the enlarger light. If you have the kind of timer that is connected to the enlarger, the light will go off automatically when the time is up. Otherwise, you will have to start the timer with one hand and turn on the enlarger light with the other, then turn off the light when the timer bell rings. The best exposure time will vary. After you develop the 10-second exposure, you will know whether you need to increase the exposure time for a darker print or shorten it for a lighter print. The printing capability of the negative, of course, is never exhausted.

You can get nearly the same results with less sophisticated equipment. Center the contact printing frame on a table 5 feet below a 15-watt incandescent bulb. Mark the position of the frame on the table, in case a second trial is necessary. Set the timer for 7 seconds, turn on the light, and proceed as above.

Developing the Print

When an exposure has been made, work by safelights only as you set the timer for the recommended developing time—often 1½ minutes at 68 degrees Fahrenheit —and start it as you slip the paper into the developing tray. Immerse the entire sheet, and agitate it gently and constantly with a pair of tongs or by rocking the tray. During developing, the image appears. When the full time is up (and not before), remove the contact sheet with the tongs, and let it drain for a few seconds over the developer tray. Then put the print into the stop bath without letting the tongs touch the solution. Use a second a pair of tongs to agitate the print so you avoid contaminating the developer. After 30 seconds, move the contact sheet into the fixer with the second pair of tongs, and continue to agitate it. After one minute in the fixer, room lights may be turned on briefly while you examine the print without removing it from the fixer. If the image is too light, you can abandon the

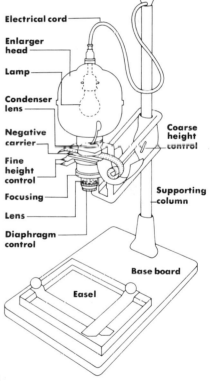

C

Figure C: The working parts of a typical enlarger include: an enlarger head containing an electric lamp that exposes the printing paper; a condenser lens that is adjusted to spread light uniformly over the negative in the carrier below it; a second lens, focused by a dial control (sometimes by a bellows) to form a sharp, enlarged image on the printing paper; a diaphragm like that of a camera, which controls the amount of light passing through the lens; and height controls to raise or lower the assembly and thus govern the size of the image cast on the easel below. The easel, which holds the printing paper flat, rests on the base board and has masking arms to determine the area of the paper that will be exposed.

print at this point and make a second one, increasing the exposure time. If it is too dark, reduce the exposure time. If it seems right, turn off the lights, and let the print remain in the fixer for the recommended time—5 to 15 minutes. Then remove the sheet and put it in the water tray until you are ready to rinse it. At the end of the printing session, move this tray to a sink, and use a tray siphon to wash all prints for 40 to 60 minutes with the running water at the recommended temperature. A 5 minute bath in a chemical called *hypo-clearing agent* will cut the final rinse time down to 10 minutes. Figure D summarizes the five processes and their durations.

To keep the print from curling as it dries, you may want to immerse it in a print-flattener solution before drying it, or you can sandwich the print between two blotters in a blotter book or blotter roll. Another alternative is to blot the prints, then dry them on a nylon window screen or an old sheet suspended from four chairs.

Why it is called hypo

When the right chemical to accomplish the fixing process was discovered in 1839, sodium thiosulfate was masquerading under the name of sodium hyposulfite. The error has since been corrected, but photographers still call the fixer hypo.

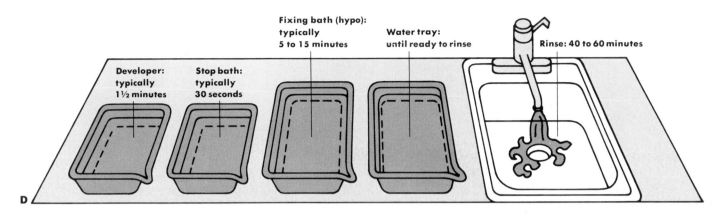

Fixing bath (hypo): typically 5 to 15 minutes

Water tray: until ready to rinse

Rinse: 40 to 60 minutes

Developer: typically 1½ minutes

Stop bath: typically 30 seconds

D

Figure D: The entire print-developing process lasts about an hour and follows the sequence of five stages shown here from left to right. The water tray is simply a holding tray, a convenience to allow you to accumulate several prints at a time before rinsing them as a group. If you use a special hypo-clearing agent after fixing, you can reduce the rinsing time to about 10 minutes.

Equipment

A negative carrier for the enlarger to hold your size of negatives

Can of compressed air, camel's hair brush, anti-static solution and soft lintless applicators (photographic wipes) for cleaning dust from negatives

Enlarging easel to hold printing paper flat and in focus under the enlarger

Grain-focusing magnifier for accurate focusing

Two pieces of 8-by-10-inch cardboard with round holes of 1- and 2-inch diameter, respectively (at the center), and the two 1- and 2-inch disks attached to stiff, non-shiny wire about 1 foot long. These are for controlling exposure on certain areas of the print (dodging and burning).

Craft knife and L-square for trimming prints

Tiny sable brush (No. 0 or smaller), for touching out dust specks with spotting dye

Mounting boards, dry-mounting tissue, and an electric iron or mounting press for mounting finished prints

Graphic Arts
Making enlargements 💲 ⬛ 🧍 🜂

Selecting negatives worthy of enlargement requires experience and discernment. In a roll containing 8 to 36 exposures, only a few are likely to be worth further attention after you make a contact print. Some pictures may turn out to be badly lighted, poorly exposed, or blurred. Others may be technically fine but uninteresting as pictures. Examine the contacts carefully with a magnifying glass in good light and select the most promising images for further work (photograph 13). Each contact print appears with the number of its corresponding negative, so it is easy to locate the strip that contains the needed negative.

The equipment and materials you will need for making and finishing enlargements are listed at left (in addition to those listed on page 1491 for developing negatives and on page 1494 for making contact prints).

The Negative Holder

You may need to raise or tilt the enlarger lamp housing (see Figure C, page 1495) to gain access to the negative carrier beneath it. In other enlargers, the carrier pulls out like a drawer. Put the strip of negatives into the holder, handling it very carefully. Align the strip emulsion side (concave and dull) down so the desired negative is framed by the window in the holder (photograph 14). Examine the negative under the enlarger light. If you see dust spots (photograph 15), clean the negative in three stages: remove small dust particles by blowing compressed air across the surface of the negative (photograph 16), loosen stubborn particles by brushing lightly with a clean camel's-hair brush (photograph 17), and if necessary, use anti-static negative cleaner applied with a photographic wipe (photograph 18) to remove fingerprints on the shiny side of the negative. Fingerprints on the soft emulsion side cannot be removed, but dust on the emulsion side can be blown away with compressed air.

With the clean negative in position in its carrier, turn the room lights off. Turn on the enlarger lamp, and open the lens diaphragm to its largest opening, typically f/4.5, to produce the brightest possible image for focusing.

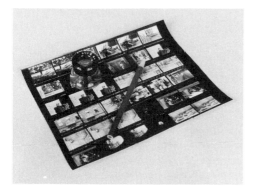

13: After you examine the contact sheet carefully with a magnifying glass, use a grease pencil to mark those pictures that merit enlargement.

14: Insert the strip of negatives into the negative carrier located below the enlarger-lamp housing and frame the desired negative in the window.

15: Under the enlarger light, examine the negative for particles of dust. Any bit of dust will cause a distracting white spot on the enlarged print.

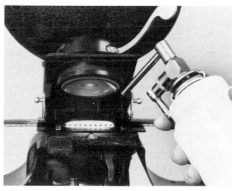

16: Remove as much dust as possible with a stream of compressed air. If there is dust on the emulsion side, lift the negative to clean it.

17: If necessary, remove the more stubborn particles with a camel's-hair brush. But be very careful not to scratch the delicate emulsion.

18: Fingerprints (on the shiny non-emulsion side only) can be removed with an anti-static negative cleaner that will also make the film repel dust.

Adjusting the Enlarger

Place the easel that will hold the printing paper on the base board below the enlarger lamp. Using the scales on the easel, adjust the movable arms to frame the size of the print you wish to make. An 8-by-10-inch print, less the white border created by the easel as it holds the paper flat, is the most common. Raise or lower the enlarger head to produce an image that exactly fills the space framed by the easel (photograph 19). This is the time to re-evaluate the composition of the picture. It is easy to eliminate unwanted areas of the photograph by raising the enlarger head so only the desired area falls within the easel opening, or adjust the arms of the easel so you print the entire negative as you saw the picture when you took it. You can also readjust the position of the easel on the base board. Printing only part of a negative is called *cropping*.

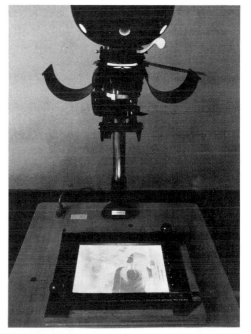

19: Raise or lower the enlarger head to adjust the size of the image until it exactly fills the space framed by the easel's masking arms.

20: When the enlarger is sharply focused, the grains in the film that make up the projected image can be clearly seen.

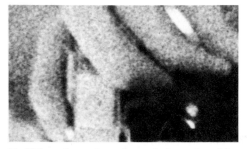

21: If the enlarger is not focused, the grains of the print are indistinct. Grain becomes much more visible in a focusing magnifier, disappearing when the image is not in focus.

22: This test print was exposed in five sections at five-second increments. By masking segments of the print in this manner for fixed exposure periods, you can select the proper exposure with ease.

Put a piece of white paper in the easel and focus the image by raising or lowering the lens. Examine the image on the easel with the grain focuser when you make the final focusing adjustments (photographs 20 and 21). The grain focuser magnifies the grains in the film that make up the projected image. If you do not have a grain focuser, look for sharply contrasting areas in the print, such as the lettering on a sign, to help you refine the focus.

Printing Papers

Choosing the right grade of printing paper is one of the most important aspects of darkroom work. Upon this depends the character of your finished print. A series of six paper types is available to create tonal gradations ranging from the softest tones (with fine distinctions among the various shades of gray) to the harshest contrasts (with hardly any shades between dense black and dazzling white). The paper grades are numbered 1 through 6. High numbers give greater contrast, with grade 2 usually being the norm for enlargements as well as contact prints. Low-contrast paper is often used in portraits to emphasize facial contours and soften blemishes and wrinkles. It is also useful for salvaging high-contrast negatives. Higher-contrast paper (above grade 2) eliminates subtle variations in tone and is used to enliven prints and sharpen a dull negative.

A second area of choice is the type of paper surface. Papers may be either glossy or matte and come in a wide variety of textures. Experiment freely with paper types on enlargements, but make contact prints on non-textured paper, since an uneven surface would interfere with viewing under a magnifying glass.

The Test Print

The proper exposure time for an enlargement is partly determined by trial and error. From past experience you may have a good idea of the right exposure, but each negative is unique and has its own requirements. You could make a few exposures, hit or miss, until you come up with the right one. But to avoid the tedium of repeated trial runs, there is a method of gathering all the information you need in a single experiment.

Reduce the diaphragm opening of the enlarger lens to a smaller f-stop. Try f/8 at first, unless the negative is badly underexposed (try f/11) or overexposed (try f/5.6). Higher numbered f-stops project less light, permitting longer exposure time. With all lights off except the safelight, remove a sheet of printing paper from its box and place it, emulsion (concave) side up, under the easel frame. Set the enlarger timer for 5 seconds. If your timer is not connected to your enlarger, use the two-handed timing method suggested for contact printing. With a piece of cardboard, cover about four-fifths of the printing paper, leaving only a narrow band on one side. Expose the strip of paper for 5 seconds. Then move the cardboard so it exposes a larger area of the paper (about two-fifths) and make a second 5-second exposure. Continue in this way, making three additional exposures—three-fifths unmasked, four-fifths unmasked and completely unmasked. You will then have samples of five different exposures, at 25, 20, 15, 10, and 5 seconds respectively, on a single sheet of printing paper (photograph 22). You could make, say, seven exposures at 3 seconds each if you wanted a different range of data. But in planning your experiment, guess what the proper exposure should be, based on past experience and the quality of the negative you are working with. Then center your experiment on that figure.

Develop the trial print as you did the contact print (refer to pages 1495–1496). Allow 1½ minutes in the developer, but this time only 15 seconds in the stop bath and only 2 minutes in the fixer (don't bother to rinse). Turn on the lights, examine the test results, and choose the best exposure time. If the darkest strip is still too light, the longest exposure was not long enough; if the lightest strip is still too dark, the shortest exposure was not short enough; in either case you will need a new test. If your range of times becomes too short to be practical, use a smaller diaphragm opening (a larger f-number). If the exposure time is approaching 60 seconds, open the diaphragm and reduce the exposure time so you do not risk damaging the negative with the heat of the enlarger lamp. (The larger the opening, the less time is required to produce the same result.)

The Finished Product

When you have selected the proper exposure time, set the timer and turn out the lights. Working by safelight only, put a fresh piece of printing paper in the easel and make the final exposure. Then develop the finished print.

About 1½ minutes in the developer tray with constant but gentle agitation should give a good result, but you can leave it in longer if the picture does not show deep tones in this time. But do not attempt to compensate for overexposure by shortening the developing time to less than 1½ minutes. Generally it is better to keep the development time constant so the only variable you have to deal with is exposure time. As with the contacts, hold the print above the tray for a few seconds while the excess solution drains off, and then transfer the print to the stop bath. Using a second pair of tongs, agitate the print continuously for 30 seconds in the stop bath. Move it to the fixer for 10 minutes, agitating occasionally. After a few minutes of fixing, you can turn on the lights to examine the print. It is now more or less in its finished form, though it will lighten a bit as it dries. After fixing, wash the print thoroughly in running water for about one hour. Again, a hypo-clearing agent can cut the rinse time considerably. The drying techniques described for contact prints apply to enlargements as well.

Equipment

Equipment and materials used for developing negatives and making prints are listed below. When you shop for the more expensive items, keep in mind that you can save by buying second-hand equipment.

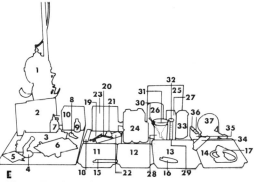

Figure E: The tools pictured and keyed are: 1) an enlarger; 2) photographic printing paper; 3) enlarging easel; 4) grain-focusing magnifier; 5) paper and pencil; 6) burning and dodging masks; 7) can of compressed air; 8) camel's-hair brush; 9) anti-static negative cleaner; 10) photographic wipes; 11) developer tray; 12) stop-bath tray; 13) fixer tray; 14) wash tray; 15 and 16) print tongs; 17) tray syphon with rubber hose; 18) contact printing frame, 19) scissors; 20) grease pencil; 21) magnifying glass; 22) glassine envelopes for storing negatives; 23) automatic timer; 24) chemicals; 25) ferrotype plate for making a high-gloss print; 26) paper toweling; 27) absorbent cotton; 28 and 29) graduates; 30) stirring rod; 31) funnel; 32) thermometer; 33) developing tank; 34) print squeegee; 35) sponge; 36) film clips; and 37) safelight.

23: Some of the tools and materials used in a home darkroom are pictured above and keyed in the drawing (top right). Specialized items are available at photographic supply stores.

Equipment summary

Basic equipment:

Two work tables (one large enough to hold a row of four trays, the other to hold an enlarger), plus storage shelves for paper and chemicals
Two 2-inch-deep stainless steel or plastic trays, 11 by 13 inches
Two 13-by-16-inch trays, 4 to 6 inches deep
Sink with hot-and-cold mixing faucet and drain
15-watt safelight with amber filter
Timer, with a range up to 60 seconds, that rings at the time set. (A watch with a second hand can be used, or an electric timer can be hooked up to the enlarger to regulate exposure time automatically.)
Photographic thermometer
One small (8- or 10-ounce) and one large (32-ounce) plastic graduate
Large plastic funnel
Two plastic stirring rods
Four half-gallon brown bottles with screw tops

Filter paper or absorbent cotton
Paper toweling
Sponge
Plastic apron
Adhesive tape and waterproof marker

For film developing:

A film developing tank
Several film clips or spring-type plastic clothespins
Glassine envelopes
Film developer, ready-mixed in powder form or liquid concentrate
Stop bath to suspend development by neutralizing developer
Fixing bath (hypo) to clear silver salts from the unexposed part of the negative
Wetting agent, to keep film from waterspotting.
Two soft photographic sponges for drying negatives

For printing:

Enlarger
Blotter books or blotter roll
Compressed air, camel's-hair brush, anti-static solution and soft lintless applicators (photographic wipes)
Enlarging easel
Scissors
Grain-focusing magnifier
Tray syphon with a rubber hose
Two pairs of tongs
Photographic printing paper
Print developer
Stop bath
Fixer
Hypo-clearing agent
Print-flattening solution
Craft knife and L-square for trimming
Fine sable brush (No. 0 or smaller) and spotting dye
Contact printing frame
Photographer's magnifying glass and grease pencil
Mounting boards, dry-mounting tissue, and an electric iron or mounting press

CRAFTNOTES: DODGING AND BURNING

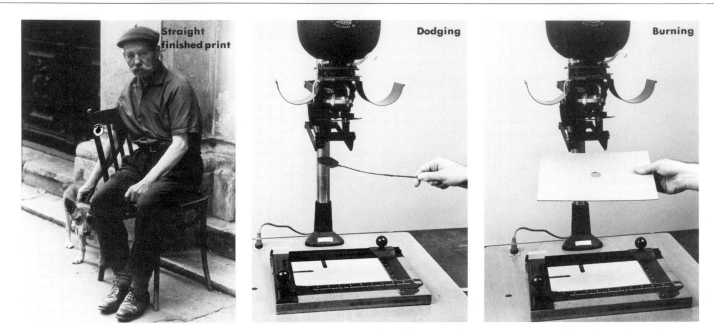

Straight finished print

Dodging

Burning

Darkening and lightening selected areas of the print

In many pictures you will find some tones that detract from the overall balance and effectiveness of the composition. The photograph above left is an example of one. In it the sidewalk and walls are too light, the man's face too dark. You can adjust the printing exposure, darkening the light areas (called **burning**) and lightening the dark areas (called **dodging**) by two simple techniques. Cut disks of 1-inch and 2-inch diameters from the centers of two pieces of cardboard, and attach them to the ends of a piece of stiff wire about 1 foot long. Use the disks, held by the wire, to block the enlarger light from the areas of the print that you want to lighten, as shown in the photograph above center; or use the holes in the pieces of cardboard to focus more light on the areas that need darkening, as shown above right. With either technique, keep the cardboard in motion, moving it around the area you are concentrating on, so its outlines will not show up on the print as a sharp change in tone. An important difference between the two techniques is that dodging is performed while the print is receiving its normal exposure of light, but burning is done by exposing light areas to additional light after the initial exposure. By moving the cardboard toward or away from the light, you can adjust the size of the area in shadow. Experienced photographers dispense with the cardboard tools in favor of using their hands to control the shadows directly. Thus the photographer becomes a handcraftsman with light itself his material. The result of successful burning and dodging is a print with balanced tones (right). The walls and sidewalks have been darkened and the man's face lightened to reveal more detail and eliminate distracting contrasts.

Improved finished print

CRAFTNOTES: RETOUCHING

Minor flaws in a picture—such as the dust spots in the photograph above—can be darkened by hand after the print is dry. Photographic-print dyes are applied directly to the finished print with a very fine (size 0 or smaller) high-quality sable-hair brush, as shown in the photograph below. For the darkest areas use the

dye at full strength. In lighter areas, dilute the dye with water until you reach the proper tone of gray. Before applying the dye, test the tone on a separate piece of paper, and compare it with the tone needed to remedy the print. Don't brush the dye on; apply it by touching just the tip of the brush repeatedly to the paper. (That's why the process is called spotting.) Mottled areas are the easiest to retouch. Even-toned areas are the most difficult, requiring great care and a skillful hand. The photograph below shows a corrected print. Lightening dark areas can be

accomplished only with a special chemical, potassium ferricyanide, which is very poisonous. This bleaching is a dangerous procedure, not recommended for non-professionals.

CRAFTNOTES: MOUNTING

Mounting boards in a variety of standard sizes come in white, black or gray and can be easily cropped to create a border of any desired size—or no border at all. To get a straight, clean edge on prints or mounts, place them on a hard backing such as a pane of glass and cut them with a craft knife guided by a steel straightedge. Prints can be mounted on exhibition boards in a number of ways. For permanence, use dry-mounting tissue —a thin, resin-based waxy sheet that adheres when heated—because it resists warping and discoloring even under the most humid conditions. Trim

the tissue to the same size as the print, put the print face-up on the mounting board with the tissue in between, and cover the print with thin cardboard. Press down firmly on the cardboard with an electric iron set at the temperature for ironing wool. An iron will not give a good result on a print larger than 8 by 10 inches; dry-mounting presses are also available to do the job of the iron more simply and efficiently.

If you are working with resin-coated printing papers, you will have to obtain a special mounting tissue and temperature control strips to prevent overheating and blistering the print. The control strips

have two temperature indicators: one melts at the melting point of the mounting tissue, the lowest temperature at which a good bond can be made; the other melts at the point that the print will blister. Mount the print at a temperature sufficient to melt the first, but not the second, temperature control strip.

Although rubber contact cement is often used and is perhaps the easiest mounting adhesive, it will eventually discolor your prints and is not recommended if you desire permanence.

For related projects and crafts, see the entries "Cameras" and "Serigraphy."

PICKLED AND CANNED FOODS
Preserving the Harvest

Margaret Backos is a kitchen assistant in the Foodservice Test Kitchen of Heinz U.S.A., Pittsburgh, Pennsylvania. At home in nearby Perryopolis, Mrs. Backos cans fruits, vegetables, and pickles for her family to enjoy all year long. All the vegetables come from the backyard garden which is her husband's pride and joy.

Useful booklets
Home Canning of Fruits and Vegetables, (20¢) Home and Garden Bulletin No. 8, and **Making Pickles and Relishes at Home** (15¢), Home and Garden Bulletin No. 92; both from the U.S. Department of Agriculture. Write to the Superintendent of Documents, U.S. Government Printing Office, Washington, D.C. 20402.

The Ball Blue Book, Ball Corporation, Muncie, Indiana 47302 ($1).

Kerr Home Canning & Freezing Book, Kerr Glass Manufacturing Corporation, Consumer Products Division, Sand Springs, Oklahoma 74063 ($1).

Home Canning Fruits & Vegetables, Extension Folder 100, Agricultural Extension Service, University of Minnesota, St. Paul, Minnesota, St. Paul, Minnesota 55101 (no charge for single copy).

If your garden produces vegetables faster than your family and friends can eat them, and you can't pass a roadside stand without stopping to buy a bushel of delicious-looking fruit, the old-fashioned craft of *putting foods up* by canning may be for you. The fact that it helps balance the grocery budget is another incentive to try this simple but effective way of preserving the goodness of nature's bounty.

Canning is preserving foods, including pickled foods, in their own juices or other liquid by sealing them in glass jars and then processing them under extreme heat. Canning may be done in cans, but glass jars are more commonly used because they can be reused, require no special sealing equipment, and make it easier to check the contents. Canned foods are processed under extreme heat to destroy organisms that cause spoilage, to kill bacteria that otherwise might produce poisonous toxins, and to render inactive the enzymes that could affect the flavor, color and texture of the food. Once canned, the foods must be stored in a cool, dry, dark place to protect their nutritional value and color.

Pickling is a form of canning in which fruits and vegetables, especially cucumbers, are put up in a vinegar-based brine, which gives a pungent flavor and crisp texture, before heat treatment. The produce can be left whole or cut to size, according to the recipe; if it is chopped, it is considered a relish. Pickled foods reach their peak of flavor only after six or more weeks in the jars.

Processing Methods
Pickles have the highest acid content of all the foods you will can because the cucumbers have a large amount of acid added in the form of vinegar brine. Less strong, but still highly acid, are rhubarb, fruits and berries, sauerkraut (fermented cabbage) and tomatoes. Foods in the high-acid category do not foster growth of heat-resistant bacteria, but they do allow growth of molds, yeasts and some dangerous heat-sensitive bacteria; therefore, they must be processed. But they can be safely processed in a boiling-water bath at 212 degrees Fahrenheit.

All other vegetables, however, are low-acid foods if they are not pickled with large amounts of vinegar. They have a low resistance to the growth of heat-resistant bacteria such as the dangerous *clostridium botulinum* which causes botulism. As a result, these vegetables must be processed at the higher temperature of 240 degrees Fahrenheit to destroy these microorganisms. This temperature can only be reached in a steam-pressure cooker or canner, usually set at 10 pounds pressure. (See chart on page 1505 for variations in pressure needs based on altitude.)

The natural acidity of the food largely determines the type of processing—boiling-water bath (212 degrees) or pressure canner (240 degrees)—needed to home-can that food safely.

In the boiling-water-bath method hot, filled and closed jars of high-acid or pickled foods (precooked or raw) are immersed in a kettle of boiling water. The jars are set on a rack so boiling water can circulate beneath them. The water covers them completely and there is space above for brisk boiling. A cover is put on the kettle and the jars are boiled for the length of time indicated in the recipe. Both jars and food are thus sterilized (Figure A, page 1504).

In the pressure-canning method, the hot, filled, and closed jars of low-acid foods (precooked or raw) are placed in a pressure canner containing only 2 or 3 inches of water. The lid is secured and the pressure builds to the figure indicated in the recipe (usually 10 pounds). The hot steam raises the temperature in the canner high enough to kill any bacteria, even those that are heat-resistant, thus sterilizing both food and jars (Figure B, page 1504).

Our grandmothers used to process foods in water that was hot, but not boiling, for many hours; this is no longer considered a safe canning method. Vegetables and fruits must now be processed by one of the two methods described above. In modern canning, the cooking time is cut while the safety of the canned foods is insured.

Home-canning of fruits and vegetables, whether home-grown or purchased during a time of abundance, is an easy and economical way to capture the taste of summer and enjoy it all year long.

Equipment

Depending on the types of foods you are canning at home, you will need all or some of the following kitchen items:

A water-bath canner for processing high-acid foods—any large, covered stainless-steel or enamelware kettle deep enough so the water will not boil over (Figure A, right). It should have a rack on the bottom. A steam pressure-cooker or canner for processing low-acid foods (Figure B, far right)—there are several types available; check the manufacturer's directions and have the pressure regulator checked periodically.

A large kettle or pot for scalding the jars and lids.

Stone, glass, pottery, or enamelware containers for foods that must remain in a vinegar-brine solution overnight or longer (metal may react to the salt and acid).

Plastic or glass trays or pans to put under jars to catch drips and overflow.

A wide-top funnel for filling jars.

Large long-handled metal spoons and spatula for stirring, skimming and filling jars. Do not use wooden spoons or a wooden chopping board which, if chipped or worn, can harbor bacteria. Also avoid rubber spatulas, which may harden and crack.

Squeeze-type tongs for lifting hot jars out of the water.

A timer (exact processing times are very important).

A food mill or blender.

Kitchen scales.

Enough potholders and dish towels to protect your hands and work surfaces from heat and stains.

(Always read the recipe through and be sure you understand all the directions. Have the ingredients and equipment ready before you start, so that no time is wasted between steps in preparing, packing, and processing foods.)

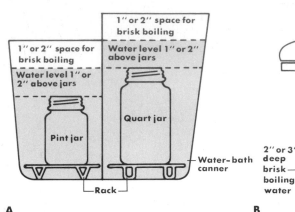

A

Figure A: A large covered metal kettle or water-bath canner is used for processing high-acid foods in a boiling-water bath (212 degrees Fahrenheit). It must be deep enough to allow the water level to reach at least 1 inch above the jars with additional room for brisk boiling.

B

Figure B: A steam-pressure canner or cooker is used for processing low-acid foods. The water level should be only 2 or 3 inches deep. Count the processing time from the moment the pressure reaches 10 pounds (240 degrees Fahrenheit). See table opposite for variations.

The open-kettle method, which involves filling sterilized jars with precooked food and sealing them without further heat treatment, is still used for jams and jellies. It is considered unsafe for use with any other foods; some of the new low-acid hybrids require more intense heat processing and bacteria entering the jars as they are filled are not killed with this method.

Processing times, as well as methods, vary according to the acidity of the foods and their density in the jars. Follow individual recipe recommendations, referring to the chart on page 1505 for variations based on altitudes.

Regardless of the type of food, canning should be done as quickly as possible after the produce is picked, instructions should be followed exactly, and the food, utensils, and the canner's hands must be scrupulously clean. Foods preserved at home should be used within a year after canning.

ESTIMATED YIELDS OF CANNED PRODUCE IN QUARTS

As indicated in the list below, the actual yield from standard measurements of produce will vary depending on the size, maturity, quality, and variety of the produce, the size of the pieces, and the manner in which you prepare and pack it into the jars. Too, the standard weight of a bushel, lug, or box may vary from state to state.

Raw produce	Weight	Yield in quarts
Peaches	48 pounds (bushel)	18 to 24
(4 medium per pound)	22 pounds (lug)	8 to 12
Pears (3 per pound)	50 pounds (bushel)	20 to 25
	46 pounds (box)	16 to 22
Plums	56 pounds (bushel)	24 to 30
(8 medium per pound)	28 pounds (lug)	12 to 15
Tomatoes	53 pounds (bushel)	15 to 20
(4 medium per pound)	30 pounds (lug)	10 to 12
Tomatoes (for juice)	53 pounds (bushel)	12 to 16
Beans (green or wax)	30 pounds (bushel)	12 to 20
Beets (without tops)	52 pounds (bushel)	17 to 24

ALTITUDE TABLES

For boiling-water bath canner			For steam-pressure canner (cooker)
The processing times given in the recipes are for foods canned at altitudes less than 1,000 feet above sea level. If you live at a higher altitude, add to the processing times as indicated in the table below. Add to the processing time if the time called for is:			The processing times given in the recipes are to be counted from the moment the pressure reaches 10 pounds (240 degrees Fahrenheit) at altitudes of 1,000 feet or less above sea level. If you live at a higher altitude, increase the pressure according to the table below in order to reach that temperature.
More than 20 minutes	**20 minutes or less**	**Altitude**	**Process at**
2 minutes	1 minute	1,000 feet	10 pounds
4 minutes	2 minutes	2,000 feet	11 pounds
6 minutes	3 minutes	3,000 feet	11½ pounds
8 minutes	4 minutes	4,000 feet	12 pounds
10 minutes	5 minutes	5,000 feet	12½ pounds
12 minutes	6 minutes	6,000 feet	13 pounds
14 minutes	7 minutes	7,000 feet	13½ pounds
16 minutes	8 minutes	8,000 feet	14 pounds
18 minutes	9 minutes	9,000 feet	14½ pounds
20 minutes	10 minutes	10,000 feet	15 pounds

The Jars

Use only glass jars that are especially designed for canning purposes, never leftover mayonnaise jars or juice bottles. There are jars available with rubber gaskets and wire bails, Mason jars with one-piece porcelain-lined screw-on lids, and Mason jars with flat lids and screw-on bands. The latter are the most popular. The jars, screw-on bands and screw-on lids may be reused; the flat lids never are. Check jars before use and do not use any with nicks, cracks, sharp edges or chips.

Jars and lids to be processed in either a boiling-water bath or in a pressure canner do not need to be sterilized before use; the food and the containers will both be sterilized during processing. The jars should be clean and hot, however. Wash jars in hot soapy water, then scald-rinse in boiling water. Jars should remain in the hot water until filled. Lift them from the water with tongs, turn them upside down on a folded dish towel to drain, then fill. Remove air bubbles by running a table knife between the sides of the jar and the food; if needed, add more liquid to cover, allowing for headroom as specified in the recipes. Wipe the top and the threads of the neck clean with a damp cloth.

Dip separate lids into hot water but do not boil. Leave them in the water until you are ready to close the jars, which should be immediately after they are filled. Fill one jar at a time and close immediately.

After processing, cool the jars by standing them upright on cloth or wood, a few inches apart, away from drafts. After about 12 hours, remove the screw bands and test the seal. If the center of the lid is down and stays down when pressed or tapped with a spoon, the jar is vacuum-sealed and safe. It can be stored without the band; otherwise, the band may be difficult to remove later. Save bands until the next canning. If the seal is not complete, reprocess the food, freeze it immediately for later use, or eat as soon as possible. If stored for some time, the contents of a jar with an incomplete seal will tend to mold and create spoilage problems.

All low-acid vegetables should be boiled in an open pot for 10 to 15 minutes before they are tasted or served. Always check for signs of spoilage—leakage, foam, or a difference in color, texture, or smell—before using any canned food. When in doubt, throw it away where children and pets cannot reach it.

About salt

When canning, use only pure salt—kosher salt or pickling salt. These come in five-and-ten-pound bags. Free-flowing salt such as table salt has anti-caking ingredients which leave a sediment in the bottom of the jar and cause the brine to cloud. Any vegetable may be canned without salt. Salt is for flavor only and is not necessary for safe processing.

About water

If possible, use soft water when canning. Extremely hard water can cause discoloration of pickles, particularly if the water has a high iron content. Some types of hard water may be somewhat softened by the following method: boil for 5 minutes, skim off the scum, and let the water stand for 24 hours. When the sediment has settled to the bottom of container, pour off the water from the top and use.

About vinegar

It is important to use only a high-quality white distilled vinegar or cider vinegar of 4 to 6 percent acidity (check the label). Wine and herb vinegars are not suitable for use in canning. Cider vinegar has a low-acid taste that gives a nice blending of flavors, but it may darken white or light-colored fruits and vegetables. White vinegar has a sharp, pungent taste and is desirable when a light color is important. Do not dilute the vinegar unless the recipe so specifies.

Pickle recipes

Bread and Butter Pickles
Fresh Pack/Boiling-Water Bath
Yield: 8 pints

Ingredients:
4 quarts washed and sliced, but not
    peeled, cucumbers
½ cup canning salt
3 cups onion slices

Brine ingredients:
4 cups distilled white vinegar
4 cups sugar
3 teaspoons celery seeds
2 tablespoons mustard seeds

Combine salt and cucumber slices (photograph 1); cover with ice-cold water; let stand overnight in the refrigerator. Next day, drain the cucumbers (photograph 2). Combine brine ingredients and bring to a boil; boil gently for 10 minutes. While brine is boiling, slice the onions.

1: Combine 4 quarts of unpeeled, sliced cucumbers with ½ cup of canning salt. Cover with ice-cold water and let stand overnight.

2: Next day, drain the water from the cucumber slices, using a slotted metal spoon. Metal utensils are safer for canning than wooden or rubber ones which may chip or crack, harboring germs.

Add cucumbers and onions to brine and bring back to the boiling point. Pack quickly into clean, hot jars to within ½ inch of top (photograph 3). Wipe top and rim of jar clean; close each jar as it is filled.

3: Using a metal funnel, fill pint jars with the boiling pickle mixture. Cook pickles in an enamelware, aluminum, or stainless steel saucepan; the acid and salt in the brine may react adversely to copper, iron, or galvanized metal pans.

Immerse filled jars in actively boiling water; boil gently and steadily for 10 minutes, counting from the time the water returns to a boil (photograph 4). Check seal.

4: Process the filled, sealed jars in a boiling-water bath. Boil gently and steadily for 10 minutes from the time the water returns to a boil.

Dill Pickle Spears
Fresh Pack/Boiling-Water Bath
Yield: About 11 pickles to 1 quart

Use 5-inch-long pickling cucumbers. Wash thoroughly, using a vegetable brush. Cut into quarters, lengthwise.

Put 1 tablespoon canning salt, 1 garlic clove, and 2 heads of dill into each clean, hot jar. Pack cucumbers into jar to fill.

Boil 1 part distilled white vinegar to 1 part water for brine; 1 teaspoon pickling spices per quart may be added. Pour brine over cucumbers in jar to within ½ inch of top.

Wipe top and rim of jar clean; close each jar as it is filled.

Process in boiling-water bath for 20 minutes, counting from the time the hot jars are placed into actively boiling water. Check seal.

Whole Dill Pickles
Fresh-Pack/Boiling-Water Bath
Yield: About 11 pickles fill 1 quart

Select small, firm, uniform-size pickling cucumbers about 1½ to 2 inches long. Wash thoroughly, using a vegetable brush; drain or wipe dry.

Place 1 tablespoon canning salt, 1 or 2 garlic cloves, and a head or 2 of dill in each clean, hot jar. Pack cucumbers into jar to fill.

Boil 1 part distilled white or cider vinegar to 1 part water for brine; 1 teaspoon pickling spices per quart may be added. Pour brine over cucumbers to within ½ inch of top.

Wipe top and rim of jar clean; close each jar as it is filled.

Process in boiling-water bath for 20 to 25 minutes, counting from the time the hot jars are placed into actively boiling water. Check seal.

The homemade pickles above are whole dills, dill spears, and bread-and-butter slices. Use only unwaxed pickling cucumbers and remove any blossoms. The brine cannot penetrate the waxy skins of eating cucumbers. Recipe for the hot peppers shown is on page 1510.

Kitchen Favorites and Celebrations
Tomato recipes

Tomatoes
Raw Pack/Boiling-Water Bath

Use only red, ripe, blemish-free tomatoes. Wash a few at a time; dip into boiling water for 30 seconds; then plunge into ice cold water. Slip skins off; core and de-vein. Cut large tomatoes into quarters; leave small ones whole.

Pack tomatoes tightly into clean, hot jars to within ½ inch of top. Be sure to push tomatoes quite firmly together so there is little air left in the jar before processing. Too much air will cause tomatoes to float on top of the liquid after processing.

Add 1 teaspoon canning salt, and sugar to taste, to each quart.

Wipe top and rim of jars clean; close each jar as it is filled.

Process in boiling-water bath for 30 minutes. (In Minnesota, longer processing times for tomatoes are recommended; check with your local county extension service.) Check seal.

Note: Low-acid (yellow) tomatoes must be processed in a pressure canner for 15 minutes at 5 pounds pressure for quart jars.

Baba's Tomatoes and Peppers
Hot Pack/Pressure-Canner Method
Yield: Approximately 8 quarts

Ingredients:
15 pounds ripe, firm tomatoes
8 pounds green (sweet) peppers
2 pounds hot peppers
6 cloves of garlic, finely chopped
4 teaspoons sugar (more or less)
canning salt and pepper to taste

Wash, core and cut tomatoes into wedges; puree in a food mill or blender. Boil the tomatoes and juice until slightly thick, then simmer.

While tomatoes are simmering, wash, seed and cut the green and hot peppers into strips (photograph 5), then chop into large pieces.

5: Cut hot peppers and sweet peppers into strips, remove seeds, and chop peppers into large pieces.

Add salt, pepper, garlic, and sugar to simmering tomatoes. Turn off heat under tomatoes and add peppers (photograph 6). Stir until raw peppers and cooked tomatoes are well mixed. (By packing the peppers raw, you can insure that they will be tender but crisp after processing in the pressure canner.)

6: Add seasonings to tomatoes, turn off heat, then add raw peppers. Peppers will be tender but still crisp after processing.

Quickly spoon mixture into clean, hot jars (photograph 7). Wipe top and rim of jar clean; close each jar as it is filled.

Process in pressure canner at 10 pounds pressure for 35 minutes. Check seal.

7: Fill clean, hot jars with the mixture; then process in a pressure canner. This recipe was handed down to Mrs. Backos from her grandmother who brought it to America from Austria in the late 1890's.

The tomato-based canned foods above are tomatoes, tomato juice, tomato-vegetable soup and Baba's tomatoes and peppers, a treasured family recipe. The recipes for canned tomatoes and Baba's tomatoes are at left; the remaining recipes are on the following page.

Tomato Juice
Hot Pack/Boiling-Water Bath

Use ripe, juicy, blemish-free tomatoes. Wash and core. Cut into quarters and put through a food mill or fine sieve to remove seeds and skin (photograph 8).

Simmer juice until most of the water evaporates, then quickly bring to a boil. Into clean, hot quart jars, add 1 teaspoon canning salt and ½ teaspoon sugar; ladle boiling juice into jars to within ½ inch of top.

Wipe top and rim of jar clean; close each jar as it is filled.

Process in boiling-water bath for 20 minutes. Check seal.

A steaming mug of homemade tomato-vegetable soup served with home-baked bread is a hearty meal in itself. Tomatoes are combined with carrots, onions, celery, parsley, and seasonings.

8: Mr. Backos helps his wife make the home-canned tomato juice by putting the tomato quarters through a food mill in order to remove the skins and seeds.

Tomato-Vegetable Soup
Hot Pack/Pressure-Canner Method
Yield: Approximately 8 quarts

Ingredients:
15 pounds tomatoes
2 pounds carrots
1 pound onions
1 stalk celery
6 sprigs parsley
¼ cup canning salt
¼ cup sugar to start (add more to taste)

Wash, core, and cut the tomatoes into wedges. Put them in a kettle and cook until soft. Clean and chop celery, onions, carrots and parsley; add to tomatoes and cook until the vegetables are tender. Cool and puree in a food mill, blender, or fine sieve.

Bring soup to a boil; add salt and sugar. Cook until thick, stirring occasionally.

Fill clean, hot jars to within 1 inch of top. Wipe top and rim of jar clean; close each jar as it is filled.

Process in pressure canner at 10 pounds pressure for 35 minutes. Check seal.

Before reheating soup for serving, mix 1 tablespoon of cornstarch per quart with enough water to make a thin paste, and add to the soup as a thickener.

Andrew Backos proudly displays a huge head of organically grown cabbage from his backyard garden. It will soon become tangy homemade sauerkraut (recipe on the opposite page).

Kitchen Favorites and Celebrations
Vegetable recipes ¢ ⌧ ☗ ⚗

Sauerkraut
Raw-Pack/Boiling-Water Bath
Yield: 2 pounds cabbage to 1 quart

The vegetables above, canned by Mrs. Backos, are sauerkraut (recipe at left), beets, and whole green beans (recipes, next page). Recipes for canning hot and sweet peppers also follow.

Choose firm, sound, mature heads of cabbage. Remove the loose, green, outer leaves. Wash and drain the inner head; cut it into quarters and core.

Shred the quarters on a vegetable shredder (photograph 9) or cut into ⅛-inch strips; try to keep strips uniform in size.

Use your hands to mix the shredded cabbage thoroughly with canning salt (photograph 10). For each quart of sauerkraut, mix 2 pounds of cabbage with 4 teaspoons of salt.

Tightly pack the cabbage by hand into clean, hot jars to within ½ inch of top (photograph 11). Press cabbage down with a spoon or your fingertips; this will cause the brine to form and cover the cabbage (photograph 12). It is necessary for fermentation that all the cabbage be kept under the level of the liquid.

Cover the cabbage with a small piece of clean cheesecloth, and cross two wooden sticks (pieces of tongue depressors) under the neck of the jar (photograph 13).

Put lids on jars and screw bands on loosely. Set jars in a shallow pan to catch any brine that may overflow during fermentation (photograph 14).

Store for about two to three weeks in a dry place where the temperature can be kept fairly constant at 70 degrees Fahrenheit. Check occasionally to see that the brine level has not fallen below the top of the cabbage. When fermentation stops, wipe outsides of jars clean and remove the wooden sticks and cheesecloth.

Press cabbage down firmly to release the last of the gas bubbles. Fill the jars to within ½ inch of top with new brine (1 teaspoon of canning salt to 1 quart of water). Wipe top and rim of jar clean; close each jar—not too tightly—as it is filled.

Process in boiling-water bath for 10 minutes. Complete seal.

9: Remove the loose outer leaves, wash and cut the cabbage into quarters, then shred or cut it to a uniform thickness.

10: Hand-mix the shredded cabbage with canning salt. Two pounds of cabbage with 4 teaspoons of salt equal approximately 1 quart of sauerkraut.

11: Tightly hand-pack the cabbage into clean, hot jars to within ½ inch of the top. Prepare one jar at a time.

12: Press down on the cabbage with your fingers or a spoon to create the brine, and bring it up over the cabbage.

13: To keep the brine covering the cabbage, cross two wooden sticks (pieces of tongue depressors) underneath the neck of the jar.

14: Set the filled jar, with lid on and band loosely screwed in place, in a shallow pan; allow the sauerkraut to ferment for about two weeks.

1509

Pickled Beets
Hot Pack/Boiling-Water Bath
Yield: Twenty pounds to 8 quarts

Cut off all but 2 inches of the beet tops; leave the roots on. Wash beets thoroughly, and sort according to size for even cooking.

Drop beets into boiling water (photograph 15), and boil 15 to 25 minutes. Remove beets from water with tongs and plunge into cold water; the tops, skins, and roots should slip off easily (photograph 16). If not, drop beets back into boiling water until they do. Cut the peeled beets into slices or quarters; baby beets may be left whole.

15: Boil fresh beets—with skins, roots and 2 inches of tops still on—for 15 to 25 minutes to loosen the skins.

16: Remove the beets from the boiling water and plunge immediately in cold water. You can easily peel off the skin, revealing the beautiful red whole beet inside.

While the beets are being prepared, simmer the brine.

Brine ingredients:
6 cups water
6 cups distilled white vinegar
6 cups sugar
4 tablespoons canning salt

(Other spices, such as whole cloves or cinnamon sticks, may be added if desired. These should be tied in a piece of cheesecloth for easy removal; they are not packed in the jars with the beets.)

Bring the brine to a good rolling boil; then turn it down to a gentle boil. Add the prepared beets, and keep the brine simmering while you pack beets and brine into clean, hot jars. Fill to within ½ inch of the top, making sure brine covers beets completely. Wipe top and rim of jar clean; close each jar as it is filled.

Process in boiling-water bath for 20 minutes. Check seal.

Note: This brine is very tart; if you like a less tart brine, reduce the amount of vinegar to 4 cups for medium tart or to 2 cups for slightly tart brine.

Pickled Green Beans
Raw Pack/Boiling-Water Bath
Yield: 1 pound to 1 quart

Choose only young, tender beans for canning. Wash, drain, string, and trim.

Put 1 tablespoon canning salt in each clean, hot jar. Fill jars tightly with whole raw beans. Cover beans with boiling mixture of 1 part distilled white vinegar to 2 parts water; fill to within ½ inch of top.

Wipe top and rim of jar clean; close each jar as it is filled. Process in boiling-water bath for 25 minutes. Check seal.

Pickled Green (Sweet) Peppers
Raw Pack/Boiling-Water Bath
Yield: 10 to 15 pounds equal 8 quarts

Select only good, firm peppers for canning. Wash; cut into strips or pieces as desired; remove seeds and stems.

Put 1 or 2 cloves of garlic, 1 tablespoon canning salt, and a sprig or two of dill into each clean, hot jar. Pack peppers tightly in jar, to within ½ inch of top.

Cover with boiling mixture of 1 part distilled white vinegar to 2 parts water.

Wipe top and rim of jar clean; close each jar as it is filled. Process in boiling-water bath for 30 minutes. Check seal.

Hot peppers are a favorite food at the Backos home, whether pickled and canned alone or with sweet peppers and tomatoes as in Baba's recipe, page 1507.

Pickled Hot Peppers
Raw Pack/Boiling-Water Bath
Yield: 15 pounds equal 6 quarts

Wash peppers; cut in half lengthwise; remove seeds and stems.

Into each clean, hot jar, put 1 teaspoon canning salt and 1 garlic clove on the bottom and a head of fresh dill on the side. Pack pepper halves tightly into jars. Add 1 cup of distilled white vinegar to each jar, and fill with boiling water to within ½ inch of top. Wipe the top and rim of the jar clean; close each jar as it is filled.

Process in boiling-water bath for 20 to 25 minutes. Check seal.

Kitchen Favorites and Celebrations
Fruit recipes

¢ 🗙 🧍 🦊

The canned fruits above are plums (front row), peaches (center), and pears (back). Fruits are packed in thin, medium, or heavy syrup, depending on the sweetness desired.

Plums
Raw Pack/Boiling-Water Bath

Use firm, ripe plums that are just beginning to soften; green gage and other meaty plums are better for canning than the juicier varieties.

Wash and drain; prick skins with toothpick. This will not prevent the skins from splitting, but will prevent the fruit from bursting.

Pack gently but closely to within ½ inch from top of clean, hot jar (photograph 17).

Cover with boiling syrup (heavy for tart plums, medium for sweet), leaving ½-inch head space. Wipe top and rim of jar clean; close each jar as it is filled.

Process in boiling-water bath for 25 minutes (quarts) or 20 minutes (pints). Check seal.

17: Whole plums are packed into the jars without precooking; skins are pricked to keep the fruits from bursting.

Pears
Hot Pack/Boiling-Water Bath
Prepare only 1 or 2 quarts at a time

Use ripe pears that are firm, not soft. Bartlett pears are considered best for canning but other varieties are satisfactory if properly ripened and cooked in plain water until almost tender before they are added to the syrup.

Wash, peel, and cut pears in half lengthwise. Use a ½-teaspoon measuring spoon to core each half.

Have prepared a mixture of 1 gallon of water with 2 tablespoons each of canning salt and distilled white vinegar. Keep the peeled pear halves in this mixture until ready to use (no longer than 20 minutes) to prevent discoloration.

Bring thin or medium syrup to a boil (see recipes at right). Drain and rinse pears and add to syrup. Boil gently for 3 to 5 minutes; do not overcook.

Pack pears in clean, hot jars to within ½ inch of the top. Cover with boiling syrup. Wipe top and rim of jar clean; close each jar as it is filled. Process in boiling-water bath for 30 minutes. Check seal.

Peaches
Hot Pack/Boiling-Water Bath
Prepare only 1 or 2 quarts at a time

Use only firm, ripe peaches. Dip into boiling water for 30 seconds, then plunge into cold water; skin will slip off. Cut in half and remove pit. Slice or quarter, as desired.

Have prepared a mixture of 1 gallon water with 2 tablespoons each canning salt and distilled white vinegar. Keep peach slices or quarters in this mixture until ready to use (no longer than 20 minutes) to prevent discoloration.

Bring medium or heavy syrup to a boil (see recipes at right). Remove peaches from vinegar and salt solution; rinse; add to syrup. Boil gently for 3 to 5 minutes; do not overcook.

Pack peaches into clean, hot jars to within ½ inch of top. Cover with boiling syrup. Wipe top and rim of jar clean; close each jar as it is filled.

Process in boiling-water bath for 30 minutes. Check seal.

Sugar syrups for canning fruits
Make syrup according to the sweetness desired.

Thin syrup: 2 cups of sugar and 4 cups of water equal 5 cups.

Medium syrup: 3 cups of sugar and 4 cups of water equal 5½ cups.

Heavy syrup: 4¾ cups of sugar and 4 cups of water equal 6½ cups.

Boil sugar and water together in a saucepan for 5 minutes or until the sugar dissolves. Skim any froth that forms on the surface. Keep syrup hot until needed, but do not let it boil down. Usually 1 to 1½ cups of syrup are needed for each quart of fruit.

Ascorbic acid: Adding ascorbic acid (Vitamin C) to the syrup at the time of canning will help prevent discoloration of the fruit. Either tablet or crystalline form may be used, following the manufacturer's directions. Ascorbic and citric acid mixtures are also available.

Substitutes for sugar: Medium syrup can also be made with mild-flavor honey or light corn syrup, using 1 cup of sugar and 1 cup of honey or corn syrup to 4 cups of water. Brown sugar may be used instead of white sugar in combination with the honey. (Use a smaller amount of brown sugar because it can darken the fruit and overpower the flavor.)

Artificial sweeteners: Some artificial sweeteners may be used in canning since the sugar is for flavor only. Check the manufacturer's recommendations on use and quantity.

Unsweetened fruits: Fruits may be canned without sweetening—in their own juice, in extracted juice, or in water. Sugar is not needed to prevent spoilage; processing is the same for sweetened or unsweetened fruit.

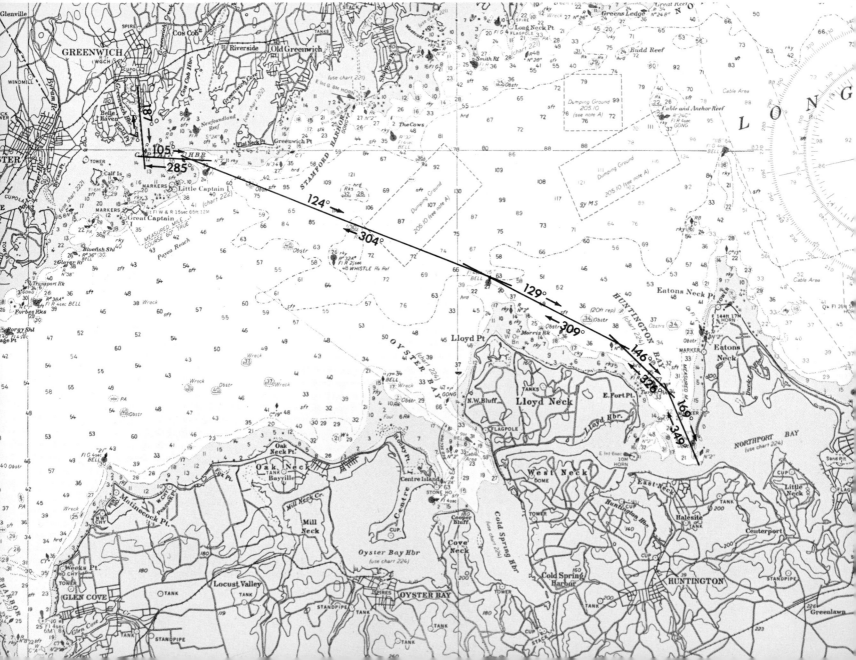

PILOTING SMALL BOATS
Finding Roads Over Water

Small-boat piloting, sometimes called dead reckoning or, in the vernacular of East Coast lobstermen, eyeball navigation, is simply the business of getting from one place to another over a body of water safely, without getting lost. What makes it exciting is the fact that there are no roads to follow over the water. To arrive at a destination (landfall, the sailors call it) the small boat pilot must blend a knowledge of wind, weather, tidal currents, charts, the compass and other navigational aids—and avoid obstructions that lurk beneath the water.

He starts applying this knowledge in the comfort of his home, well before his cruise begins. There he plots a course on a nautical chart, playing a fascinating game of strategy with nature which takes into account the latest weather information and the direction and speed of currents that will affect him. The roads he plots for his boat consist of a series of compass-direction readings (called headings) that take him from one checkpoint to another safely, until he reaches his port.

On pages that follow I have set up a model trip, including most of the variables a small-boat skipper might encounter in planning a short cruise. Once you have looked over my shoulder, so to speak, while I work out this theoretical trip, you will have a better understanding of how charts are used to plan safe, comfortable cruises, whether one lives near the ocean or an inland lake. The basic principles of navigation apply on all waters and to both sail and power boats. But you don't need to own a boat to enjoy and benefit from watching me chart and run this course. It will make you a better skipper when you do acquire a boat and, in the meantime, an interested and more helpful passenger on someone else's boat.

To become an expert small-boat pilot takes years of practice and some training as indicated at right. But the essentials of navigating from one point to another within a few miles of shore are not difficult to learn. Advanced techniques such as celestial navigation (using a sextant to find a position) may be useful for sailors who must cover great distances on the open sea, but they are not needed for small-boat piloting close to shorelines where navigational aids proliferate.

Navigational Charts

The basic tool for plotting a course is a nautical chart. It is never called a map. A nautical chart reveals much more than maps (Figure A). It gives a profile of the land beneath the water. It shows obstructions such as rocks and wrecks. It shows the location of lighthouses, how high they are, and from what distance they can be seen in clear weather. It tells at a glance whether water is shallow or deep. It shows whether the coastline is sandy or rocky, mangrove swamp or steep bluffs. In short, the nautical chart tells sailors what they must know about the area they will be cruising. With the chart, a pair of binoculars (7x50 or 7x35 are best for boating), and a compass (photograph opposite), the navigator can determine his position on the water at any given moment (see Craftnotes, pages 1520 and 1521).

In addition to nautical charts of the cruising area, small-boat pilots use a copy of Chart No. 1, which is not a chart at all but a booklet listing and explaining the abbreviations and symbols found on nautical charts (Figures B and C, page 1514). This shows, for example, that *Fl R 4sec BELL* indicates a bell buoy with a red light that flashes every four seconds, or that *Fl 2sec 101ft 16M* means a lighthouse that flashes every two seconds, is 101 feet high, and can be seen from 16 miles away. A nautical chart is usually printed in three colors: yellow for land, blue for shallow

Stuart James, *formerly editor of* Rudder *magazine and outdoors editor of* Popular Mechanics, *grew up with boats and has written many articles about different boating techniques, from canoeing to power boating and sailing.*

Getting started in boating

The good small-boat skippers are the prudent ones. They know the marine "rules of the road" and how to handle their craft before setting out. They make sure their boats are fully equipped and in prime operating condition. They never challenge foul weather in small craft. They chart a course to avoid tricky currents or other hazards their boats cannot handle.

If you have never piloted a boat, the best way to get started is to take a course offered by your local United States Power Squadron, a voluntary organization that gives courses in the correct operation of both power and sailboats. You should also read some books on basic navigation and boating rules and techniques. One good source is **Piloting, Seamanship and Small Boat Handling**, by Charles F. Chapman (Motor Boating, N.Y.C.). Another is the **Time-Life Library of Boating**, published by Time-Life Books. When you have absorbed what the courses and books have to offer, make a point of taking an experienced local skipper on your first cruises in local waters. This will get you off to a safe, enjoyable start in boating.

A good skipper can use a handheld compass like the one in the inset (top, opposite) to find his position or to check the accuracy of the steering compass mounted in his boat. Both techniques are explained in the Craftnotes on pages 1520 and 1521. Boating waterways are studded with buoy markers and lighthouses like the one pictured at left that help a skipper find harbors and avoid obstructions.

Figure A, opposite: Here is how a short cruise is plotted on a nautical chart. This is the model trip—from Greenwich Harbor in Connecticut to Northport Bay in Long Island—described in the text. Each leg of the trip over and back is marked with the compass direction (heading) for that leg and an arrow indicating the direction the boat will be moving.

Aids to Navigation on Navigable Waters except Western Rivers and Intracoastal Waterways

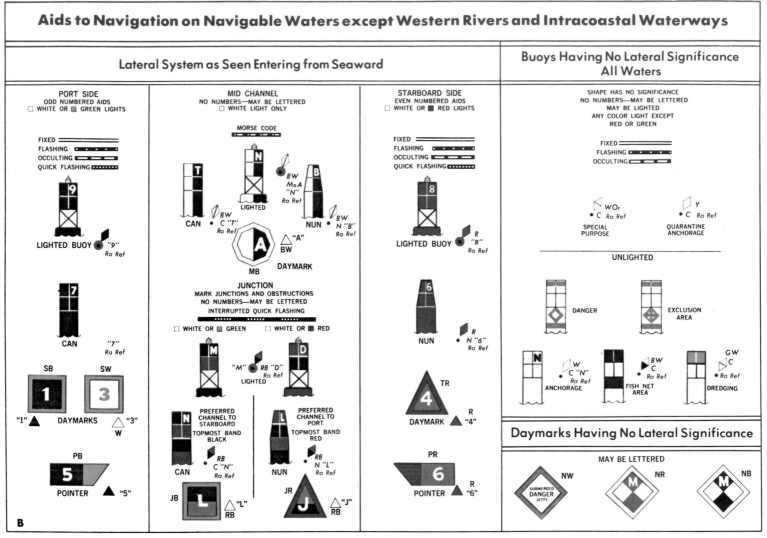

Lateral System as Seen Entering from Seaward

PORT SIDE
ODD NUMBERED AIDS
□ WHITE OR ■ GREEN LIGHTS

FIXED
FLASHING
OCCULTING
QUICK FLASHING

LIGHTED BUOY "9" Ra Ref

CAN "7" Ra Ref

SB SW
1 3
"1" ▲ DAYMARKS △ "3"
W

PB
5
POINTER ▲ "5"

MID CHANNEL
NO NUMBERS—MAY BE LETTERED
□ WHITE LIGHT ONLY

MORSE CODE

T N B
CAN BW C "T" Ra Ref
LIGHTED
NUN BW N "B" Ra Ref
BW "A"
MB A DAYMARK

JUNCTION
MARK JUNCTIONS AND OBSTRUCTIONS
NO NUMBERS—MAY BE LETTERED
INTERRUPTED QUICK FLASHING
□ WHITE OR ■ GREEN   □ WHITE OR ■ RED

M D
"M" RB "D" Ra Ref
LIGHTED

N L
PREFERRED CHANNEL TO STARBOARD
TOPMOST BAND BLACK
PREFERRED CHANNEL TO PORT
TOPMOST BAND RED
CAN RB C "N" Ra Ref
NUN RB N "L" Ra Ref
JB L "L" RB
JR J "J" RB

STARBOARD SIDE
EVEN NUMBERED AIDS
□ WHITE OR ■ RED LIGHTS

FIXED
FLASHING
OCCULTING
QUICK FLASHING

LIGHTED BUOY R "8" Ra Ref

NUN R N "6" Ra Ref

TR
4
DAYMARK ▲ R "4"

PR
6
POINTER ▲ R "6"

Buoys Having No Lateral Significance
All Waters

SHAPE HAS NO SIGNIFICANCE
NO NUMBERS—MAY BE LETTERED
MAY BE LIGHTED
ANY COLOR LIGHT EXCEPT
RED OR GREEN

FIXED
FLASHING
OCCULTING

WOr C Ra Ref
SPECIAL PURPOSE
Y C Ra Ref
QUARANTINE ANCHORAGE

UNLIGHTED

DANGER   EXCLUSION AREA

N W C "N" Ra Ref
ANCHORAGE
BW C Ra Ref
FISH NET AREA
GW C Ra Ref
DREDGING

Daymarks Having No Lateral Significance

MAY BE LETTERED

SUBMERGED DANGER JETTY NW   M NR   M NB

B

Figure B: Here are some typical shapes, colors, and markings of buoys used on United States boating waters. Daymarks and pointers are usually shore-based markers that substitute for water-based buoys. *No lateral significance* means the buoy can be passed on either side. The small symbol and abbreviations beside each pictured buoy indicate the way that buoy is shown on a chart. Thus the purple circle for the lighted buoy shown at upper left indicates the buoy is lighted, the 9, its number, and the *Ra Ref*, that it is a radar reflector. *Occulting* means a light interrupted by brief periods of darkness.

Rock	Rock	
Sand and mud	Sand and mud	
S	Sand	
M	Mud; Muddy	
HW	High water	
LLW	Lower low water	

Rk; rky	Rock; Rocky
⚓ ⚓	Anch; Anchorage (small vessels)
※	Rock awash. Dotted line emphasizes danger to navigation
5½ Wk	Wreck over which depth is known
+ rky +	Limit of rocky area
BELL BELL	Bell buoy
WHIS	Whistle buoy

RB RB	Isolated danger buoy (RBHB)
	Riprap surrounding light
	Bkw Breakwater
	Dock
R TR	Radio tower
TR °Tr	Tower
TANK °Tk	Tank
NWS SIG	Nat. Weather Service Signal Sta.

C

Figure C: This is a small sampling of the symbols and abbreviations used on nautical charts. The complete listing of them is given in a booklet, *Chart No. 1*, published by the National Ocean Survey. *Riprap* is a pile of stones around a marker—a warning not to come too close.

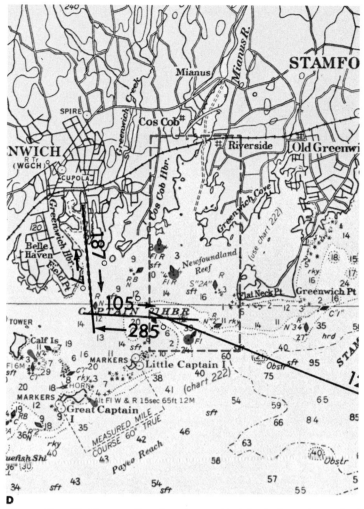

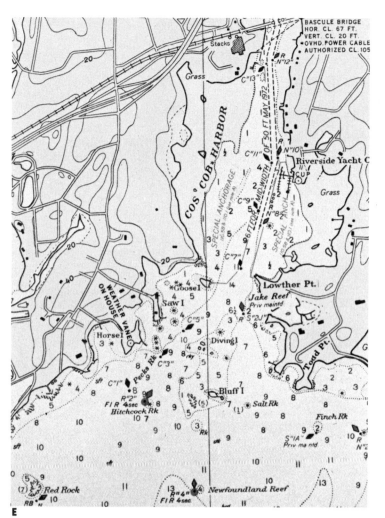

D

E

Figures D and E: These sections from two nautical charts show why good sailors always get the most detailed chart available of any harbor to be entered. The red dashed lines on the chart at left outline the area shown in the chart at right. The section at left shows the red navigation flashers but not the small islands, the privately maintained nun *1A*, and the rocks at the Cos Cob Harbor entrance; all of these are detailed in the section at right.

water, and white for deep water. It is covered with numbers that give the depth of the water in feet at low tide. All buoys are marked with their type, color, and number. Land details are limited to those that could be important to a sailor, such as whether the shoreline is sandy or rocky, the clearance of a stationary bridge in a channel, and the location of landmarks that can be seen from the water (smoke stacks, church spires, storage tanks and the like).

The nautical chart also gives locations for the display of storm-warning flags, the frequencies of local radio stations, the times of weather broadcasts, and a scale in nautical miles. To make it easy to determine compass directions the chart has a compass rose printed in several places, showing both magnetic and true north (see Craftnotes, pages 1520 and 1521).

Another vital piece of information given on nautical charts is the difference in feet between mean low water (an average of low-water depths over a period of time), and the low low-water extremes, which occur when there is a full moon or a new moon. At these times, the tides, known as spring tides, are both lower and higher than at other times. So the underwater obstruction whose clearance is shown as 8 feet at mean low water may be only 4 feet beneath the surface—if the extreme low water is 4 feet lower than the mean low water. For the same reason, a bridge with plenty of clearance for a sailboat mast at mean high water may not have quite enough at extreme high water. A good sailor always gives himself an extra clearance margin and allows for the differences that accompany the spring tides.

The red nun at left marks the right-hand boundary of a harbor entrance. A typical bell buoy with white flasher is at right. Both show on a chart, but at night, plotting a course on the flasher will bring a sailor close enough to the unlighted nun to pick it up with a searchlight.

1: The time to plan a boating trip is the night before it will be taken. This is when the course is plotted on a nautical chart of the area that will be traversed, using a pencil, straightedge, dividers, and parallel rules—as explained in the text. The good boatman also listens to the latest weather forecast, and if he is sailing, plans to compensate for tidal currents he will encounter.

Nautical charts are prepared by the National Ocean Survey Unit of the National Oceanic and Atmospheric Administration (formerly the National Coast and Geodetic Survey), and are available at most marine supply stores. In addition to charts that cover a sizable cruising area, detailed charts of specific harbors are available (Figures D and E, page 1515).

To supplement the charts, sailors use a copy of *Coast Pilot*, a paperbound booklet published by the National Ocean Survey. The nine editions of *Coast Pilot* cover various areas of the Atlantic and Pacific Coasts, and the Great Lakes. Each gives detailed information on the sections of coastline it covers. For example, regarding the harbor at Greenwich, Connecticut (Figure A, page 1512), *Coast Pilot* reports, "Greenwich Harbor, on the north side of Captain Harbor and northeastward of Field Point, is entered through a dredged channel that leads northward 1.2 miles to the head. The channel is buoyed for about 0.8 mile. In 1968, the controlling (minimum) depth was 12 feet. Two anchorage basins, one at the head and the other just southward, are off the west side of the channel. Depths of 5 feet are available in the northerly basin in 1966." The book even gives an approach to the harbor, with compass directions, distances, and tidal currents between checkpoints. And it warns about danger spots that small-boat pilots should stay away from: "Nantucket shoals should be entirely avoided by deep-draft vessels when possible and by light-draft vessels without local knowledge, on account of treacherous currents. In calm weather at slack water these shoals are sometimes difficult to see."

What Buoys Tell

Coast Pilot instructions may not always be available to a sailor cruising unfamiliar waters. But he can still work his way in and out of a strange harbor if he knows some basic rules about the buoys that mark the harbor channel (Figure B, page 1514). The black buoys (usually cylindrical and called cans) mark the left or port side boundary of the harbor channel being entered; from seaward the red buoys (usually conical and called nuns) mark the right or starboard side boundary. The idea is to stay between these two sets of markers. When a sailor enters a harbor, he keeps the red nuns on his right (hence the phrase *red right returning*) and the black cans on his left. As he leaves a harbor, he keeps the black cans on his right, the red nuns on his left.

On entering a harbor or channel, the red buoys on the right may have even numbers that increase as the boat moves into the harbor; the black buoys on the left may have odd numbers that increase toward shore. Any lights on buoys will be red or white on the right (starboard) side, white or green on the left (port) side.

Mid-channel buoys usually have black and white vertical stripes (Figure B), and buoys marking junctions or obstructions have horizontal red and black bands. The latter may be passed on either side, but the color of the top band tells which side is safer; red indicates left (port), black indicates right (starboard). Chart No. 1 also indicates variations in buoy shapes and markings which appear on some inland waters, as well as the types of buoys used to identify speed limit zones, anchorages, dredging operations, fish nets, and other special areas.

Plotting a Model Course

The start of any cruise begins with plotting a course that will enable the navigator to steer in the right direction. For this he needs: a chart, a pencil, a straightedge, a pair of dividers, and parallel rules (photograph 1). The chart is spread on a table and with the straightedge, lines are drawn from the starting point, through each checkpoint where the course will change, to the destination.

To illustrate the procedure, this is how I plot my model trip. Using chart No. 1213 of the western end of Long Island Sound (Figure A, page 1512), I start at the head of Greenwich Harbor and plot a course that will take me, in several legs, to the mouth of Northport Bay, Long Island. The first leg is straight down the channel to the red nun buoy at the mouth of Greenwich Harbor. From here I can draw a line from the red nun past the black can buoy *1A*. This line will get me safely past the rocks and shallow water off Little Captain Island. (I don't draw such lines through the buoy; I draw them close to the side I intend to pass.) Using the dividers, I measure this leg (photograph 2), check it against the distance scale on the chart (photograph 3), and find it is 8/10th of a nautical mile. The next leg is across Long Island Sound to bell buoy *15*. Next comes a slight change of course to red nun *6*, then to red bell *8*, and from there to the mouth of Northport Bay.

After these lines are drawn lightly on the chart, I measure and note down the length of each leg. Then, as shown in photograph 4, I place the parallel rule along the line of each leg in turn, and walk it (holding one rule on the line, expanding the other) to the nearest compass rose on the chart. The center of the rose should be bisected with the edge of the second rule. Reading the markings on the inside circle (magnetic scale) where the rule cuts through the circle, I find the compass direction—the heading—that must be steered on that leg of the cruise (photograph 4). As I find the compass heading, I make a pencil notation of it above or below the line representing that leg of the trip, with an arrow indicating the direction the boat will be heading. The run down the channel out of the harbor has a heading of 187 degrees. Although the channel is well marked, if I note this heading it will give me a chance to check the accuracy of my compass when I am under way (see Craftnotes, pages 1520 and 1521). The next leg is 105 degrees, but I should be able to see black can *1A* easily. The course for the next leg is 124 degrees to bell buoy *15*, then a slight change to 129 degrees to make the *6* red nun, then 146 degrees to the *8* red flasher bell, and 169 degrees to the mouth of Northport Bay.

Those are the basic steps of plotting a course. If I follow the same course on my return trip, my compass headings will change 180 degrees from the readings going out, since I will be traveling in the opposite direction (Figure A, page 1512).

Tidal Currents and Wind Drift

My plotted course makes a fine road for my trip, but since I am sailing, I will have to adjust for the water moving under me, and the wind that blows over it. If I were to use a powerboat, water currents and winds would not seriously affect my navigation. I would use more gas if I had to buck winds and currents to maintain my course, but all I would do is crank in more power to overcome their effects. In a sailboat, however, winds affect the tacking needed to maintain course and speed. And currents can affect not only speed but the course to be steered to arrive at a destination. Information on tidal currents is contained in the Tidal Current Charts published by the National Ocean Survey (Figure F, page 1518).

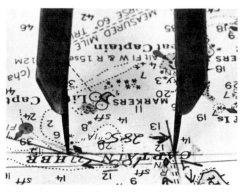

2: To measure the distance on a chart of any leg of a trip, the dividers are spread between the two checkpoints forming each end of that leg.

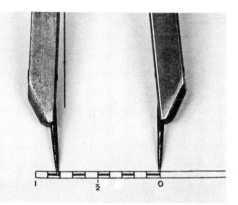

3: Then, without changing the span of the dividers, their spread is checked against the scale of nautical miles to find the distances covered by that leg of the trip.

4: To find a compass heading, one of the parallel rules is held along the course line, and the other rule is spread until it bisects the center of the nearest compass rose on the chart. Where the second rule crosses the inside (magnetic) circle on the compass rose will be the compass heading in degrees for that leg of a trip. If the parallel rule won't stretch far enough to reach the compass rose in one step, a line is drawn parallel to the course line along the edge of the second rule; then the rule is extended from this line to the nearest compass rose.

Figure F: This section from a tidal current chart shows the currents that affect the trip from Connecticut to Long Island described in the text. Each tidal chart shows tidal currents prevailing at a specified hour after slack (when the tide changes from ebb to flood or flood to ebb). The tidal figures are based on averages compiled over the years and may be altered by weather conditions prevailing at the time of the trip. A careful sailor checks the tidal current effects on a course when under way, as described in the text.

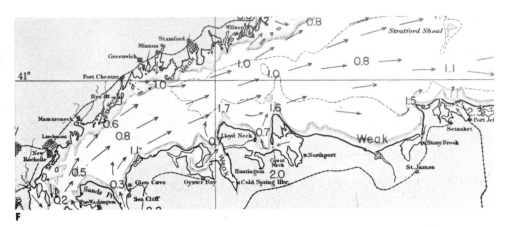

F

This is how the tidal charts would be applied to my theoretical Greenwich-Northport Bay cruise. From the tide chart, I learn that the tide in Long Island Sound ebbs in an easterly direction, running strongest about three hours after the ebb begins. My tide table for the area and date tells me that the ebb will begin about 6:30 A.M. at Greenwich, and since I am sailing east and want to take advantage of a current that gets up to 1.7 knots on the Long Island side of the Sound, I plan my departure for 9:30 A.M. The winds, I learn, are from the southwest, a pleasant 12-knot breeze. This is a good wind for my course, because I can reach all the way to Northport Bay. But there is going to be some drift to the leeward—the direction the wind is blowing—that I must compensate for.

Since there is no way of knowing in advance the exact speed of the current, or the amount of drift caused by the wind, I put some guesswork in my compensation. I know that if I steer the 124-degree leg of the course I have plotted, the current and leeward drift will carry me to the east of my checkpoint at bell buoy 15. It is logical, therefore, to plan to sail a compass course slightly below the original plot; so I decide to try 130 degrees. If that is not the right compensation, I can correct it after I get under way.

When I leave the light buoy off Greenwich Harbor on the 124-degree leg of my course (Figure A, page 1512), I can use either the black can 1A or the 15 bell to try to pick up a range, where one object lined up directly behind another provides a check on my course heading. I sight over the stern with a handheld compass (inset photograph, page 1512) to see if I can line up some landmark on shore directly behind one of the buoys. It can be a spire, a large tree, anything that allows me to line up the two objects. Say there is a flagpole, rooftop, chimney, large tree, or other landmark that lines up directly with the buoy at 304 degrees. I now bring the boat onto the 130-degree course and continue on that for 10 or 15 minutes. If my guess is correct, the buoy and the landmark will still be lined up behind me, and if I sight on them with the hand compass I should still get a reading of 304. If I should happen to get a reading of 290, I know that the current and leeward drift are stronger than I had estimated, and I change course again, perhaps to as high as 135 degrees, checking again after 10 minutes or so.

This is the same as swimming across a river that has a strong current. You can point yourself directly across the river and swim in that direction, but you will land some distance downstream. In the sailboat I steer at 130 or 135 degrees to maintain a course close to the originally planned 124 degrees. But if I simply angle slightly across the direction of the current, I should wind up close to my planned destination. When I get close enough to the buoy to see it with my binoculars, I can adjust my course to it.

Speed and Distance Calculations

Before going cruising, a sailor needs to determine how far he has to go and predict how long it should take him to get there. He wants to make sure he has enough reserve fuel for the trip and can make it there and back before any threatened weather changes occur.

Since all charts have a scale of nautical miles, computing distance is simply a matter of adding up the lengths of the various legs of the trip and comparing them to the scale. The procedure is to lay a strip of paper along the line of the first leg and mark it. Then mark it again, adding on the second leg and so on (as in photograph 5).

When this has been done, the strip is measured from the beginning edge to the last mark. For example, on my model trip, the distance from the head of Greenwich Harbor to the mouth of Northport Bay is 11½ inches on the chart. When measured against the scale printed on the chart, this comes to just about 12.7 nautical miles.

Speed is quite another matter. There are two kinds of speed for a vessel—the speed through the water and the speed of the water across the bottom. Since the water the boat is moving through is also moving, these speeds differ.

If I were traveling through the water at 5 knots *against* a 3-knot current, my progress in terms of over-the-bottom distance would be 2 knots. If I were traveling *with* the current, still moving through the water at 5 knots, I would be making 8 knots across the bottom. What interests me for navigation purposes is my speed over the bottom. One way to figure this is to use the speed scale shown on many charts. With my dividers, I place one point on the distance run and the other on the time (in minutes) it took (as in photograph 6, below). Without changing the span of the dividers I place one point on the 60 and read off the speed (in knots) at the other point (as in photograph 6, below). For example, let us say I made a run of 1 mile (about the distance from my mooring in Greenwich Harbor to the red nun at the harbor entrance, Figure A, page 1512), and it took me 20 minutes. I place one point of the dividers on the 1 (for 1 mile) at the left side of the scale and spread the dividers until the second point touches the 20. I then move the first divider point to the 60, which is the far right of the scale, and the other point will rest on 3. So I am making 3 knots across the bottom. To convert that to miles per hour, I multiply by 1.15, which gives me 3.45 miles per hour. That puts me comfortably under the harbor speed limit of 5 miles per hour.

5: To measure the length of a trip, a strip of paper is placed with its edge at the starting point and the length of the first leg is marked. Then the length of the second leg is added to the strip and the same is done for the remaining legs. The strip is then measured from its beginning edge to the last mark against the nautical mile scale.

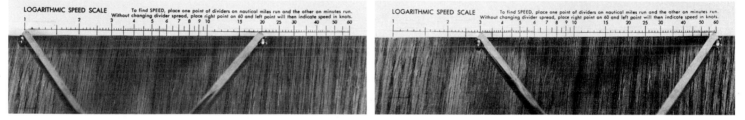

6: To use the speed scale on a chart, one point of the dividers, is placed, as at left, on the distance run (1 mile in this case) and the other point on the time it took (20 minutes in this case). Then, as at right, without changing the span of the dividers, one point is placed on 60 and a reading is taken where the other point touches the scale (at 3 in this instance). This is the speed in knots.

To make periodic checks of speed and distance traveled, I would use the charts to measure the distance between two objects (two buoys will do) and check the time it takes to travel between them. I can even compute my speed roughly by clocking how long it would take my boat to pass an object in the water. Let's say I have a 30-foot boat and it takes the full length of the boat (from bow to stern) 4 seconds to pass a buoy. There are 6,076 feet in a nautical mile, so I divide 30 into it to come up with 202.5 boat lengths in a nautical mile. I multiply this by the time it took one boat length to pass the buoy (4 seconds) and I come up with 810 seconds, or 13.5 minutes it would take me to travel a nautical mile. I run this through the speed scale and get a speed of 4.4 knots.

It is possible to navigate from one point to another without knowing the distance or calculating the speed. But a good sailor likes to know where he is at any given moment and when he can expect to make landfall. This is good insurance against getting lost, running out of fuel or being caught cruising in bad weather.

All sailors should observe one caution about buoys. The anchor of a buoy is fixed in the position shown on the chart. But the buoy itself, attached to the anchor with a chain, is free to move around the anchor point in small circles when pushed by currents or the wind. So I never pass too close to a buoy; if it is an obstruction marker, it may have swung closer to the obstruction at the time I passed it. For the same reason, for a really precise fix of a position, I can take more precise bearings on objects that are not floating but fixed, such as a church steeple or a lighthouse.

Here are some basic exercises in the use of a compass that all pilots of small boats need to master:

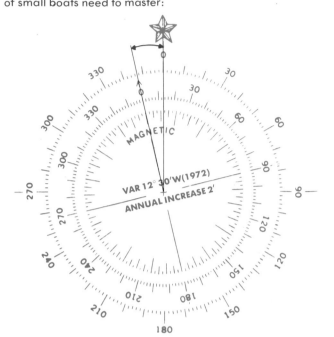

Determining compass variation

The most important instrument on a small boat is the compass. Combined with a chart, it enables a sailor to turn a featureless plain of water into a network of roads of his own design.

The compass rose printed on all nautical charts shows two kinds of north—true north, as shown on the outside circle, and magnetic north, as shown on the inside circle. The star at true north points to the North Pole and the arrow indicating **north** on the magnetic scale points toward a magnetic field in northern Canada. The difference between the two points is called variation. On a chart of western Long Island Sound, the variation printed on the compass rose is 12 degrees 30 minutes west (12° 30′ W) as shown above. On the Pacific Coast, the variation is to the east.

The compass on a boat is a magnetic compass and will always point to magnetic north. To transpose a magnetic course to a true course, the navigator can subtract the variation for his area from the magnetic course for variation west or add it to the magnetic course for variation east. But this is rarely necessary. He will usually find it simpler to use the compass rose on the chart, which gives the magnetic and true course for every direction with the variation already computed. In the drawing above, for example, if the navigator runs a line through the center of the rose and the 0-degree inside (magnetic) scale he will get a true reading of 347 ½ degrees if his course is northward.

Small boats always steer a magnetic course, but some literature used for navigational aid, such as **Coast Pilot,** will give directions in true bearings, which must be converted to magnetic bearings. Taking an area with 12° 30′ W variation, if the **Coast Pilot** tells a sailor to ". . . steer 054° to pass 100 yards east of West-Southwest Ledge Lighted Buoy, and thence 014° to pass about 100 yards eastward of the breakwater light in entering the harbor," he runs a rule across the compass rose and reads 054 degrees true as 066 degrees magnetic and 014 degrees true as 026 degrees magnetic.

Correcting for compass deviation

Steering compasses are not automatically accurate. The amount of inaccuracy is called compass deviation. This is the effect that metal objects, radios, magnets and electric currents have on a compass, pulling the needle away from magnetic north. There is hardly a boat that does not create some deviation in a compass, so it is essential that the sailor compensate for this deviation before the compass can be trusted for piloting.

Most steering compasses have built-in compensators (small magnets) operated by two adjustment screws as below. The side screw adjusts for north and south, the fore-and-aft screw adjusts for east and west. The compass is first mounted in a permanent place on the boat as far as possible from radios, engines, electrical equipment or even plastic steering wheels (they may have steel cores). It is mounted with its sighting line (lubber line) parallel with the keel of the boat.

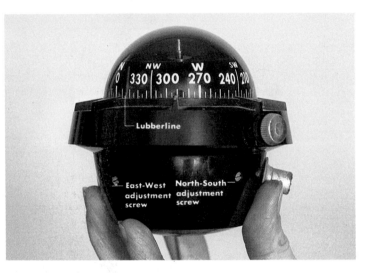

Swinging the compass

After the compass is mounted, it is swung, which means adjusted, to compensate for deviation on the four major points—east, west, north, and south. It is not enough to adjust for deviation on one or two points. It must be on all four.

Using his chart the sailor finds a course about half a mile long that the chart tells him runs exactly east and west on the magnetic scale, and another course that runs exactly north and south. For each course, he needs two objects directly in line, perhaps two buoys, or one buoy and a spire, tower or lighthouse on land. He can range on them (right above), keeping one directly behind the other, or he can keep one directly off the center of the stern and the other directly off the center of the bow. (If he has difficulty lining up two objects for either the east-and-west or the north-and-south courses, he can run a course from a fixed object for half a mile and drop a disposable buoy over the center of the stern. Then he swings the boat around and runs the reciprocal course using the buoy and the fixed object for his two lined-up markers (right, center).

If he runs his charted east course and the compass is not 090 degrees, he turns the fore-and-aft compensating screw to move the compass needle **half** the distance between 090 degrees and the compass reading. The distance is halved because the deviation on a reciprocal course is roughly opposite and equal.

AND USING COMPASSES

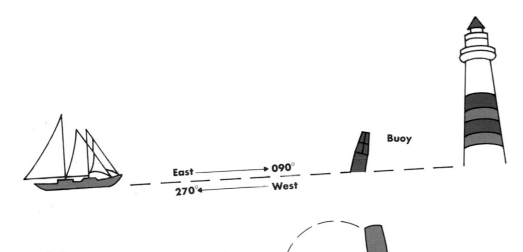

East ——→ 090°
270° ←—— West

Buoy

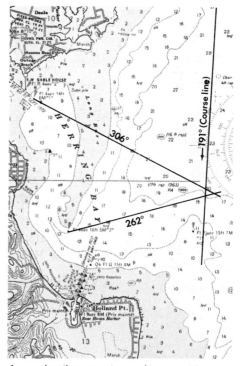

Disposable buoy
(plastic bottle)

South
000°

180°
North

Sailors use a nonmagnetic screwdriver for adjusting the screws. They can demagnetize a metal screwdriver by having a local electronics repair man run it through a bulk magnetic tape eraser or a color-TV degaussing coil.

The next run is made on the charted 270-degree course (west), and again half the error is removed. Both the east and west course runs are repeated, halving the difference each time, until the corrected compass reads 090 degrees running east and 270 degrees running west. Then the 0-degree north and 180-degree south courses are run as were those for east and west, and the side adjustment screw is used to halve the adjustment each time until the needle is in line with the course.

The sailor then checks the final adjustments on a variety of courses, running between buoys, ranging on stacks and bridges, wherever his charts establish a known course. If his compass is not exactly on course, he swings it again.

A compass can get out of adjustment if it, or metal equipment on the boat that can affect it, is moved. One way a sailor checks a compass when he is under way is to test it against a handheld compass (inset photograph, page 1512). With the compass held as far as possible from any metal or electrical objects that might affect it, he sights through its center (lubber) line along the center line of the boat. Then he compares its reading with that of the steering compass mounted in the boat. If they don't agree, he adjusts the steering compass to match the reading on the handheld compass.

Finding a position

Suppose a sailor knows he is on a heading such as the 191-degree course shown at right, because his compass confirms it. But he is not sure of his speed and would like to know where he is at the moment. With the handheld bearing compass, two stationary objects and a chart, he can pinpoint his position.

Let's say he can make out a lighted buoy with his binoculars and is able to find it on the chart. He sights on the marker with the handheld compass, and reads the direction in degrees to the buoy from his boat. Then he draws a line representing that compass bearing on his chart. The line should cross the line of the course he is sailing. He takes another bearing on another marker to the right or left of the first marker, and draws a line on the chart for that second bearing, as below. Where the three lines intersect is his approximate position. Because he is moving and his sightings are not going to be perfect, the intersecting lines will not cross each other in the same place; instead they will make a small triangle. In seaman's jargon this triangle is known as a **cocked hat,** and it is his approximate position. It should be close enough to let him know about where he is, how far he has progressed from his last checkpoint, and at about what speed he is moving.

A good sailor practices taking position fixes in familiar water. It will give him a feeling for navigating, and if the time should come when it is vitally important for him to know where he is, he can run through the procedure quickly.

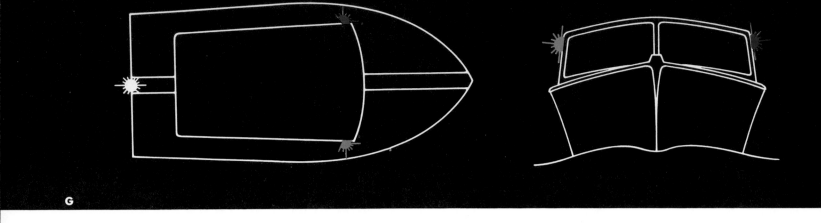

Figure G: At night, a good sailor can tell which way another boat is moving by watching its lights, which are located as shown above, left. If both red and green are getting closer, he knows the boat is coming toward him (above, near center). White stern lights are also required but are not always visible from the front (though larger craft must carry an additional white light on the mast). If he sees green and white only (above, far center), a boat is moving toward his right; if red and white only (far right), it is moving toward his left. The red and green lights may be placed at the bow or along the cabin or sides of a boat.

Navigating at Night

Novice boatmen fear traveling at night (when objects and shorelines may be obscured by darkness), but night navigation is largely a matter of reading the many lighted signposts that guide the sailor and keep him out of danger. In some ways, I find that piloting a boat at night is easier than in the daytime. Less traffic means fewer wakes to contend with. On a clear night (the only kind prudent sailors go out in), navigation lights are much easier to see than buoys on a hazy day.

Good sailors travel slowly at night and keep a sharp lookout for floating debris and unlighted lobster pots and buoys. The charts will tell them where to look for unlighted channel and obstruction buoys, but not for the mooring buoys that are so plentiful near or in harbors. Here the wisest course is to go slowly and scan ahead constantly with a good searchlight or superpowered flashlight.

A person of average eyesight, standing in a boat 6 feet above the water, can see an object 3 miles away in clear weather. When that object is a flashing light against a dark background, he cannot miss it. The running lights of other boats are also easy to see in clear weather. Since the red light will be on the left (port) side and green light on the right (starboard) side of a boat, with white at the stern, a sailor can determine what the other boat is doing by watching the movement of the lights (Figure G). When he sees both red and green moving closer, he knows the boat is coming toward him. Good sailors are also wary of an unlighted boat moving or at anchor in open water. It is illegal for the boat to be without lights, but the main thing is to avoid it.

Of great importance at night is the sure knowledge that one's compass is accurate and working properly, and a familiarity with the light symbols on the chart. Most pleasure boating is done in waters where there is a profusion of navigational aids; so piloting at night is mostly buoy-hopping. But a sailor still must be able to trust his compass in case he has to locate an unlighted marker.

After my daytime sail to Northport Bay, Long Island, let us say I am returning at night. The tidal currents are for a slack time, with negligible currents running. If they weren't I could compensate for them as I did on the trip over. I go over the chart with a magnifying glass (every pilot should carry one) and make a list of the lights to follow into Greenwich (Figure A, page 1512). A 4-second green flasher *1* is at the harbor entrance, where I will be making a right turn out of Northport Bay. My course plotting shows a heading of 349 degrees from the green flasher to a 4-second red flasher with a bell (listed on the chart as *R 8 Fl R 4sec BELL*). I will see it in the distance and count the intervals of darkness between flashes of red: one-and-two-and-three-and-four, and on four the light will flash. The distance between the green and red flashers is about 1.2 miles, and I can check my speed by timing the run between the two lights and computing it on the speed scale.

The next light is a 4-second white flasher (*Fl 4sec 15 BELL* on the chart). I may be able to see it from the red flasher 8 but I plot my course on a 326-degree

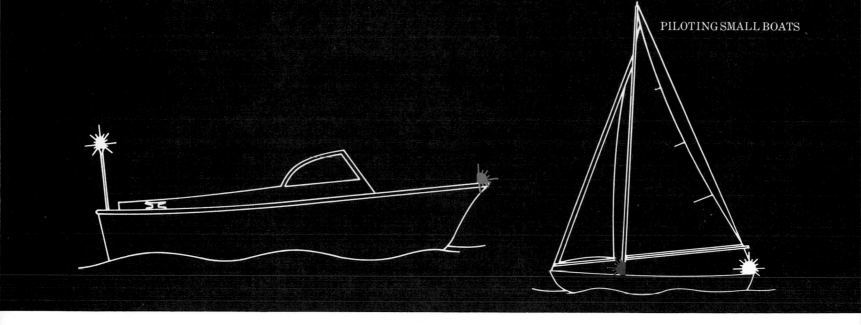

heading to the red nun *6*, to make sure I will clear the rocky, shallow areas east of Lloyd Neck safely. The distance from red flasher *8* to red nun *6* is about a mile and, having checked my speed, I will know about when to scan for the unlighted nun with my searchlight. When I spot it and clear it, I know that it will be safe to change course to 309 degrees and aim for the white flasher *(Fl 4sec 15 BELL)*, where I change course to 304 degrees. When I reach the white flasher I should be able to see the light from the lighthouse on Great Captain Island clearly, with its alternate white and red flash every 15 seconds. My landfall course will be east of the lighthouse, but it is there in the distance if I need it for homing.

The next light is a 2½ second red flasher with a whistle *(R 32A Fl R 2 1/2 sec WHISTLE)* on the chart. If I maintain the course heading I have set for this leg (304 degrees), this red flasher should be well to my left when I pass it. From there it is a straight shot on the same course past the white flasher bell *1* east of Little Captain Island to black can *1A*. From the white flasher, I will work my way past can *1A* and the red nun at the entrance to Greenwich Harbor, using my searchlight to find these unlighted markers. At the red nun, I will make a right turn into the harbor, and I am home safely.

Any night cruise in an area where there is commercial marine traffic calls for a knowledge of the running lights used by commercial vessels. A good reference work for this is *Piloting, Seamanship and Small Boat Handling* by Charles F. Chapman. If I happen to cross a shipping lane at night, for example, I should know when a tugboat is pulling a barge. I might see both the tugboat and the boat behind it, but if I were to try going between the two, I might hit a taut cable. The lights would warn me of this situation.

A good rule to follow in a small boat is to give a wide berth to all commercial traffic. I never assume that a small boat has the right-of-way over a large ship. I might be right, but I might not be around to argue the point later. There are rules of the road about which boats have the right-of-way under varying circumstances. A good sailor learns them so that he will know what other skippers expect of him. But sometimes the other fellow doesn't even see an oncoming boat. My single safety rule is to give *all* other boats the right-of-way. It may not be the textbook way, but it has worked well for me during many years of boating.

While it is remarkable how many objects can be seen in the water on a clear night without a searchlight, good sailors know that small islands and isolated rocks tucked in close to shorelines are difficult to distinguish. They always use the detailed chart of any harbor they plan to enter. Such charts give more information on local obstructions (Figure E, page 1515). They follow these charts closely and scan with a light for markers or landmarks that will help in avoiding the obstructions, while working slowly around them.

For related entries, see "Canoeing," "Kayaks," "Maps and Pathfinding," "Sail Making and Repair."

PIÑATAS
Bursting at the Seams

Javier Romero is a law student at the University of Mexico City. In his spare time, he and his sister, Rosa, enjoy modernizing traditional Mexican piñata designs. Between semesters, Javier visits friends and relatives living in the United States.

The piñata is one toy that is made to be broken, and when it is, be prepared to scamper to get your share of the surprises hidden inside. Outside, it may resemble a star or a sailboat, but inside will be candy and perhaps other treasures. In Mexico, the breaking of piñatas such as the ones shown in the photograph opposite and on page 1529 is a traditional and hilarious party game. The piñata, tied on a rope, is hung from a courtyard rafter. Each guest is blindfolded, spun around three times, and given a stick. The comedy begins when the piñata is pulled up and down by the host over the heads of the blindfolded guests while they flail away at it, and sometimes at each other in the excitement (although they are supposed to take turns). A successful hit on the piñata sends the contestants scrambling to gather candy or small toys spilled on the floor.

A similar game is played in Spain, but there the colorful piñata is kept intact because it is formed over a cardboard carton that has a tissue-paper bottom. In this case, when colored ribbons on the bottom of the piñata are pulled, goodies shower out like rain. The wishing well, doll, and sailboat piñatas on pages 1531, 1534 and 1535 are of this type.

In the days of the Roman Empire, piñatas were clay pots filled with fruit. Workers in vineyards of the countryside would smash the pots to mark the end of the harvest season. Caesar's troops took the ritual to Spain, and when the Spanish explored the Antilles in 1492 and conquered Mexico in 1521, the piñata went along. Nowadays piñatas are used in both Spain and Mexico as decorations, table centerpieces and souvenirs for all sorts of social gatherings, but they continue to be a very special part of the children's celebration of the Christmas season.

Toys and Games
Star of Bethlehem ¢ ▯ 🏃 🕯

In the villages of Mexico, many months of preparation go into Christmas festivities, which have a blend of pageantry and ceremonial ritual that lasts for 21 days. A piñata such as the Star of Bethlehem still plays its traditional role. On Christmas Eve there is a joyous feast that is climaxed by singing, dancing, fireworks—and the smashing of the piñata. Later, on January 6, the Day of Kings and the last day of the Christmas celebration, children present a Nativity play to mark the coming of the Wise Men and then participate in the piñata game.

Materials
To make the Star of Bethlehem, shown in color opposite, you will need these art supplies and household items: one 18-by-24-inch sheet of tracing paper; one 18-by-24-inch sheet of carbon paper (or several smaller sheets of carbon paper taped together); five 18-by-24-inch sheets of bristol board; nine 15-by-20-inch sheets of red tissue paper; one yard of silver gift wrap; one ½-inch nylon brush; white glue; an empty 2-quart soda bottle; transparent tape and masking tape; scissors; pencil; mixing bowl; spoon or butter knife; 16-inch cord; 6-foot rope; hammer; nail; screw-eye; screwdriver; old newspapers; and two packages of plaster of paris bandages (available at drug stores—they are usually used to make casts). To prepare for the piñata party game, you need to know how many children will participate so you will have the right number of broomsticks and blindfolds. Fill the piñata with a generous assortment of wrapped treats such as candy, cookies and gum, and if you like, party favors such as balloons, whistles, miniature plastic toys, or small packaged games.

It may pain you to break the bottom cone off this star piñata covered with silver foil and red tissue paper curls. But you will feel better when you chomp on the sweets stashed inside.

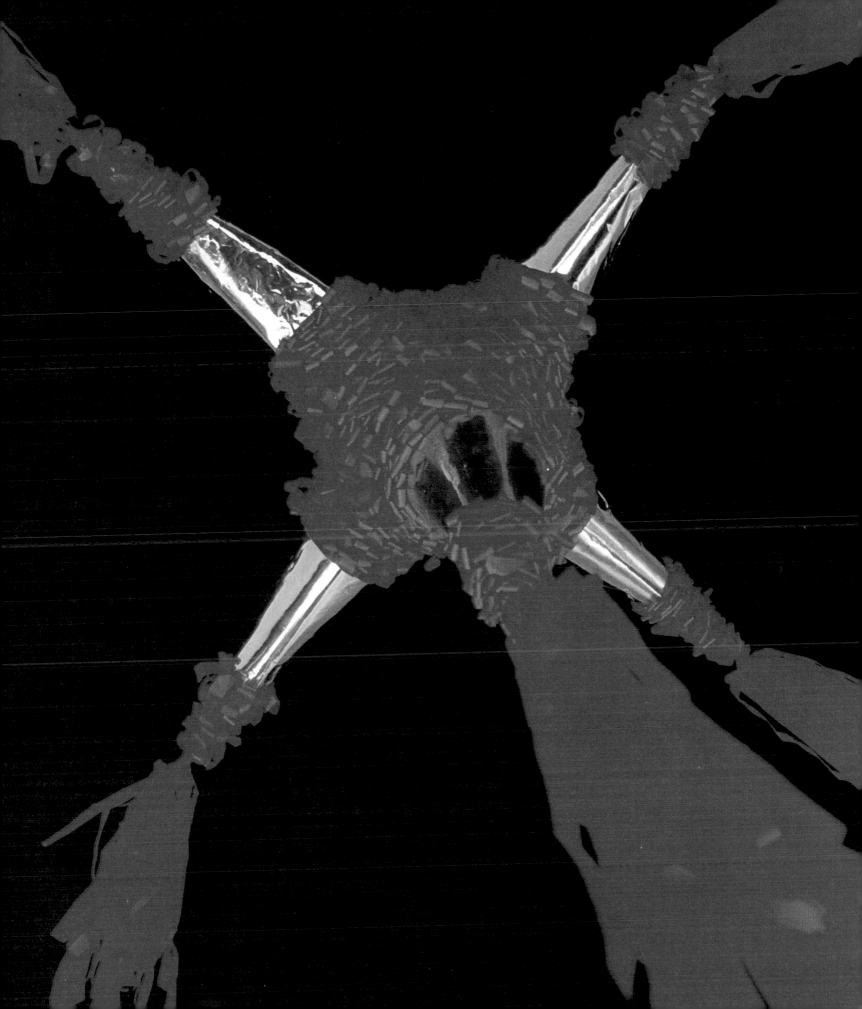

The Container

Earthenware pots provide the core for authentic piñatas, but broken clay fragments flying through the air could endanger players. I suggest that you replace the clay pot with a stiff cylinder made by wrapping newspapers, then plaster of paris bandages around an empty 2-quart soda bottle (which will be removed, of course). To begin, cover the work table with several layers of newspaper. Fold two dozen newspaper sheets into long strips about an inch wide. Tape these strips up the sides of the bottle, covering the surface evenly so that it follows the shape of the bottle. Do not cover the bottom of the bottle. Fill the mixing bowl with lukewarm water. Cut a roll of plaster of paris bandages into 8-inch-long strips. Dip each strip in the water to activate the plaster of paris adhesive and wrap it about the newspapers fastened over the bottle (photograph 1). Build up three layers of these bandages to make a plaster form 8 inches high and even all around the top and bottom rims. Set the wrapped bottle aside until the bandages are completely dry. Then pull the bottle out of the open-ended plaster cylinder and stuff the form with crumpled newspapers to cushion it until you are ready to assemble the piñata. (Craftsman's hint: the paper decorations that will be attached to the cylinder will stick better if a smooth layer of newspaper is glued over the plaster surface; to do this, brush the outside of the form with white glue, then cover with small newspaper strips.)

Follow the instructions with Figure A at left to enlarge the star-point pattern on an 18-by-24-inch sheet of tracing paper. Then put the carbon paper over an 18-by-24-inch sheet of bristol board, carbon side down. Put the tracing over the carbon paper and go over the pattern lines with a pencil to transfer the pattern. Stack four 18-by-24-inch sheets of bristol board evenly beneath the transferred pattern and cut through all five layers with a craft knife or scissors. To keep the sheets from shifting as you cut, bind the corners with masking tape. When you have cut out the pieces, make short cuts along the dotted lines at the curved edge of each piece. Make sure that the cuts are of the same depth.

To prepare the stiff bristol board to hold a cone shape, roll each piece across its length and width several times. Brush glue along the edges of each piece (see Figure A) and shape it into a cone (photograph 2). To hold the bottom of the cone in place as the glue dries, clip a clothespin onto the seam. Rub the seam line from both outside and inside as the glue sets. When the glue is dry, reinforce the seam on the inside with several small pieces of masking tape. Remove the clothespin, bend out the flaps that line the bottom edge of the cone and stand it upright. Glue the remaining pieces into cones the same way.

To decorate the cones, cut five 8-by-10-inch sheets of silver gift wrap. Shape a piece of foil paper around the middle of each cone. Where the foil overlaps, cut away most of the excess, leaving a narrow seam (photograph 3). Close the seam with transparent tape and slip the foil off the cone. The foil will be uneven. Cut away the excess to make a 6-inch band for the middle of the cone with parallel top and bottom edges. Then put the foil back on the cone and use clear tape to hold it in place.

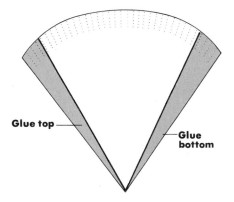

Glue top

Glue bottom

A

Figure A: To make the five cone shapes for the star piñata on the preceding pages, first enlarge this pattern onto a sheet of 18-by-24-inch tracing paper, letting one square equal 1 inch. For the rabbit-foot piñata shown on page 1529, let one square equal 1¼ inches. For either design, transfer the pattern to an 18-by-24-inch sheet of bristol board with carbon paper, cut it out, and cut along the dotted lines to make flaps at the base of the cone. The tinted areas on both edges of the pattern indicate where to put glue to close the seam.

1: To make a cylinder for the piñata core, paste plaster of paris bandages around a newspaper-padded bottle. Leave the bottom uncovered and keep the top edge low enough so you can slide the bottle and papers out when the plaster hardens.

2: Put white glue on the two edges of each cone piece marked for glue application in Figure A. Bend the shape into a cone so the glued edges overlap. Rub up and down this seam line with your fingers until the glue sets.

3: Roll an 8-by-10-inch piece of silver paper around the middle of the cone. Cut paper so the seam overlaps ¼ inch and seal it with transparent tape. Slip off the foil and trim it so the top and bottom edges are parallel.

4: To form a fringe, make 1¼-inch-deep cuts every ¼ inch along the length of each 2-by-15-inch tissue-paper strip.

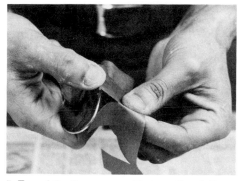

5: To curl the tissue-paper fringe, pull each flap over the edge of a butter knife or the bowl of a spoon in a swift, steady motion.

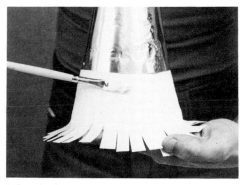

6: Brush white glue from the base of the cone to the bottom edge of the silver foil band before you begin wrapping the tissue-paper curls.

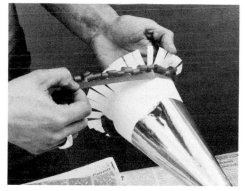

7: Turn the cone as you wrap curls over the glued surface. At the end of one row, tear the strip and begin a new row directly above it.

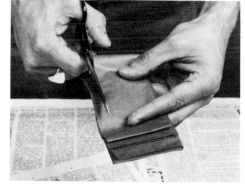

8: Fold three stacked sheets of 15-by-20-inch tissue paper down to a 2-by-4-inch size. Then cut fifty ¼-by-15-inch strips for each tassel.

9: Tape 50 tissue-paper strips at one end to make a tassel, brush glue over the tape, and insert the end into the small opening at the cone tip.

Curling and Wrapping

Stack five 15-by-20-inch sheets of red tissue paper evenly, and cut them into ten 2-by-15-inch rows. Fringe the edge of each row of strips with cuts 1¼ inches deep at ¼-inch intervals (photograph 4). Then separate the strips. Use the edge of a spoon or butter knife to curl the fringe downward as you would curl a ribbon with a scissors blade (photograph 5). Tissue paper is more delicate than ribbon; so handle it with care. Experiment with a few strips until you get the feel of it.

When all the fringe is curled, you are ready to wrap the cones above and below the foil. Brush white glue over the base of the cone to just below the foil (photograph 6). With curls facing away from the cone and next to the base flaps, wind a tissue-paper strip around the cone (photograph 7) turning the cone as you wind. When you complete one full row, tear off the excess tissue paper and begin a new row directly above the first, overlapping rows so the curls are closely packed. (A lazy susan will let you wrap and turn in one easy motion.) Cover the cone to the bottom edge of the foil; then cover the top in the same way beginning at the top edge of the foil. Repeat for each of the other cones.

To make tassels for the cone tips, fold three 15-by-20-inch sheets of red tissue paper along their width several times so you cut many strips at once. Then cut these into ¼-by-15-inch strips (photograph 8); you will get about 250 strips. To make each tassel, bind about 50 strips at one end with a piece of transparent tape. Put glue on the taped end and insert it in the small hole in the cone tip; if necessary, cut off the tip to make a small opening (photograph 9).

Attaching Cones

Remove the newspaper stuffing from the plaster cylinder. Use a screwdriver or an awl to punch two holes 1 inch below the top rim and opposite each other. To support the piñata, thread each end of a 16-inch-long cord through a hole; then pull each end over the rim and tie it onto itself (photograph 10, page 1528).

10: Use a screwdriver or awl to punch two holes for the supporting cord opposite each other and 1 inch below the top rim of the cylinder.

11: Turn the decorated cone upside down and spread white glue evenly on the bottom of the ring of flaps that you have folded outward.

12: Glue the first cone on one side of the cylinder, anywhere near the bottom rim. Reinforce the flap joints, if necessary, with transparent tape.

13: Fill in spaces between cones with leftover pieces of curled tissue-paper strips, cutting them to fit. Parallel the base of each cone with the rows.

To assemble the star, turn a cone upside down and put white glue on the flaps (photograph 11). Center and glue the cone anywhere along the lower edge of the plaster cylinder (photograph 12). Use transparent tape over the flaps to reinforce the joint. Glue the next cone in the same way opposite the first. Glue two more cones between the two in place. Finally, invert the cylinder and glue the fifth cone to the bottom (cordless) rim. Do not reinforce the last cone with tape if you want the children to knock it off easily. Candy used to fill the piñata will filter through the cylinder and lodge itself in the cone centered at the bottom of the piñata. When this cone is hit squarely it will fall off letting the candy pour out. Less accurate hits bounce candy out of the top of the cylinder if you fill the piñata full enough.

Double-check all other joints. To cover the flaps and to fill in the spaces between cones, glue on the remaining curled tissue-paper strips (photograph 13). The lengths of these strips will vary depending on the area being covered. Try to follow the curved form with neat rows, keeping all the curls facing the same direction. Let the glue dry for one hour.

Hanging a Piñata
You can hang the piñata from a tree, a rafter, an exposed pipe, or a hook or screw eye put in the ceiling where you plan to play the game. You will also need a hook to which you can tie the piñata rope until it is time for the game. Tie one end of a 6-foot cord to the cord across the top of the plaster cylinder. Thread the free end of the long cord through the ceiling hook. Adjust the height of the piñata so you can reach its open end to fill it. Tie the free end of the cord to a second hook in the wall. Pour treats through the open end into the bottom cone of the star. Once the piñata is filled, you are ready to pull on the cord and set the piñata in motion. If the blindfolded children take turns batting at the piñata, it is unlikely that anyone will get hurt. If the players are unable to knock off the bottom cone, the top opening is large enough so that ultimately treats will spill out as the container swings back and forth over their heads.

Toys and Games
Rabbit-foot piñata

¢ 🗓 👫 📻

Another popular Mexican design is called the rabbit-foot piñata. Although it looks more like a carrot, it brings good luck like a rabbit's foot. You will need the materials listed on page 1524 except that this design calls for one 18-by-24-inch sheet of bristol board; three 15-by-20-inch sheets of green tissue paper and four 15-by-20-inch sheets of orange tissue paper.

To begin, make the plaster cylinder shaped around an empty 2-quart soda bottle following the instructions on page 1526. When the plaster is dry, remove the bottle and stuff the cylinder with crumpled newspaper. Then glue a layer of newspaper strips smoothly over the plaster surface. Punch two holes on opposite sides, an inch below the rim. Thread with a 16-inch cord and knot (page 1528).

The basic shape of this piñata comes from one large cone. To make it, enlarge the pattern as directed in Figure A, page 1526, on 18-by-24 inch tracing paper, noting the change in scale. Trace the enlarged pattern on the bristol board. Cut out the pattern. Follow the dotted line to cut flaps along the bottom edge. Roll the bristol board across its length and width to ease the stiff paper so it can be shaped into a cone. Apply glue along edges as indicated on the pattern (Figure A). Shape the cone and rub the glued seam until it dries. Then reinforce the seam inside and out with clear tape. Bend out the flaps at the base of the cone for it to stand.

Rest the plaster form on its top rim. Then invert the cone and brush white glue along the ring of bent flaps. Turning the cone upright, center it over the rim of the plaster cylinder (photograph 14). Do not reinforce the flap joint any more than necessary to hold it temporarily if children will be trying to knock the cone off.

This piñata is decorated with orange and green tissue paper. Stack two 15-by-20-inch sheets of green tissue paper evenly and cut ten 2-by-15-inch rows. Make fringing cuts 1¼ inches deep along the length of the strips at ¼-inch intervals. Curl the fringe downward with the edge of a spoon or butter knife. Then cut and curl two 15-by-20 inch sheets of stacked orange tissue paper.

Begin at the cone tip and brush white glue down one third of the cone. Starting at the tip, cover the glue with the green curled strips (photograph 15). With the curls at the top of the strip, turn the plaster form as you glue the green tissue in place. At the end of each row, tear off excess paper and begin a new row directly below it. Use orange tissue-paper curls in the same way to cover the rest of the piñata.

To make the tassel for the tip of the cone, fold a 15-by-20-inch sheet of green tissue paper in half, so it measures 10 by 15 inches, and cut it into fifty ¼-by-15-inch strips. Bind the strips at one end with a piece of transparent tape. Brush glue over this end and insert it into the cone tip.

Screw in an overhead hook where you want the piñata displayed; if you have a plaster ceiling, you may need to use a toggle bolt or molly anchor. Then place a second hook on a nearby wall so you can latch the rope until game time arrives. Tie a long cord to the cord across the piñata opening, thread the free end through the hook, put in the treats, and tie the cord to the second hook.

14: To make a one-cone piñata, rest the cylinder so its bottom rim (the one without a supporting cord) is up. Set the glued flaps over the opening.

15: Brush glue over the top third of the cone tip. Wrap the glued area with one color of curled tissue-paper strips.

Though this rabbit-foot piñata looks like a carrot, there is no doubt that it will bring good fortune to the players who break it open.

Making a wishing-well

Yolanda Hidalgo and her husband Miguel came to the United States from Cuba. Yolanda has a degree in rehabilitation therapy from Havana University and has worked as a physical therapist privately and in a New York hospital. Several years ago a friend asked her to design a piñata for a special occasion. Ever since she has been creating designs for private parties.

The Spanish-style piñatas opposite and on the pages that follow are all made over cardboard cartons. I particularly enjoy making this type of piñata, since it is not destroyed during the party game. It is made with a false bottom of crepe paper, with ribbons attached. Party guests gather under the piñata, each holding a ribbon. When the ribbons are pulled, the bottom is torn out and the candy rains down. This more sedate version of the piñata game leaves the decorated part of the piñata intact for use another time.

The wishing-well piñata opposite is a simple design that demonstrates the basic techniques I use to make piñatas. To duplicate this piñata you will need a cardboard carton about 6 by 15 by 20 inches; if it has flaps, cut them off so that one of the two larger sides is open. If the carton is too tall, the sides can be cut down as was done in this example. You will also need: one ¼-by-16 inch dowel and two ¼-by-17-inch dowels; a craft knife; masking tape; staple gun; a 1-inch nylon brush; white glue; scissors; one 4-by-6 inch cardboard pattern; a sail needle (one with an eye large enough for ¼-inch-wide ribbon); a 2½-by-3½-inch plastic flower pot; a 2¼-by-3¼-inch block of plastic foam; a 4-foot length of nylon fishing line and a screw eye. To decorate the box, you will need: two rolls of festooning paper (colored tissue-paper fringing that is sewn to a tissue-paper band); ½ yard of heavy-stock crepe paper (2 sheets of thin crepe paper glued together will do); two 10-inch chenille pipe cleaners; ¼-inch-, 1½-inch-, and 2-inch-wide rolls of satin ribbon to match the festooning paper; and two dozen plastic flowers with spear ends (available at variety stores). I used yellow festooning paper and ribbon, and green crepe paper, but you may substitute any colors that you prefer.

Examine the inside of the carton to make sure that it is tightly sealed. Turn the carton so the open side is down and the sealed side is up.

The Trap Door
To be able to fill the completed piñata with candy and toys, you will need to make a trap door in one side of the box. To do this, rest the carton so its open side faces you. Put the 4-by-6-inch cardboard pattern on the box with the long dimension parallel to the open side. Use a craft knife to cut around three sides of the cardboard pattern—all but the hinge edge nearest the open side (photograph 16). Use the back edge of scissors to score the hinge edge and bend the flap up and back (photograph 17). (The trap door will serve to identify the back of your piñata-to-be; the side with the sealed flaps will be the top, and the open side will be the bottom.)

Turn the carton sealed side up. Punch a hole at either end to hold the dowels. Put one of the ¼-by-17-inch dowels in each hole, inserting it about 1½ inches. Secure the dowels inside the box with masking tape and use a staple gun to tack them to the outer edges of the box. Then place the 16-inch dowel across these posts and bind it on with masking tape (photograph 18).

16: To make a trap door on the back of the box, position a 4-by-6-inch cardboard pattern 2 inches in from the right hand edge and the top. Cut along the sides and top of the cardboard pattern.

17: Use the back of a scissors blade or table knife to score the uncut edge of the trap door. Then fold the flap outward. You will load the piñata with treats through this opening.

18: Insert the two 17-inch dowels into holes punched in the top of the box, then put the 16-inch dowel as a crossbar between these posts. Hold the crossbar in place with masking tape.

Your wish is sure to come true when you pull the ribbons to tear the false crepe-paper bottom from this piñata. Since the wishing-well design remains intact, it provides a warm remembrance of a shower or a graduation get-together.

False Bottom

Heavy-stock crepe paper is used to make a false bottom over the open side of the carton because it is strong enough to support the candy and small gift items that will be put in the piñata. Center the carton open side down on a sheet of crepe paper. You need a 2-inch border of crepe paper all around; anything more than that should be cut away since it is hard to glue tissue paper to crepe paper (photograph 19). Carefully stretch the crepe paper taut as you staple it every couple of inches to the sides of the box. Cut off any paper that extends more than 2 inches up the sides (photograph 20). Make sure that the crepe-paper border is even on all sides.

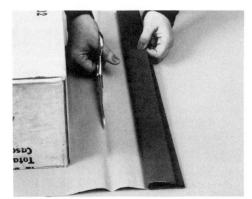

19: To make a false bottom for the piñata, place a sheet of heavy-stock crepe paper beneath the open side of the box. Cut the paper so it will lap up 2 inches around the box.

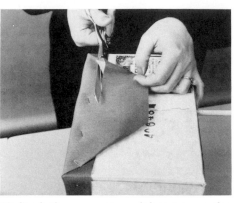

20: Staple the crepe paper so it is taut across the bottom of the box. To facilitate adhering festooning, trim away any excess paper that extends more than 2 inches up the sides of the carton.

Covering the Carton

All sides of this piñata except the crepe-paper bottom are covered with rows of festooning paper. I fasten it on with white glue thinned slightly with water. Cover the sealed side of the carton first, working out from the middle (photograph 21). Unravel some of the roll of festooning and thread it through your fingers as you glue it to the carton. When you reach an edge, cut the strip free of the roll. Glue the next row close to the first. Continue until the sealed side is covered. Cover the other four sides, one at a time, gluing horizontal rows of festooning in place from the top down. Be sure to cover the 2-inch crepe paper border (photograph 22).

To make the decorative loop of ribbon that you will use to identify and open the trap door, cut a 6-inch length of 1½-inch-wide satin ribbon. Fold this into a loop and center the ends on the inside of the bottom edge of the trap door. Use a stapler to fasten the loop in place (photograph 23). Cover the trap door with short strips of festooning glued on horizontally so the door can be opened. Finally, glue on a strip to cover the narrow space beside the trap door. Since the festooning may have been crushed as it was wrapped over the box, fluff up the paper fringe with your fingers.

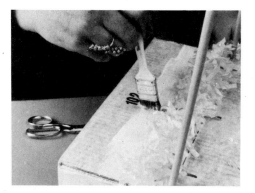

21: Brush slightly thinned white glue from the center of the box toward the edge nearest you. Then begin covering the box with festooning paper in horizontal rows.

22: Glue festooning paper to the sides of the box, working from the top to the bottom edge. Cover the crepe-paper border with festooning, but do not cover the trap door until later.

23: Since it will be hard to find the trap door once it is covered with festooning, fold a 6-inch loop of 1½-inch ribbon and center it underneath the edge of the trap door, then staple it in place.

Cover the crossbar and vertical dowels by coating each with glue, then winding a 24-inch length of festooning around it (photograph 24).

A small plastic flower pot hung from the crossbar makes the wishing-well bucket. To make a hanger for the pot, fold two chenille pipe cleaners in half. Twist their ends twice to close. Hold one closed loop perpendicular to the center of the crossbar. Then bend the other loop over the crossbar and through the first loop. Twist this pipe-cleaner loop once to close.

Using an awl or screwdriver, punch two holes on opposite sides of the plastic flower pot, ½ inch below the rim. Cut a 12-inch length of ¼-inch satin ribbon. Snip one end on a slant and knot the other end. Thread the slanted end through one hole so the knot is on the inside (photograph 25). Brush glue over the outside of the flower pot, rim to base, and cover it with festooning (photograph 26). Then glue festooning to the bottom of the pot.

Hang the pot from the crossbar by running the free end of the ribbon through the pipe-cleaner loop hanging from the crossbar. Then thread the ribbon through the other hole in the pot's rim and knot it on the inside. To conceal the excess pipe cleaner, wrap it around the crossbar.

Fill the pot with a 2¼-by-3¼-inch piece of plastic foam. Insert the stems of 10 artificial flowers in this foam block. Slide stems of the remaining flowers beneath festooning strips anywhere along the dowels and on the top of the box.

To decorate the sides of the box, cut one dozen 6-inch strips of 2-inch-wide satin ribbon. Roll each strip into a loop. Staple the loop closed from its inside as you attach it to the box (photograph 27).

Place the box on its side so you can attach piñata ribbons to the crepe-paper bottom. Cut as many 36-inch lengths of ¼-inch-wide ribbon as you need—one for each child who will play. Space the ribbons evenly; for ten children, I might lay out

24: Brush white glue over the crossbar. Then wind it with a 24-inch length of festooning to cover it. Do the same on the upright dowels. Begin at the top of each dowel and work down.

25: Use a screwdriver or awl to punch two holes in the rim of a plastic flower pot, the bucket of your wishing well. Thread a 12-inch length of ¼-inch ribbon through a hole so the knot is inside.

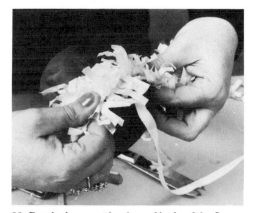

26: Brush glue over the rim and body of the flower pot. Cover the flower pot by wrapping it with small strips of festooning.

27: Cut 6-inch lengths of 2-inch ribbon. Fold each into a loop and staple along the sides of the box for added decoration.

28: Thread a slanted end of a 36-inch length of ¼-inch ribbon through the eye of a sail needle and sew it to the crepe-paper bottom of the piñata. Do the same with as many ribbons as there are to be guests. Space them evenly over the crepe paper.

A little girl would love this dolled-up piñata. Other toys could be substituted to personalize the piñata for a birthday party.

three rows of ribbon; four across one end, two in the center and four across the other end. Thread each ribbon through the eye of the sail needle and stitch it to the crepe paper (photograph 28). When all the ribbons are in place, open the trap door and fill the piñata with goodies. To hang the piñata, tie a length of nylon fishing line to the top of the chenille pipe-cleaner loop at the center of the crossbar. The length of this line will depend on how high you wish the piñata to be. Make sure the children can reach the ribbons to rip out the crepe-paper bottom. Tie the line holding the piñata to a rafter or a hook in the ceiling.

Toys and Games
Piñata pageantry

To make a piñata that resembles a miniature parade float, display a doll, toy or cartoon character at its very top. Even after the party, such a piñata will make a charming keepsake for your child's room. This piñata requires the same kind of trap door, false bottom and festooning decoration described on the preceding pages.

For the doll piñata in the color photograph at left you will need: a 6-by-12-by-14-inch carton with the smaller side open; a ¼-inch dowel 17 inches long; a 2-by-4-by-6-inch block of plastic foam; ½ yard of heavy-stock crepe paper; 2 rolls of festooning paper; three 10-inch chenille pipe cleaners; ¼-inch-, ¾-inch-, and 3-inch-wide satin ribbon; a craft knife; masking tape; stapler; white glue; a 1-inch nylon brush and a 4-by-6-inch cardboard pattern.

Decorating the Piñata

With the box open-side down, cut a trap door on the right side of the back of the box, following the directions on page 1530. Use a screwdriver to punch a ¼-inch hole in the center of the top of the box. Insert 2 inches of the dowel into the foam block. Brush white glue around the hole inside the box and on the top of the dowel support. Push the dowel through the hole from the inside of the box; press the foam block against the glued area inside the box. Hold it until the glue sets.

Put the box open-side down on a square of crepe paper large enough to turn up 2 inches on all sides, and staple it in place as directed on page 1532.

Cover the top and sides of the piñata with festooning paper and attach a ribbon pull to the trap door as directed on page 1532.

Turn the covered box so the trap door is in the back. Bend a chenille pipe cleaner in half. Glue and staple 2 inches of its ends to the top of the dowel. Use masking tape to bind the ends of the pipe cleaner to the dowel. Then brush white glue over the dowel and wrap it with a 24-inch length of festooning.

Cut two 48-inch lengths of ¾-inch satin ribbon. Align the ribbons and put them both halfway through the pipe-cleaner loop. Twist the pipe-cleaner loop once to hold the ribbons and keep them from slipping. Place two ribbon ends to the right and two to the left of the dowel. There will be excess ribbon that drapes over the sides of the box. Roll this excess into a loop at the end of each ribbon and staple it from the inside of the loop to a corner of the box just below the top.

To make a bow for the dowel, fold another chenille pipe cleaner in half and cut a 50-inch length of 3-inch satin ribbon. Fold one end of the ribbon to make a 10-inch loop. Pinch the middle of the loop with your thumb and forefinger. Then loop the remaining ribbon through these two fingers every 10 inches until the ribbon resembles a doubled bow tie. Twist the folded pipe cleaner twice around the middle of the gathered ribbon where you are pinching it. Use the pipe cleaner ends to fasten the bow to the dowel ½ inch below the top. As you fasten this big bow to the dowel, use the pipe cleaner ends to pull up any slack in the ribbons attached to the corners. Conceal any excess pipe cleaner beneath the bow.

Make four more bows the same way from 50-inch lengths of ¾-inch satin ribbon. But instead of holding each bow together with a pipe cleaner, staple it in place, one at the center of each side of the box.

Stand a doll or other figure 8 to 12 inches tall in front of the dowel. Wrap a pipe cleaner (choose a color that blends with the figure's outfit) around its waist and the dowel. Twist the pipe cleaner several times to close the loop.

Toys and Games
Surprise sloop

Sometimes alterations can be made in the shape of the box, producing unusual piñatas such as the sailboat below.

To make the surprise sloop you will need: a sealed box with flaps intact at the narrow ends, 6½-by-7-by-16½ inches; a roll of solid-color festooning; one yard of multi-colored festooning; one yard of heavy-stock crepe paper; 10- and 17-inch lengths of ¼-inch dowels; one 2-inch square block and one 2-by-4-by-6-inch block of plastic foam; two chenille pipe cleaners; 2 yards of ¼-inch satin ribbon of one color and ¾-inch satin ribbon in another; pencil; ruler; craft knife; masking tape; white glue; a 1-inch nylon brush; and a 4-by-6-inch cardboard pattern.

Say "bon voyage" and send your friends on a cruise with this sailboat piñata. Or try your hand at making one that resembles an antique airplane or an automobile for other occasions.

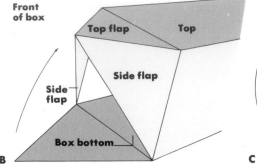

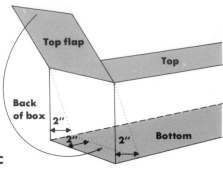

Front of box

Top flap

Top

Side flap

Side flap

Box bottom

B

Top flap

Top

Back of box

2"

2"

2"

Bottom

C

Figure B: To make the bow (front end) of the sailboat, open one flap end of a long box. Pull out the four flaps. Cut the top flap from the center of its outer edge toward both corners of the top of the box, making it a triangle. Then cut the two side flaps diagonally from their outer top corners to their inner bottom corners to support the top flap. Push the bottom flap against the cut side flaps. Cut it to fit against the others.

Figure C: To make the stern (back end) of the sailboat, open the opposite end of the box. Remove all of the flaps except the top one. Draw a line across the bottom of the box 2 inches in from its outside edge. On the sides of the box, connect the ends of this line with the top corners. With a craft knife and ruler, cut the box on these lines. Bind the top flap to the cut sides with masking tape. Then remove the box bottom.

Bow and Stern Construction

To make the bow (front end of the boat) open the top, bottom and side flaps at one end of the box. To cut the flaps at the proper angle, follow the diagram (Figure B). Bind the cut edges of the flaps together with masking tape to form the angular bow.

Open the opposite end of the box to make the stern (back end of the boat). Extend the top flap out and remove the side and bottom flaps. Use a pencil and a ruler to draw a straight line across the bottom of the box 2 inches in from its back edge. Extend this line just above the box edges on its two opposite sides. Use a pencil and a ruler to connect these marks on both sides of the box with the back corners of the top of the box (Figure C). Use a craft knife to cut along the lines on the sides and the bottom of the box. Fold the top flap down and tape it to the side edges of the back of the box. Then use the craft knife to remove the box bottom.

Cut a trap door 2 inches in from the stern end on one side of the boat. Staple a ribbon loop to the center of the underside of the trap door.

To lengthen the bow of the boat, use a scissors point to cut a ¼-inch hole in the tip of the bow. Shape the 2-inch foam cube to fit the inside of the bow tip. Insert the 10-inch dowel into the foam block. Run the dowel from the inside of the box through the hole in the bow. Glue the foam block to the inside of the bow to hold the dowel; reinforce with masking tape. Cut a ¼-inch hole in the center of the top. Push the 17-inch dowel mast into the 2-inch width of the 2-by-4-by-6-inch foam block. Glue the foam inside the box to hold the mast in the same way.

Fit and staple a piece of crepe paper across the bottom of the box to make a false bottom (page 1532). Cover the top and sides of the box with festooning. Fold a chenille pipe cleaner in half. Glue 1 inch of the ends to the dowel tip and bind in place with masking tape. Brush both mast and bow dowels with glue and wrap them with festooning. Fold a 36-inch length of the multi-colored paper in half and use clear tape to fasten it at its midpoint to the tip of the mast.

Cut eighteen 6-inch lengths of the ¾-inch ribbon. Roll two pieces into a loop. Place each over an end of the multi-colored paper. Staple them both to the stern.

Roll each of the remaining ribbons into a loop and staple three on each side of the boat's top, four on each side and two at each end of the boat.

Fold a 28-by-28-inch square of blue crepe paper into a triangle. Use clear tape to hold one of the folded ends to the mast tip and the other to the bow tip. Then tape the corner opposite the folded edge to the base of the mast.

Cut a 50-inch length of ¾-inch ribbon. Garther it into a bow (page 1534) by wrapping a folded pipe cleaner about its center. Tie it to the mast tip.

Cut as many 36-inch ribbons as you need for the children. I attached 9 ribbons with a sail needle, using three rows of three ribbons each.

For related projects and entries, see "Birthday and Christmas Celebrations," "Papier-Mâché," "Toys."